"A treasure trove of information, insights and practical ideas that you can use to become a well-rounded practitioner of the case method. Scott Andrews is a master case method tutor and takes you through the nuances of case writing and teaching in his inimitable style. I am impressed by the comprehensive coverage of the book that walks the reader through the traditional aspects of case method, and through to the present times when both case teaching and writing has evolved and adapted to keep pace with the advancements in digital technologies."

**Debapratim Purkayastha**, *Professor & Director,*
*ICFAI Business School Hyderabad, India*

# THE CASE STUDY COMPANION

The Case Study method of teaching and learning, adopted by business schools and management centres globally, provides an important function in management education, but employing it effectively can often be a challenge. This book provides practical insights, tools, and approaches for both case teaching and writing, drawing on perspectives from expert practitioners around the world.

This book aims to critically examine different approaches to using case studies in group-based, participant-centred learning environments, exploring good practices for case teaching and learning. It provides guidance for case writers on various approaches to structuring case data, presentational formats, and the use of technology in the construction of different types of cases. It also demonstrates the use of the case method as a tool for assessment, supporting students' own development of cases to demonstrate good practice in organisations. The final section of this book showcases some of the resources available, providing links and reviews of additional material that can support future case teaching and writing practice, including publication.

*The Case Study Companion* is designed for lecturers using cases within their teaching across all management disciplines, as well as those training for Professional Development and Management Education qualifications. It will also be useful for postgraduate, MBA, and Executive Education students wanting to make the most of case studies in their learning and assessments.

**Scott Andrews** is a Principal Lecturer in Leadership and Business at the University of Worcester, UK. He is an experienced case teacher and writer, having run over 150 case development programmes across more than 30 countries. He has been appointed a Senior Fellow of the Higher Education Academy in recognition of his contribution to the global development of the Case Method.

# THE CASE STUDY COMPANION

Teaching, Learning and Writing Business Case Studies

*Scott Andrews*

Routledge
Taylor & Francis Group

LONDON AND NEW YORK

First published 2021
by Routledge
2 Park Square, Milton Park, Abingdon, Oxon OX14 4RN

and by Routledge
52 Vanderbilt Avenue, New York, NY 10017

*Routledge is an imprint of the Taylor & Francis Group, an informa business*

Access the Support Material: www.routledge.com/9780367426965

*British Library Cataloguing-in-Publication Data*
A catalogue record for this book is available from the British Library

*Library of Congress Cataloging-in-Publication Data*
A catalog record has been requested for this book

ISBN: 978-0-367-42697-2 (hbk)
ISBN: 978-0-367-42696-5 (pbk)
ISBN: 978-0-367-85449-2 (ebk)

Typeset in Bembo
by Taylor & Francis Books

Dedicated to my mentor, John
A learning facilitator who kindly and patiently led me
on a voyage of discovery.

# CONTENTS

# FIGURES

# TABLES

# ACKNOWLEDGEMENTS

The long-awaited production of this *Case Study Companion* would not have been made possible without the 25 years of friendship and support from the whole team at The Case Centre, and especially from Richard, Kate, Hazel, Antoinette and Gemma.

My thanks are extended to those case writers and scholars who kindly permitted me to use their material for this manuscript including Todd Bridgman, Anne-Marie Carrick, Pierre Chandon, Direnç Erşahin, Sandra Vandermerwe, Tsai Terence and Tao Yue.

I am hugely grateful to the editorial team at Routledge who persevered with me throughout the drafting of the manuscript and supported its production, as well as the ongoing encouragements from Rachel, Harry, Lois, Esme and Martha.

# FOREWORD

As Director of The Case Centre, I lead an organisation dedicated to supporting the acceptance, growth, and development of the case method – one of the most powerful pedagogical approaches available to the business educator. Our members are located in more than 80 countries and in business schools and universities of all shapes and sizes. We host probably the most diverse case collection in the world, curate the annual World Case Teaching Day, provide resources and support to case practitioners everywhere, and offer professional development pathways in case teaching and case writing. So I know a good resource when I see one.

It is widely accepted that the case method has a huge beneficial impact on student engagement and learning, bringing the experience of real-life decision-making into business school classrooms around the world. The leading business schools invest heavily in supporting case research, writing, and teaching. Dedicated case publishing teams of professional researchers, writers, and educational designers often support their faculty. It is a powerful indication of how they value the case method.

The problem is that although schools dedicating such resources to support practice can be seen as an indicator of commitment and value, this can also be seen as a barrier to entry by non-case schools or individual faculty wishing to adopt the case method for the first time. Seen from the outside, the case method can seem like a pedagogy confined to a single, standardised model reliant upon having access to the resources, practices and students of the top schools.

And without their experience, or resources, where to start?

This book shows you how to enter the water of the case method and how to adopt and adapt it to suit your own experience, your classroom, your students, and resources: how to swim.

I know Scott Andrews as a committed and experienced case scholar. I have seen him lead workshops on the case method at schools and conferences over many years. I know how much his input is valued by participants and have seen them growing in confidence and dexterity over the course of a workshop. By sharing his own insights and the practical, real experience of case practitioners operating in many different circumstances, this book provides aspiring case practitioners at all levels insight into leading case discussion in the classroom and the practicalities of creating cases to meet the needs of you and your students. In it you will discover that the case method is not monolithic, but thrives on diversity. You will be supported as you move your teaching practice from lecturing to facilitating case discussion, and your writing from full disclosure to just enough disclosure. You will find it essential reading, and I hope that it supports you in creating case studies reflecting the lived experience of academics and business professionals on the ground, wherever that might be. Good luck. I wish you success and enjoyment in exploring and adding to the richness of the case method.

Richard McCracken
Director, The Case Centre: the independent home of the case method
www.thecasecentre.org

# INTRODUCTION

If you are using case studies in your programme, this book is for you. If you used to use case studies but you are no longer sure that they work as well as they used to, then his book is for you. If you have never used cases in class but are intrigued to know how to do so, then this book is also for you.

I have worked with lecturers, researchers, scholars and practitioners from around the world, who have explored the use of the case study for teaching and learning in management education, and it has been my privilege, over more than 25 years, to see and hear stories of how the case method has adapted and morphed from its origins as a discovery-learning tool from Harvard Business School more than 100 years ago. Today, I see many different types of academic, scholar, and writer adapting case methodologies for undergraduates, postgraduates, apprenticeships and professional development programmes for employers, as well as for the traditional executive MBA learner. I have seen the development and adaptation of many digital tools to support technology-enhanced learning through the case method, and I have seen a further blurring of the lines between the case study and other valuable learning tools that we can bring into the classroom – both literally and remotely. I have seen cases adapted for many different cultural contexts, in places with very different traditional philosophies on teaching and learning, delivered by enthusiastic researchers and writers from China to Kenya to Germany to Turkey. This is reflected in the many quotes that are cited in this text, to each of which I have left the country of origin to showcase the diversity of creative thinking about the case method.

The use of the case study or case method in management education was first developed at Harvard Business School in the early 1900s, in response to a growing need for new ways of thinking about teaching and learning in management education, with the first book of written cases published in 1921.[1]

Those original pioneers and scholars of the case method at Harvard looked to their Law School and Medical School for inspiration. For centuries physicians have kept "case notes" which have formed the basis of modern medicine as we know it today. Similarly, in the Western world, legal systems have been formed through the development of what has become known as 'case law'. So, it is not surprising that Harvard management scholars noted these approaches and adapted them for the management case study approach, which has become so popular today. The *management case* or *teaching case* has become a constructivist-oriented pedagogic tool, which is widely employed to promote students' active participation so they can form their own learning.

> 'Thinking out original answers to new problems or giving new interpretations to old problems is assumed in much undergraduate instruction to be an adult function and, as such, one properly denied to students'.[2]

As can be seen from this historical quote from Harvard in 1940, the 'case' was originally conceived as a tool for management education for postgraduate/post-experience learners. However, since then approaches to the case method have been adopted and adapted in many different ways by practitioners from business schools and management centres across the world. Today, it is fully embedded in many institutions as part of the professor's/tutor's/facilitator's toolbox for classroom delivery. Once the preserve of the postgraduate's classroom, nowadays the case method is equally as popular with undergraduate learners, post-experience, and executive learners, as well as work-based learners; and its use is constantly being adapted to meet the ever-changing needs of the learner in different cultural contexts across the world. For example, one popular case distribution centre boasts a membership of more than 500 institutions across six continents.[3]

Whether we regard ourselves as lecturers, class demonstrators, tutors, teachers, or trainers of management, we have probably adopted the case study in one form or another into our teaching and learning armoury. This book explores examples of good practice captured from case study facilitators, scholars, and practitioners from across the globe and considers how you can adapt your style of delivery to best suit your specific learning environment. Topics to be explored include different approaches to case class design, the format by which case information is received by the learning community, the scope for using live cases, and effective use of technology enhanced learning.

Having developed and delivered more than 150 case teaching and writing programmes in more than 30 countries across five continents over 25 years, one of the most repeated concerns raised by case users is the need for more localised cases, written with the local context and culture in mind, by writers who are familiar with the local learning environment. With this in mind, the second section of this book explores approaches to writing your own cases and provides guidance based on experiences derived from case writing centres across the world.

Case studies are frequently used as vehicles for student assessments and it has become quite commonplace to invite students to develop and present their own research-informed, evidence-based case studies. Often these types of cases are less concerned with management education *per se* and tend to focus more on approaches to organisational research and showcasing good practice. The third section of this book explores case assessment, including approaches for guiding learners to develop their own cases.

The global growth in the use of the case method for learning has led to a growing network of organisations dedicated to supporting the development of the case method. The final section of this book showcases some of the resources available from these organisations, providing links and reviews of additional resources that can support you in your future case teaching and writing practice. This section includes some sample cases, a teaching note and links to an annotated example of case analysis.

In my work with scholars and professors across the globe, looking to teach with cases or to write cases, I have come to appreciate that we all have our own preferred styles, terms and language that accompanies our work. This is no better exemplified than in the terms that we use for our class groups. My peers refer to their target group as readers, students, learners, participants, and co-workers, to name but a few. For the purposes of this text, and respecting the various terms that have been employed in my conversations with case scholars, I have intentionally chosen to intermix these terms within the narrative of each chapter.

Each chapter contains insights that have been gleaned from a host of different case users and institutions from across the world, as this book does not seek to deliver a solitary view or a singular approach to the case method. As my experiences have shown over the past 25 years, the case method is adopted in a multiplicity of ways by different user groups across the world, and this book seeks to *celebrate* and, where appropriate, to *showcase* that diversity. Intermixed with the issues raised in each chapter, you will find sections where *lessons learnt* from my own experiences have been shared to reinforce a key learning point. In addition, there are opportunities throughout the book for you to *pause for a moment* and reflect with an invitation to take part in an exercise of your own, to help you to seek to develop your own case teaching and writing skills.

Chapter 11 includes four actual case *openers* from previously published award-winning cases, and Chapter 20 contains three distinctly different case studies and a teaching note for further reference.

One of the key things that I have discovered as I have worked with scholars of the case method is that *approaches* and *methodologies* are constantly changing and adapting to the changes in our classroom contexts. When I first started using case studies as a young lecturer, I worked with an experienced case mentor who used to refer to himself as a *learning facilitator on a voyage of discovery*. At first, I thought perhaps he had watched too much *Star Trek*; yet slowly and surely, I started to understand what he meant. As a firm believer in lifelong learning, it has been a privilege to be part of that same learning journey, which has truly been a voyage of discovery and which continues to challenge me to be a better scholar. So too, I hope that this book will open your eyes to the possibilities for learning through the case method and encourage you to push boundaries and be part of the next paradigm shift in the ongoing evolution of the case study as a tool for management education.

So, let's get started.

## Notes

1  Heath, 2015
2  Gragg, 1940, p. 2
3  www.theCaseCentre.org

# SECTION I
# Case Teaching

# 1

# WHY USE A CASE STUDY?

What have scholars from around the world had to say about their use of the case study?

'The case method is not only the most relevant and practical way to learn managerial skills, it's exciting and fun. But it can be confusing if you don't know much about it'.

*USA*[1]

'The case method is a powerful approach to teaching and learning business subjects. Its main advantage is that it is a 'question-oriented,' as opposed to 'solution-based,' approach to teaching. It allows students to participate in 'real-life' decision making processes'.

*Hong Kong*[2]

'A case is the description of a real situation with a protagonist who has to decide something. The data in the case are likely to be incomplete, as data often are in the real world'.

*Switzerland*[3]

'The style of a teaching case is vivid, realistic, and convincing. It compels students to take the role of the decision maker in the organization, think as if they were him or her, and be analytical and creative'.

*The Netherlands*[4]

This section explores the following questions:

- How do your students learn?
- What motivates your learners in their studies?
- How do we know that learning is taking place and what can be done to ensure learning is effective and impactful?
- Is student learning through case studies genuinely meaningful and relevant to the needs of the current and future workplace?
- What could we be doing differently to enhance the participant's capacity for learning with cases?
- How does the case fit into your programme planning?

The case study provides hands-on, practical opportunities to explore real-life management situations in organisations through examination and analysis, to enable learners to draw conclusions about management that they can take back into their real world once the class session has ended.

However, if the impact of the case session is to be effective, we first need to explore how the case approach engages with the learning process. No doubt the questions listed above, or many more like them, have crossed our minds at some point as we reflect on how we can build on the experiences and techniques that we currently deploy in our classrooms and management training centres with our learners. The case method has been widely used in a range of different contexts in management education across all management disciplines and at all college, university and professional levels.

Mini-cases are frequently presented in subject-themed management textbooks to provide practical applications to help students to unpack and explore the theories and models that the textbooks are promoting. Although this provides useful insights into learning with cases, these short narratives tend to focus more on showcasing good practice rather than providing a learning journey through which students can engage with the stories and situations, within a larger organisational context. These are normally structured to enable students to draw upon management knowledge, skills and behaviours to unpack learning through knowledge-input, discovery and reflective practices.

That the case method continues to be valued as a tool for learning is not in doubt (given that case studies have remained a core part of the staple diet of the management scholar for more than 100 years); however, their usage has more recently diversified across different developmental and competency levels, as well as across geographic and cultural boundaries.

The real question is not *why use a case study*, but rather *how* can you ensure engagement with the case method provides an effective, supportive and productive learning experience that motivates your specific group of learners, embedding lifelong learning and developing key employability skills that will play a vital role for future career enhancement?

## 1.1 How do your students learn?

'Case method provides the means for allowing students to either develop theory or make their own theories-in-action explicit in a forum where they can be re-examined in ways that are not likely to happen elsewhere'.

*USA*[5]

Before we tackle the intricacies of developing teaching approaches with case studies, it is important to reflect on *learning* itself and more specifically how the learners whom we encounter each week in our classrooms engage with the notion of learning (be they in real classrooms studying face-to-face or in virtual spaces). We all learn differently, and yet as scholars we often tend to deploy generic, homogenous learning approaches to most forms of student programme delivery.

If we are to truly embrace effective impactful learning in the classroom then we need to ensure then it is tailored to the competencies, needs, and capacities of our specific learners. To do this, we need to know how they learn best and how the 'secret histories' that they bring into the classroom can be used to help and inform their approaches to learning through case methodologies. In other words, we need to really *know* our learners. Only then can these case class sessions be *tailored* to the known learner-types as they present themselves in our classrooms. There is no single approach to delivering through the case method, and it is highly likely that some approaches to case delivery will be more effective than others in different contexts. It cannot be stressed enough how important it is to know your learners' backgrounds, habits, preferred styles of learning and general interests. The more we can understand about our learners, the more we can tailor our approaches to meeting their best preferred style of learning.

---

### LESSONS LEARNT

We often learn best through our own classroom mistakes. I have a vivid memory of an awkward moment in a classroom many years ago when I had been asked to present a case study to a group of first year undergraduates studying globalisation as part of a marketing degree programme. I was no more than ten minutes into the case discussion, which focused around the challenges facing the CEO of a major global business which was about to adopt a new marketing project, when one of the students raised her hand and called time on the discussion. She told me how she had only been at university for eight weeks, was 18 years old, had never previously had a job, nor left home, and was not only unaware of how global businesses operate, but also, she did not even know what a 'CEO' meant. It became immediately clear that I had pitched this case far too high for this individual who, understandably, was not at the developmental level needed to be able to address the issues raised in the case discussion, on the basis of the viewpoint that we were exploring. I asked her what she wanted to do when she graduated, and she said she would like to be a marketing executive. So, I invited her (and her class colleagues) to rethink the context from the perspective of a marketing executive: to imagine she had just graduated and was in her first role as an executive in a large business that had offices located in many different countries. I informed her that one of the 'big bosses' had requested that as a new team of marketing executives, she and her colleagues were being asked to take on a new marketing project for the company. On hearing this, the troubled student and her colleagues immediately engaged with this revised context and happily put their creative minds to the challenges that had been proposed. It was clear to me that I had not sufficiently endeavoured to understand the former knowledge and life experiences of the group in the classroom prior to starting the course, to be able to satisfactorily pitch the case discussion. A lesson quickly learnt.

When case tutors have been asked for their opinions of how students learn, the following list includes commonly repeated responses:[6]

- Case learning is dependent on the learner's age and experience of management in the workplace.
- People learn differently in different cultures.
- We only learn what we are interested in learning.
- Learning depends on a desire and willingness to learn.
- We learn best when we are free to create our own response to a situation.
- Learning depends on not knowing the answers.
- We all learn in our own way.
- Learning is largely an emotional experience.
- To learn is to change.

Undoubtedly, not everyone will agree with all of these statements, but they reflect common points of view which have subsequently informed approaches to case delivery.

> PAUSE FOR A MOMENT: take another look at this list of viewpoints and ask yourself to what extent do you agree or disagree with each statement. Then ask yourself how your views on these statements are reflected in your own teaching style.

Arguably if at least one of the following three criteria is achieved at the end of a case session, then we might agree that an individual has learnt:

- The individual knows something they did not know before; or
- They can do something (or do it better) than they could before; or
- They have formed a view about something that they did not hold before.

So, before you being to plan the case delivery schedule, pause to consider how the construction of your programme is going to affect learning, specific to the features of your known learner group.

## 1.2 Motivating learners

One of the frequently raised questions when meeting with case scholars is how do we meet the challenge to motivate learners to engage with the case study process? In contrast to more traditional and passive approaches to teaching and learning, the case method relies on a certain level of engagement and participation on the part of student – both before, during, and after a case class discussion-session. If the student is not prepared, then it is more likely that the learning benefits of the case session will diminish, and this can serve to further demotivate the learner, forming an ever-diminishing return which can easily spiral out of control. Therefore, it is important to ensure that there is student engagement and participation from the onset. Both the choice of case and the approach to case delivery play key roles in ensuring that the learner is motivated and better predisposed to the intended learning outcomes of the session. This could involve investment in case writing to provide resources that are more familiar to the learner and potential use of digital technologies that promote engagement with the case narrative.

In more traditional contexts, case studies have been perceived as lengthy paper-based exercises that require a strong commitment to reading, extensive pre-class analysis, and exercise work. If a student is not used to this style of learning then introducing the case concept with a 40+ page document of an in-depth, complex management situation, based on a large company located a long way from the student's home, might not be the most motivating starting point. Chapter 3 explores *types of case study* and will provide insights into the best ways of selecting a case to ensure the balance is struck between maintaining student motivation and ensuring the key learning objectives of the programme are achieved with the technology available. Chapters 5 and 6 examine different approaches to engaging with the case learning session, to foster curiosity and interest with the student group, which promotes engagement and participation.

## 1.3 Capturing effective and impactful learning

One of the perils of the case method is closing the session with an assumption that the programme's intended learning objectives have been achieved. Just because a student has participated in a case study that explores, for example, key aspects of change management, this does not meant that the student has necessarily learnt the key principles or practices of change management by virtue of participation. Although the case study will provide an opportunity for the learner to wrestle with issues related to change management, it is important to consider how the student has processed this experience and, as a result, how it has contributed to their learning.

### LESSONS LEARNT

As a very young lecturer, I recall one of my highest performing students leaving the classroom at the end of what I had considered to be a well delivered case session. She turned to her classmate and said: "Yeah, Yeah, interesting case study, interesting story, so what?!" and she left the room. While feeling initially deflated by the comment, I quickly resolved to ensure that future case sessions positively encouraged learners to address the "so what?" question for themselves. In doing so, not only did the case discussion therefore promote opportunities for discovery-learning, but also concluded with an opportunity to capture reflective learning. This occurred more than 20 years ago and has framed my approach to incorporating reflective practice into my case classes ever since.

Although your students might enjoy the case discussion and contribute positively to the issues raised in the discussion, this is no guarantee that they have assessed for themselves how this is contributing to their learning. A few carefully crafted questions at the end of the case discussion, which are oriented towards personal reflection, can assist the learner to ensure that they have had the opportunity to *capture and bank* the learning objectives for themselves. Their responses to these questions will also enable you, as the facilitator, to determine whether or not all the intended learning outcomes have been fully achieved.

There is no guarantee that case participants are going to fully assimilate all the intended learning outcomes from a case session, so it is helpful to allow sufficient opportunities within programme planning to ensure the same key learning outcomes can be revisited and reinforced throughout the programme. In that way, if the objective was not captured by all the students on their first case experience, then it is likely that it would be seized in its second outing. This is discussed in more detail in Chapter 4.

## 1.4 Relevant and meaningful learning for future employability

There is a growing demand in Western higher education to ensure that university programmes are more reflective of the real needs of the current or future workplace. This has been evidenced with greater investment by programme leaders in thinking around 'employability' criteria, which now regularly feature in module specifications. This is of particular importance where cases are used for teaching as part of an apprenticeship, work-integrated learning programme, or as part of a work-based learning initiative, especially if the employer is the sponsoring organisation. It is perhaps not surprising that employers want to be assured that there is a return on their investment that is reflected in the benefits to the workplace. Although case studies can provide valuable true-to-life experiences for learners, the impact can be less obvious if the context for the case is too abstract. It is therefore important to ensure alignment of case selection with the organisation(s) that are likely to be engaging with your students in the future.

Universities often draw on the support of employers through employer advisory boards or forums which can, if managed correctly, be a useful resource when thinking about using cases in your programmes. Employer forums can provide really helpful insights into the issues facing local organisational contexts, which could help to inform case choice. They can also identify potential willing contributors who could provide a rich resource for case writers looking to develop cases based on localised issues of significance to employers. Chapter 9 provides further insights into identifying useful sources of case data.

## 1.5 Enhancing the learning experience.

Learning is dependent on many factors, but two frequent challenges to learning through the case method are the individual's *motivation* and their *developmental level*. The case facilitator needs to determine the best approach to delivering the case session, which accounts for these two factors. This means that the same case could be approached differently with diverse case groups where the class demonstrates different levels of motivation and competency in their subject matter. These two factors account for the groups' prior experience of the case method, their level of commitment to the learning process, willingness to co-operate, prior knowledge, and people skills. The approach adopted by the case facilitator would also be affected by their prior knowledge of and professional relationship with the learner, or, in other words, the level of familiarity between the tutor and the class.

### Directive tutoring

This is often the starting point for the case tutor, working with learners for whom their knowledge of the case method is either limited or unknown. It will be the approach most probably adopted for students who have not prepared their case materials or have no knowledge of how to prepare for a case discussion, or where the topic for discussion is unfamiliar to the learner. For example, imagine a student group is exploring a case rich in quantitative financial data, as part of a complex financial analysis to determine an organisation's readiness for a new financial venture. A novice student in this context is unlikely to yet know what to do with the case tasks, so the tutor might need to provide specific directive guidance, with clear instructions, to effectively *direct* them through the number-crunching, to develop and reveal an approach that is consistent with common good practice. This approach requires a high level of supervision. In general, it is likely that this approach forms the starting point with many less experienced (or less motivated) undergraduate groups.

### Engaging and facilitating approaches

As case tutors start to form professional relationships with the case group, they are more able to draw insights from each individual learner's personal contexts and secret histories. This informed facilitation enables tutors to more specifically orientate students to the data in the text, often inviting learners to compare and contrast aspects of the case narrative with their own personal insights. This engaging and facilitating approach assumes that the learner knows what to do, but lacks

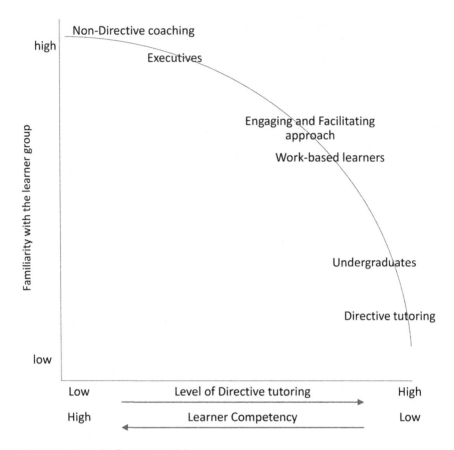

**FIGURE 1.1** Case Facilitation Model
Note: This figure illustrates suggested approaches to delivery and facilitation, based on the motivation and developmental level of the learner group.

practice, experience, and perhaps the required skills to undertake the case tasks competently on their own. Tutors might therefore need to be on hand to explain and persuade and to address questions where uncertainty arises. As a result, this approach continues to assume a limited level of competency on the part of the learner, but over time, with careful coaching or guiding, the case class will develop greater confidence in their capacity to address the issues in the case. Learners can then be encouraged to step into the shoes of the protagonist in the case, in order to better engage with the issues facing the company. This relies on the student having first prepared for a class discussion with a growing familiarity with the approach to learning through the case method. As the learner progresses along this curve, they develop new skills, knowledge, and experience to manage the case tasks (but might still sometimes lack confidence or motivation). Often work-based learners can provide a higher level of motivation and competency, given their work-based experiences, which can brought into case class discussions. The tutor will need to listen, discuss, and encourage the learners to make decisions. By this point, case tutors can facilitate a *learning journey* through carefully crafted questions, towards key learning objectives, while continuing to pursue a highly relational approach to guiding the learning experiences of the class.

### Non-directive coaching

As the learner develops higher levels of competency and motivation a less directive approach to case tutoring can be adopted. This approach is dependent on a highly responsive, committed, and experienced learner group, often captured in executive education. The role of the case tutor can be reduced significantly, and the approach adopted can become less personalised. The level of responsibility for learning in this context sits extensively in the hands of the learner. This approach works well with highly competent learners, who perform well intuitively, without even thinking about it. Case tutors will trust learners to take control of the case journey, keeping out of the way as much as possible, to enable learners to make their own decisions. This approach might also be favoured when using cases as part of a distance learning or e-learning programme.

In reality, case tutors can find themselves adopting a range of different responses across all parts of the case facilitation curve, at different times during the delivery of a case-based programme, depending on the nature of the cases, the key learning objectives, and the competency and commitment of the learner group.

## 1.6 How does the case fit into programme planning?

The purpose of this book is by no means to present the case study as the panacea for all teaching and learning challenges. Although a small number of management programmes deliver exclusively through the case method, the vast majority use the case as one of a range of tools in the tutor's toolbox. There are certain areas in management education where the case study will be logical learning approach and other areas where there might be alternative approaches that are more effective. In this way, the case method can be considered as one of a number of options available to tutors, which can be utilised with their learning community to fulfil useful pedagogical objectives (noting that these can relate to knowledge, skills, and professional behaviours). Figure 1.2 provides an illustration of the types of areas where each tool in the tutor's toolbox might be considered to be most effective.

Some institutions tend to deliver programmes that are entirely case based, while others tend to prefer a programme with a mixture of different approaches to class delivery. Although no single approach is ideal, it is reasonable to assume that your best approach depends on the overall pedagogical objectives of the programme and both the motivation and developmental level of the learner.

The important challenge from this illustration, when developing your own teaching plan, is to consider the learning objectives that you are seeking to achieve from your programme and then to devise a sequence and approach that best enables you to

| Learning Objective | Training on the job | Lecture | Group Discussion | Case Study | Business Simulation | Role Play | Application Project | Reading Assignment |
|---|---|---|---|---|---|---|---|---|
| Motivation | Good | Average | Average | Average | Good | Average | Good | Poor |
| Active Involvement | Good | Poor | Average | Good | Good | Good | Good | Average |
| Individual thinking | Good | Poor | Average | Average | Average | Average | Good | Average |
| Sequencing and structuring | Average | Good | Average | Average | Average | Poor | Average | Good |
| Providing feedback | Good | Poor | Average | Average | Good | Good | Good | Poor |
| Knowledge transfer | Good | Poor | Average | Average | Average | Average | Good | Poor |
| Analysis and Critical Thinking | Average | Poor | Average | Good | Good | Average | Average | Poor |

Legend: Level of impact in achieving objective:

| | |
|---|---|
| ◼ | Good |
| ◼ | Average |
| ☐ | Poor |

**FIGURE 1.2** Classroom Toolbox

achieve these objectives, using the 'learning tools' available to you, while bearing in mind the past experiences of the learner and their developmental level.

> PAUSE FOR A MOMENT: take another look at this Classroom Toolbox illustration and replace the top row with the tools that are most familiar and available to you. These should include all the approaches that you are most confident about using in your classroom. Then consider a specific course for which you are responsible and list the knowledge, skills, and behavioural objectives that you are seeking to achieve. Finally, plot the impact of your chosen 'tools' against the 'objectives' to reveal the scope for framing your own programme.

Now that you have completed this chapter, you should know that:

1. The case is a useful tool for encouraging participant centred learning but in order to be successful you need to match the correct choice of case, with the right teaching approach to best suit the type of learner in your programme.

2. We all learn differently, and so the case method needs to be used in a manner that enables the widest possible scope for individuals to engage with the discussion and learning processes.
3. The level of directed guidance provided by the case tutor depends on the motivation and developmental level of the learner group.
4. Carefully crafted questions that support *reflective practice* can take place towards the end of a case discussion to evaluate the degree to which the case discussion has enabled the learner to truly capture the intended learning outcomes.
5. The case is one of a number of different tools that can be used effectively to achieve key pedagogical objectives. Your sequencing of these tools needs to reflect the learning objectives for your specific programme and the motivations of your learner group.

## Notes

1  Hammond, 2002, p. 1
2  Farhoomand, 2004, p. 103
3  Schmenner, 2002, p. 5
4  Yue, 2016a, p. 1
5  Clawson, 1995, p. 3
6  Adapted from Heath, 2015

# 2

# WHAT MAKES A GOOD CASE STUDY?

'Good cases are like onions – the more you peel away the outer layers, the more you discover inside'.

*Switzerland*[1]

This section explores the following questions:

- What are the ingredients that make an effective case learning experience?
- How do cultural differences impact case learning?
- How long should a good case be?
- How might cases differ from other published outputs?

Imagine a mixing bowl, into which you pour in the ingredients for the dish you are about to prepare. As you pour in the ingredients then start to stir in the mixture, an essence starts to emerge from the bowl. Now imagine that the mixing bowl is your learning community or classroom and the essence that you are looking to create is *learning*. What are the key ingredients that you need to pour into your bowl in order to achieve effective learning with the case method? This question has been raised with case scholars across five continents on more than 100 occasions, and the most common responses have been used to frame this chapter. The response begins at Harvard University, travels across Europe into the Middle East and Africa, on to India and China, before ending in Australia.

## 2.1 Tell a story

Professor Malcolm McNair was a renowned Harvard Scholar, Professor of Retailing and 20th Century pioneer of the case method in management education. However, his earlier scholarly experiences were in Shakespearean literature. As a result, it is perhaps not surprising that his knowledge of Shakespearean approaches to participant engagement were used to inform his practices in the classroom with case study groups. McNair became a strong advocate for the function of storytelling as a fundamental component of the case method.[2] Storytelling has been widely acknowledged as a powerful learning tool,[3] as the narrative structure forms one of four key structures that determine what many regard as the essential dimensions of effective case study development.[4] Although storytelling forms an important part of the narrative structure, it might be worth considering the particular role that it plays when using case studies with younger and less experienced undergraduates, to support and motivate the learner to engage with the narrative through what Samuel Taylor Coleridge first referred to as a *willing suspension of disbelief.*[5] Confucius once stated: Tell me and I will forget, show me and I may remember; involve me and I will understand.[6] When we tell a story well, we do not just listen to the story, but we join in, immerse ourselves and become *involved*. It was this literary approach that first made the Shakespearean experiences so popular and engaging, and, similarly, the same approach works well in case learning. As a journalist once pointed out:

> 'Stories matter. They are where we lose ourselves in order to risk other possibilities, where we can escape and play, or confront and confess. We do not listen to stories; we join in and in accompanying the players of that story we meet many sides of ourselves that we can take back to our lives when the playing is over. But good stories need to be told well if they are to envelop us. Flair, humour, truth and insight are all tools that must be well honoured'.[7]

## 2.2 The Key learning objective

The peril of the case method is the tendency to lose oneself in the narrative and forget the point of the experience. The first priority of the case tutor is to tell a good story, but the story needs to have a point, or as is commonly referred to in the US – *the takeaway*. It might be easier to consider this as the '*so what?*' question that the tutor needs to ensure has addressed by the learners to bridge the gap between merely participating in an engaging discussion and ensuring that learning has actually taken place. The '*so what?*' response often takes the learner to the *Key Learning Objective* (KLO) of the case exercise. The case experience has already been repeatedly referred to as a journey, and the KLO often forms the *destination point* of this journey. As Stephen Covey once stated, the best journeys begin with the end in mind,[8] so planning a case journey with the KLO clearly in sight is a vital ingredient of a good case study experience. In addition, a case journey may also capture *interesting visiting points* (IVPs) on the way to the destination. These IVPs might also contain key learning objectives that contribute to the overall learning derived from the case discussion. Developing IVPs as part of the case writing process is discussed further in Chapter 6. In summary, KLO's define the purpose of the case and, although many different examples exist, as a general rule, a good case should contain no more than 3–5 KLOs.

## 2.3 The Case Focus

The Case Development Centre at Rotterdam School of Management uses the *case focus* as the starting point for new case writing ventures.[9] Although the case itself might describe an interesting situation or sequence of events, which tackle a relevant and important issue, it is also important to make clear the main *focus* of the case. Is its focus on Leadership? Management? Branding? Quality? Decision making? Stakeholders? or Strategy? The narrative style and the expository structure of the case ought to draw attention to this *focus*, and the details of the *focus* should be included in the tutor's teaching note to ensure the tutor is able to communicate this focus effectively when briefing the learner group.

## 2.4 The Data

A good case study draws attention to the relevant data required to make the case effective. Traditionally, the case method was formed on the basis that everything you needed to know to address the issues raised in the case study could be derived from the data contained within the case, or as Prof. Abell from IMD once stated: 'a good case should be able to stand alone', and the author needs therefore to 'make sure the case has the data required to tackle the problem – not too much, and not too little'.[10] However, more recently this philosophical approach has been challenged by changes in classroom culture and the advent of digital technologies in management education. It is now commonplace for students to attend classes armed with digital capabilities to enable them to undertake their own searches of vast databanks of information which could be drafted into a case discussion. As a result, it is no longer necessary to ensure that the case study contains all the data to tackle the problems raised by the case situations, but rather a new type of case is emerging that provides signposting to enable learners to undertake their own searches to gather data for problem-solving. Nonetheless, as a general principle a good case should contain sufficient relevant data (and signposting to further data) to enable the learner to adequately engage with the issues captured in the case narrative in such a way as to promote analysis and, where appropriate, decision making. The case itself is of limited value if it draws attention only to itself and the organisation represented in the text. The main themes and generalisations captured in the case should be presented in such a way as to draw out useful contrasts and comparisons to other similar scenarios. In other words, the learner ought to be able to draw out key discussion points from a case session to enable them to apply the lessons learnt to their own organisational contexts.

## 2.5 The Controversy

A good case is a controversial case. Case studies often examine complex management situations involving decision making between individuals, to which there are normally more than one probable response. It is these decision points that offer opportunities for conflicting opinions to arise in class discussion, and it is often during such discussions of points of conflict and controversy that a deeper level of learning is achieved. This works on the premise that 'learning is an emotional experience and not simply a cognitive one'[11], and as a result, controversial decision-making engaging the emotions of participants can foster a deeper level of learning that gets *locked in* for life.

## 2.6 Keep it short

How long should a case be? This is one of the most commonly raised questions by tutors in case development programmes. The answer is always: *it depends*!

---

### LESSONS LEARNT

I was invited some years ago to deliver a case study workshop to the Thai Institute of Directors in Bangkok. As I was preparing my materials in anticipation of a challenging audience, my host requested that any case study that I chose to bring to the workshop as an example or illustration should be no more than one sheet of A4 paper in size. This was an unusual request and would require significant alterations from my initial plans. When I enquired about the reason for such a request, I was informed that all the participants are directors of large organisations from across Thailand and Central Asia. They have marketing managers deciphering complex marketing reports, finance directors analysing large financial data sets, operations chiefs working out complex logistical plans, and these are normally summarised in short, succinct strategy reports to the directors, from which they are expected to make strategic decisions. Any case study above a page of A4 paper would not be an appropriate reflection of reality for such directors.

---

If a case study is to represent a slice of reality, then the length of the case needs to be considered too. Sometimes *less is more*! Often, a short case can provide a significant opportunity for discussion and exploration, where the participants have to manage assumptions based in the gaps that are caused by the lack of available data, and argue the adequacy of these assumptions that they are making. By contrast, a complex case might contain many different types of data, including potentially unimportant or misleading data. The initial challenge for participants is to separate the relevant data from the less relevant data. Given that we live in such a data rich environment, this capacity to identify and separate relevant data is itself a useful management skill. If students are using cases for finance, business planning and accounting type programmes, then it is highly likely that these will be data-rich and therefore contain larger number sets for analysis. There are hints and tips for case tutors on how to select sequential cases that break down cases with larger data sets, for students who might normally be find them demotivating; these can be found in Chapter 3.

In 1996 The Case Centre (which holds the world's largest collection of management case studies) reported that the average size of the case studies submitted to their global collection was 27 pages long. By 2019 the average size had reduced to just 12 pages. There are many possible reasons why this has reduced by more than 50% over the course of 23 years, which might include the growth in demand for cases to use with undergraduates, the wider global circulation of cases into countries with educational systems that are less predisposed to working with large case resources or the general trend in youth culture towards shorter, bite-sized methods of communication. The use of social media platforms by undergraduate learners as part of universities' technology-enhanced learning strategies is growing. The use of short or limited-text communication tools, such as Snapchat and Twitter, has changed the way that young people have adapted to online communication and is subsequently influencing undergraduate learning.[12] As a result, the evolution of shorter cases, with less text and a greater use of video imagery, that can be adapted for use on social media platforms, presents new opportunities for engagement and learning, particularly in undergraduate management contexts.

> PAUSE FOR A MOMENT: take another look at your own classroom – what digital and social media tools are your learners using and how are they currently being exploited for teaching and learning purposes? How could such tools be integrated into the case classroom to enhance levels of participant engagement? For example, I recently heard of a University which had a large contingent of overseas students who were particularly uncomfortable with traditional approaches to case study discussion. To remedy this, the case tutor set up a Twitter live-feed, which provided messages onto a screen in the room, so that these overseas students could tweet responses and questions that could contribute to the ongoing discussion in the case class.

## 2.7 A well-structured and easy to read case

One of the stumbling blocks to case learning is the use of management language that is unfamiliar to its target learners. It is sometimes wrongly assumed that if a student is registering to study management, then terms which are commonplace to the management scholar should be known and understood by the student group. Those of us who claim to be management scholars are also well versed in writing for scholarly journals in a style fit for the wider academic research community. However, as McNair reminded us earlier in this chapter, the first responsibility of the case writer is to tell a story and tell it well. This therefore suggests that an approach to case writing might be significantly different to the approaches adopted for other forms of writing and as such, often require the writer to un-learn their normal practice of writing to rethink the process of storytelling. Case structures are discussed in greater detail in Chapter 11, drawing insights from the narrative (storytelling) approach, managing the balance between the unearthing and hiding of data, the development of plot structures and presented a clear chronology of events.

Moreover, the style of writing needs to reflect the requirements of the reader, such that complex management terms might sometimes need to be sacrificed for plain language that sets data out in an easy-to-read format to promote curiosity and interest in the case situation. As my case study mentor once pointed out to me, the case itself should be a *journey of discovery with some interesting surprises along the way*. If we seek to honour this approach in our case writing (and our case selection), then we are more likely to experience an engaged, prepared and motivated learning group.

## 2.8 The Personal Touch

'An instructor must not strive to replicate another teacher's style or approach. He should, instead, develop a style with which he is comfortable. Otherwise, the instructor will not be effective'.

*India*[13]

In a research project involving more than 700 scholars from across Australia, the case study repeated scored highly as one of the most preferred teaching methods to promote innovation in learning.[14] There is no single right or wrong way to use the case study for teaching and learning, but the importance of applying a personal touch has been widely recognised as a necessary pre-requisite to effective case use. There are plenty of online video examples of cases being taught in classrooms, but these are not your classrooms, and the students on the screen are not your students. As much as it is important to know your own learner group, it is also important to ensure that your own personal delivery style is reflected in your approach to handling the case study.

As the case method continues to be adopted by more and more groups across the world as a tool for learning, cultural adaptations and innovations in design, construct and delivery are continuing to exploit new technologies and broader varieties of learning styles, in support of the lifelong journey of discovery and learning.

Now that you've completed this chapter, you should know that:

1.  The case study can be used in a variety of different ways to promote effective learning opportunities, exploiting cultural differences and learning styles.
2.  Case choice and selection need to reflect a clear understanding of the motivations and experiences of the target learner group – the more we can discover about our class group, the more targeted we can be in our use of the case method.
3.  A good case needs both to tell a story and to fulfil key pedagogical objectives.
4.  We all learn differently, and so the case method needs to be used in a manner that enables the widest possible scope for individuals to engage with the discussion and learning processes.
5.  A good case study should support learning as an emotional experience and not simply a cognitive experience derived through rational and objective reasoning alone.

## Notes

1 Abell, 1997, p. 3
2 Greer, 1985
3 Fawcett and Fawcett, 2011
4 Heath, 2015
5 Coleridge, 1817
6 Bramley, 2015
7 Clark, 1996
8 Covey, 1999
9 Yue, 2016a
10 Abell, 1997, p. 5
11 Schmenner, 2002, p. 3
12 Mollett, Moran and Dunleavy, 2011
13 Vedpuriswar, 2003a
14 Ballantyne, 2006

# 3

# CASE SELECTION

'A case study is a distinct literary form. It is obviously not a poem. It is not purely a narrative, but it has important elements of narration. In is not purely an exposition. It is not just argumentation, but it may have important elements of argumentation. It is not just fiction, but ….. it may have important elements of a detective story'.[1]

This section explores the following questions:

- What should you look out for when searching for the right case?
- How do you evaluate the anatomy of a case study?
- What are the different types of case study?

Every case study is different – in design, content, context, written style and purpose. Anybody who has had to undertake a case search will have no doubt found themselves overwhelmed with the different options and choices available to them. However, if you were to make a closer inspection of cases, you would start to see commonalities that enable cases to be grouped into different types. Each type of case can be used to fulfil a different type of learning opportunity, and so it is important to develop a clear understanding of the different types of cases that exist and their potential for *learning* in different contexts, so that case tutors can streamline their searches to focus on specific criteria to achieve specific outcomes. Most of the larger global case collections provide well-developed search engines that allow tutors to shortlist cases for review by:

- General subject area
- Keywords
- Size (pages)
- Geographical location

- Type of organisation
- Age of case
- Digital format
- Previous popularity (no. of adoptions)
- Data source
- Language
- Availability of tutor notes/teaching notes

Before examining the different types of cases, it is helpful to consider the anatomy of the case in the context of the classroom session.

## 3.1 The Anatomy of a Case Study

Before starting a case search, it would be beneficial to consider answers to the following six basic questions:

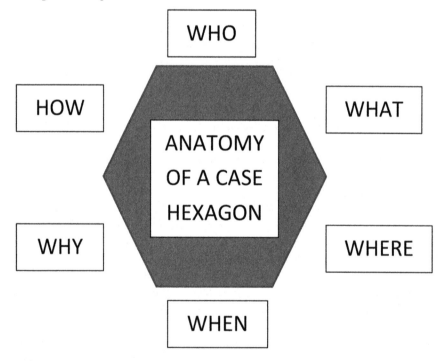

FIGURE 3.1 Anatomy of a Case Hexagon

### WHY are you using a case at this point in the programme?

Although there is no single logical order to addressing the six questions in the anatomy hexagon, it might be helpful to start by asking WHY? For what purpose are you choosing to use a case at this stage in the course programme and what objectives is it there to fulfil? Cases may be used to:

- Create interest and foster curiosity.[2]
- Bring a slice of reality into the classroom.[3]
- Serve a specific learning objective.[4]
- Explore new approaches, techniques and philosophies.[5]
- Confuse, explain, suggest and review.[6]
- Identify, analyse and solve issues.[7]

Undoubtedly, your response to this question will be a combination (if not all) of these suggested functions and might contain others too, including the application of theory to practice, to explore new ideas and relationships, to formulate hypotheses and to build on those all-important employability skills of decision-making, effective communication and team work. Yet it is worth reflecting, as you prepare to search and select your case, to first consider for which specific purposes each case is needed.

### WHO are your target students?

This was the main theme of the opening chapter which reminds us that the more insight we can capture into the 'secret histories' that our learners bring into the classroom, the more we can tailor our case selection to appeal to their best learning and pedagogical needs. It is reasonable to assume that the *developmental level* of the learner will affect their probable capacity to respond to the challenges within the selected case, so with a little reverse-engineering, it is easy to anticipate likely reactions of our learners to any given case, from which to then ensure that the right case is selected for the right purposes for any given learner group.

### WHAT subject area and learning objectives are you seeking to fulfil?

It will soon become clearer in the next section of this chapter that the type of data and the way that it is presented in the case can elicit and develop any number of different skills and behaviours from the learner. One factor to consider here is the type of data that should be embodied within the case: should there be little, or should there be lots? Should it be made explicit, or should it be provided in a more implicit form within the case narrative? This then determines the level of work that the learner will need to undertake to *search, identify, analyse* and make *judgements* on the data provided. Traditionally, cases contained large volumes of data to enable learners to extract relevant from less relevant data, before reformulating it to enable conclusions to be drawn. Nowadays, popular cases tend to be less data-heavy, with many designed to more systematically focus on a single form of data analysis rather than on multiple complex sets of different data to achieve numerous purposes. The developmental level of the learner and the degree of direction provided by the tutor will have a clear bearing on the type of data contained in the case and in what format it is presented. (*Directive* and *less-directive* styles of delivery are considered further in Chapters 4 and 6).

### WHERE does the 'story' of the case take place?

The setting of the story that forms the context for the case can have a significant impact on learner motivation, case preparation and engagement. In other words, if the setting is familiar to the learner, then there is often a greater likelihood that the learner will be persuaded to participate and engage with the case session. It might therefore appear logical to ensure that cases are selected based on student familiarity, but this might come with added complications. If a student is perceivably over-familiar with the case situation, then they migh begin to control the flow of discussion in a manner that could undermine engagement with other students. Or alternatively, an over-familiar story might appear to offer nothing new to the learner beyond that which they perceive that they already know, and as a result, this could undermine the 'discovery' element of the learning process. In many instances, it is not the conclusion that really matters, but rather the true learning that is contained within the journey taken to reach the conclusion, but this might be lost if the context is over-familiar to the learner.

### WHEN in the course programme will this case be used?

It is important to consider when the case is to be scheduled as part of the course/module/programme, as this will provide an indication of the student's developmental level, based on their knowledge and subject awareness; understanding of the tools, models and theories that can be used to inform practice; and prior exposure to case method participation.

If the case session is scheduled towards the start of the course, then a more directive approach to case facilitation might be needed. Shorter cases often tend to work better in the earlier part of a course as students develop a familiarity with the case method, during which a more inductive learning approach can be popular.

### HOW do your students learn best, and HOW are you planning to deliver the case session?

When considering the HOW? question, three issues should be considered:

a. HOW will you treat the data? As discussed above, an *inductive* (theory-developing) approach can be quite popular if the case is to be introduced in the early stages of a programme, where the learner's knowledge of management theory might be somewhat limited. Similarly, this can also be a popular approach among more experienced learners where they can be challenged to conceptualise, develop and adapt their own theories or models towards problem-solving. A more classical learning response that follows an input-discovery-reflective style of course delivery might support a *deductive* treatment of the data (applying known theory). For example, you might run a number of more formal lectures to introduce a theory and then provide a case that invites learners to apply the theory to the situation in the case, before drawing conclusions (takeaways) that can be noted as reflective learning generalisations. *Convergent* treatment of the data takes place when there are large data sets that invite a more analytical approach to case delivery, whereas *divergent* treatment of the data encourages a more creative response to treating case data, which might include scenario-setting or action research approaches to case development.

b. HOW will analysis be undertaken? The case tutor's role is to navigate a journey through the case data towards the fulfilment of key learning objectives, ensuring a balance between *breadth* and *depth* of enquiry from the learners. *Breadth* of discussion promotes movement towards the goal, while the issue of *depth* involves analysis. Within most cases there ought to be some elements of the journey where learners are invited to think at a deeper level about the issues that they are confronted with; perhaps to consider other perspectives on the same situation, alternative responses to a decision that needs to be made, or different ways of interpreting the numbers within the data. It is often in these places of analysis (or at the *interesting visiting points* as they are referred to in Chapter 6) where emotional intelligence kicks in and students discover more about their own skills, behaviours and perspectives, which they can take back to their real world once the case discussion has ended.

c. HOW much discussion time is needed? We all have a limited capacity for engagement on any given case issue, and yet sometimes it seems that we can try to squeeze every ounce of juice out of a case for what appears to be hours of class discussion and delivery. Some of the most experienced case schools across the world tend to limit the case discussion time to no more than 50–70 minutes, which means that time needs to be managed well. If a particular case study is found to be so rich in content that it merits longer then it might be worth considering taking more than one 'journey through the case' at different scheduled intervals, to avoid a prolonged and extensive case session beyond 90 minutes, as the capacity for student engagement and memory recall will be seriously compromised. And remember, just because the issue has been covered in class, it does not mean that *learning* has taken place in an effective way.

## LESSONS LEARNT

I was determined to get the most out of a new award-winning case study that I had recently introduced to my undergraduate marketing programme. Whilst some textbooks provide careful explanation of the four 'Ps' of marketing (and some even of the five Ps), this case study, based on a popular online retailer, provided an opportunity to explore 13 Ps of marketing through an extensive and data-rich journey, with plenty of opportunities for analysis. However, it was not long before I started to notice the tell-tale signs of fatigue on the faces of a growing number of my students. While there were easily more than ten different stages of analysis that we could engage with as part of the class discussion and group time, it became only too clear to me that I needed to limit the number of 'interesting visiting points' to no more than three or four within a class session, and that rather than schedule the case to run over three hours, one hour for a discussion was plenty enough. At first, I was left feeling that I had not made the most of the data in this case, but then it struck me – I could segment the case and provide the data in smaller bite-sized segments, through directive student guidance, to allow three separate 'mini' journeys to take place on three separate occasions. This allowed the students to steadily feast on the data in the case without suffering from premature case indigestion.

PAUSE FOR A MOMENT: take another look at the case anatomy hexagon and have a go at applying it to the case that you are planning to use for your next class discussion. See if you can address the *who, what, when, where, how* and *why* questions for yourself, and see if this leads you to reconsider any of your approaches to your use of the case.

## 3.2 Types of Case Study

Having considered the anatomy of the case, we can move on to explore how different types of cases can therefore be adopted to achieve different types of learning opportunity, with different learner groups, by utilising different treatments of data at different times in the learner's programme, according to their developmental level. There are three ways to explore *types of case study*, either by content, source of case data or by presentational design and structure. Although content remains relatively unchanged over time, source and design have changed significantly in line with the growth in the use of digital technology in classes and the massive expansion of access to data.

### Content

My father was a detective, who worked for the police force. As a child I used to ask him what did he used to do in his job? And his response would commonly be: 'I solve cases'.

It is therefore not surprising that when we think of what to do with case studies, the first answer is often to *solve* the case or to *solve* a problem. The role of the detective involves far more than just solving the case. Indeed, many of the other actions needed in the job can be contrasted to other attributes of the case process, besides just problem-solving skills, including:

- Problem-identification and analysis;
- Looking at things from multiple perspectives;

- Handling assumptions;
- Decision-making;
- Evidence-based judgements between different courses of action;
- Relating theory to practice.

In much the same way as the detective needs to gather, analyse and assess the evidence about the case, so too does the learner need to consider the case content and the valuable evidence and insights that it provides to enable the learner to treat the data, which might even sometimes lead to a case being solved. There are commonly seven different types of evidence that forms the case content.

One of the most traditional and popular forms of case has been the *situation case*, which tends to include a description of a situation or a sequence of events and activities for which there is likely to be more than one probable set of responses and subsequent outcomes. These situation case studies remain the most popular type of case in management education and are frequently found in Strategy, Marketing, Human Resource and Operations Management programmes.

In these types of cases, it is quite common for case tutors to ask the students to identify what went wrong in the situation? Or how could the protagonist within the case have responded or behaved differently? This classic case approach invites participants to step into the shoes of the key protagonist within the story and to consider the various options available as the situation unfolds.

Another similar type of case is the *complex case,* which have traditionally been produced as very large paper-based case studies, frequently used particularly in postgraduate study. In complex cases, the case content incorporates data highly relevant to the case situation intermixed with less significant data, or even some data that may be irrelevant. The principle purpose behind this form of case is to challenge the learner to make judgements regarding the quality of the data and to determine relevant data from the less relevant data before then considering a response to the challenges set by the case objectives. The usefulness of these types of lengthy paper cases is questionable today, given that, to a certain degree, the World Wide Web presents similar challenges for learners who need to search for relevant evidence from the vast quantities of less relevant data available online. A remedy for the pitfalls of a complex case, would be to ensure the case narrative is able to signpost learners to online resources from which they can decipher the relevant data from less relevant online data. The complex nature of the case study remains the same, but the context is shifted from the paper to the screen.

As a detective, my father would often find himself in court cases where decisions needed to be taken based on the evidence that had been revealed from his investigations. In a similar way, case studies that provide descriptions of situations often lead the learner to a point where the protagonist is required to make a decision. The classic *decision-making* case study would normally provide at least two or three likely and feasible approaches to a certain issue facing the organisation. The challenge for the student is to exercise judgement to determine the most appropriate option, while considering the merits and pitfalls of the other options, in order to present a balanced argument, to enable the organisation to respond to the context raised within the case.

Many of these types of decision cases involve people, opinions and data. Those with larger data sets tend to require far more in-depth analysis and number-crunching. These quantitative cases are often referred to as *exercise cases* and tend to prove highly effective in subject areas, such as accounting, finance, business planning and big data analytics.

By contrast, a more descriptive case can lack plot, people and the need for decision-making. These types of cases, which are often referred to as *background cases*, tend to be more popular as scene-setters, when looking to develop a broader understanding around a particular theme. For example, the tutor might wish to run a module, which explores a number of strategic decisions made by different motor manufacturers, and so they might have selected appropriate cases from a range of different companies. The background case can serve as a popular prerequisite with which to explore an over-view of the motor industry – its trends, themes, mergers and acquisitions over time. These exploratory cases enable all the class participants to come to a certain point of knowledge and awareness, through macro environmental and economic analysis, from which to then begin exploring the individual organisational cases.

The *incident case* is a highly popular short, often single issue, case that the tutor can bring into a lecture or class discussion. These types of cases tend to require no pre-planning on the part of the students and can often serve as a useful breakout exercise, to change the pace of study in what might otherwise be a lengthy lecture session. They tend to allow the learner to apply a single concept or approach in a specific context and can be useful tools for discovery, application and reflection.

More recently there has been a growing body of case researchers contributing to what has become known as the *dark side of business*. The rationale for these cases is based on the following premise:

> 'Case libraries are almost exclusively devoted to "best practice" cases or diffi-cult decisions by basically well-managed firms. When we want to talk to our students about the more typical cases, let alone the really scandalous practices of the worst firms, the cupboard is almost entirely bare. It's almost impossible to even find a reasonably rich case on a labor/management conflict'.[8]

The *dark side* series emerged from the Critical Management Studies Interest Group at the Academy of Management and has grown to become a regular annual com-petition. The Academy's Dark Side Competition was established to build interest and participation in case writing, to develop new cases for teaching based on a broad range of themes, including the integration of sociopolitical issues with orga-nisational dynamics, with a specific focus on organisational and management pro-blems within capitalist systems. Many of these cases draw insights from business ethics and explore the notion that so-called 'ideal-type' cases also need to recognise the wider social, political and economic factors that shape managerial decisions.[9] Although originating in the USA, this network has grown to attract cases from across the world, including New Zealand, Canada, France and South Africa. Further details about this can be found in the final section of this book.

Finally, the *live case* presents a very vivid and real challenge to the learner, often through introducing real people to bring their own organisational issues to the class:

> 'In a typical live case, a leader or team from a local company visits the classroom and presents a business problem the organization is facing. Students are then tasked to develop solutions. Sometimes they do so in a consulting team throughout the semester and then present their solutions to the professor, their classmates, and company representatives'.
>
> *USA*[10]

> 'Live case studies [are] an approach that has wide currency in business education and as a method where students are emotionally and behaviourally involved in experiential learning'.
>
> *Australia*[11]

These types of cases are highly popular for leadership, change management and consultancy class groups. The success of these fast-emerging approaches to the case method have been evidenced across the world from the USA to New Zealand, and research has demonstrated that across cultures, this type of case study provides a genuine, engaging and realistic insight to learners, who are able to capture a vivid real picture, in contrast to a hypothetical or distant business situation from a paper-based case.[12] Disengaged students often point to a lack of genuine applicability when faced with a large paper-based case study that centres on historic situations facing a distant organisation, which is unlikely to provide viable future employment for the learner group, given the proximity of the company to the learner. By contrast, a live case fixes the context for the case on a situation that outplays itself right in front of the learner group, and which can therefore be shaped around localised agendas, culture, traditions and approaches. Although all previous forms of case content are rooted in the past, live cases are often presented in the current or even future tense. Live cases are discussed further in Chapter 8.

> PAUSE FOR A MOMENT: take another look at the seven different types of case listed above and consider which ones might be most favoured by your learner group. What types of cases do you currently tend to employ in the classroom, and, on the basis of the details listed above, are they the best choices for your current teaching and learning challenges, given both your learner's developmental level and the nature of the subject matter that you are delivering?

## Source of Case Data

When exploring sources of data for the case study, there are principally three types: Field research, Desk research and Personal experience (or Armchair cases). The traditional notion of the case study in management education emerged out of *field research*, with the adage that everything that you needed to know to address the issues in the case could be derived from the data found within the case. Hence, originally, cases emerged as large data-rich papers, full of field research. However, with the emergence of greater access to online data, the desk-based research case study evolved to compete with more traditional field data. The merits of both are compared and contrasted in chapter 9, but it is worth pointing out at this stage that there has been a growth in popularity of desk-based case studies. Research from IMD, conducted in 2009, identified that 35% of cases adopted from a global repository were formed from desk-based research and just over 50% were from fields research.[13] By 2019 data from the same repository identified that the popularity of desk-based research had risen to 41%.[14]

What is also worth noting is that *desk-based* cases are by no means second in quality to research cases. Evidence from case competitions, based on both quality and frequency of adoption for teaching, demonstrates a growth in desk-based case award winners. There could be several explanations for the growth in desk-based cases. Firstly, the authorship of cases has broadened internationally over the past 20 years to become a global phenomenon, promoting case writing from very remote contexts, sometimes with limited access to primary field data. Secondly, access to secondary, online data has enabled case writers to utilise their creative writing skills to develop highly engaging case narratives, often from geographically remote contexts, to incorporate significant insights into organisations which create the illusion that the case is the result of field data. Thirdly, the use of field research requires formal release authorisation from the organisation involved, and, in an increasingly litigious world, companies are becoming more resistant to co-operating in case study development.

This has led to a growth in the third type of case study – the *personal experience* or *armchair case*. When companies have been unwilling to provide release authorisation for case data, case writers are faced with the choice of either disguising key aspects of the company or its data, or producing entirely fictitious narratives based on personal experiences that provide a *reflection of reality*, while safeguarding the author from any libellous repercussions. Research draws attention to subjects such as finance and business ethics where researchers, who might find it impossible to gather real data from organisations, turn to fictionalised companies in order to produce credible materials for class use.[15]

## Design and Structure

Although the traditional presentational format of the management case study has been based on a *single, linear, print formatted output*, there have been many recent adaptations and variations to the case in both design and format.

Given that one of the objectives of the case, from a pedagogical perspective, is to promote *discovery* learning,[16] then a phased release of the data related to a situation might provide preferable terms for discovery, enabling the steady unfolding of a story. This is particularly favourable for learner groups that might be less willing to invest in extensive preparation by critiquing lengthy case texts. Hence, the *sequential case* has grown in popularity, as it provides bite-sized segments of data for the learner to digest before moving on to the next phase or stage of the case journey. Tutors who prefer to use sequential cases can control the pace at which students are able to progress through case data to prevent some running too far ahead of their peers. By adopting a sequential, phased release of data, tutors can ensure that the learning is fully captured from one stage of the case before permitting the whole group to progress on to the next stage, as illustrated below:

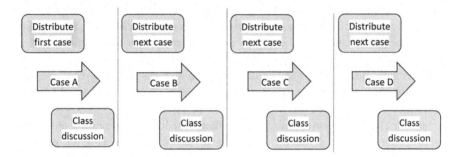

**FIGURE 3.2** The Delivery Schedule for a Sequential Case

There has been a long-standing tradition of incorporating role-play into cases, particularly as they are intended to provide a *willing suspension of disbelief* that the student is in a classroom and rather encourage the learner to immerse themselves into the narrative of the case situation.[17] This can be achieved through many different approaches, depending on the willingness of the group to participate, their developmental level and prior experience, as well as the resourcefulness of the case tutor. There have been occasions where professional actors have been incorporated into case class scenarios to emulate the live case situation, in much the same way that medical schools sometimes utilise actors to stage medical incidents and mock emergencies for trainee practitioners. If the case tutor chooses to break the group into role-play situations, then this enables learners to take different perspectives on any given situation, which is particularly valuable when looking at cases with multiple stakeholders. For example, I have frequently used a case that tells the story of a small business leader preparing to appeal to his shareholders to request further investment in the company's future. I would normally treat the data by breaking the class into two groups, with half playing the role of the business leader and his management team, while the other half plays the role of the shareholders. In scenarios like this it is common to see two very different viewpoints emerging, which enables the learners to appreciate the benefits of multiple viewpoints on any given situation, and that such management opportunities are rarely black and white.

*Digital-media cases* have steadily grown in popularity over the past 20 years, which is not surprising, given the general switch from paper to screen as a function of technology-enhanced learning. However, there are challenges and pitfalls to this switch, especially in terms of participant engagement and memory recall. Research has identified that the capacity for learning is enhanced when taking notes, and that taking notes by pen and paper enhances learning further than the use of a keypad.[18] The other challenge is to ensure that the shift to digital media still encourages an attitude of engagement, curiosity and endeavour among learners in contrast to passive observation. Video cases exist in various formats, but the challenge for the tutor is to determine how to 'treat the data' in such a way that ensures that learners can work critically with it, rather than simply listen to it. More complex digital cases have emerged, which provide a wider variety of access points in the case with different options for navigation through the data. The gamification of case data has enabled the formatting of information to be more reflective of a department store with different floors (levels) and aisles of data in different formats. Learners can choose their own entry point into the case data and can navigate through the different *aisles, departments* and *floors* to access the content in whichever order they choose.

From a class management perspective, digital media cases provide some other useful benefits. Through careful co-ordination it is feasible to track the route(s) that learners take as they navigate through more complex digital cases, to provide a unique insight into learner-engagement with the case analysis process; and which can also provide tutors with opportunities to prompt learners with encouragement where they might appear to be struggling with the navigation or finding themselves at a cul-de-sac. Critics of the gamification of cases might question the degree to which genuine learning might possibly be undermined by the desire for learner entertainment. Certainly, such digital cases should not replace the opportunity for learning through group discussion, whether that is face to face or through other remote learning platforms. The culmination of the digital case is the *simulation case study*, which places the learner into a real-time scenario where they have to analyse, plan and implement decisions in order to address a compelling issue within the case.

> 'Case-sims may help in moving toward double-loop learning as students are able to move away from a teacher-constrained scenario to one that allows freely questioning their own mental models about a particular situation'.
>
> *Panama, Norway and Costa Rica*[19]

Although often requiring some considerable preparation on the part of both the tutor and the learners, these have proven to be extremely popular among learners of all developmental levels, as they provide a genuine context for practical engagement that yields immediate responses, often prompting both a collaborative and competitive dimension for learners at the same time. There are many case development organisations across the world that are significantly investing in simulation and complex digital cases, details of which can be found in Chapter 19.

---

## LESSONS LEARNT

When designing your programme and selecting your cases, it is important to be aware of the IT requirements and any further support that might be needed to ensure all learners or participants can access the same data in the same format that you can. On many occasions I have selected multi-media cases for future programmes only to discover on the day that learners are using different types of devices with different platforms that present the data in different formats, and many of which did not even permit data to be opened. How many times have I been confronted by a frustrated learner showing me their screen emblazoned with the words: 'cookie blocker' or 'you do not have administrator access?' The platforms that we use are changing rapidly to enable greater digital agility, and we need to ensure that our selected cases are suited to the increasingly complex platform requirements for today's learners.

---

*Live cases* have already been described in the earlier part of this section, but they complete the list of cases by *design and structure* insofar as they might not involve any text or digital narrative, but tend to focus on the words of key individual(s) from within an organisation, together with any supportive documentation that they might bring. Tutors can choose to supplement the content of these live contributions with text or other media resources, but the main construct of the case focuses on the words, opinions, motives and actions of the individual subject(s).

Now that you have completed this chapter, you should know that:

1.   Different types of case study can be used in a variety of different ways to promote learning in different contexts.
2.   Before selecting the case, it is helpful to work through the case anatomy hexagon, to be confident you are maximising the potential of your chosen case to achieve all your learning objectives.
3.   Case selection can be broken into three different sets of criteria – by type of content, source of case data, or by presentational design and structure.
4.   Although a shift away from paper towards digital media content can prove to be very enticing to learners, this also brings complex challenges for the learner, the tutor and IT support teams when ensuring that it can be accessed in a consistent and workable format.
5.   The tutor should manage the distraction of *entertaining* the learner with the need to ensure that continued engagement with case material provides genuine scope for development and challenge.

## Notes

1   McNair, 1971
2   Heath, 2015
3   McNair, 1971

4   Corey, 1998
5   Shapiro, 1984
6   Hammond, 2002
7   Erskine, Leenders and Mauffette-Leenders, 2003
8   Adler, University of S. California, quoted in Raufflet and Mills, 2017, p.4
9   Bridgman, 2010
10   Rapp and Ogilvie, 2019
11   Schonell and Macklin, 2018, p. 1
12   McKenna, 1999
13   Yemen, 2012
14   The Case Centre, 2019
15   Yemen, 2012
16   Heath, 2015
17   McNair, 1971
18   Mueller and Oppenheimer, 2014
19   Perez-Bennett, Davidsen and Lopez, 2014, p. 1803

# 4

# ROLES OF THE CASE TUTOR

'The essential fact which makes the case system .... an educational model of the greatest power is that it arouses the interest of the student by making him an active rather than a passive participant'.

*Wallace B. Donham, Dean of Harvard Business School 1919–42*[1]

'We have more weapons that just our voices....the atmosphere is terribly important to student learning and we must pay attention to how the class itself employs its own talents in the pursuit of what it learns. Your body language and the tone of your voice can be as important as the words coming out of your mouth'.

*Switzerland*[2]

This section explores the following questions:

- What are the essential roles of the case tutor before, during and after the case class session?
- When should you adapt your style to suit a changing learner context?
- How do you know when to change your approach?

When I first started teaching with cases, I valued the extensive knowledge and support of my case mentor who, with more than 30 years of experience of case teaching and writing, introduced the notion of the case tutor as *a learning facilitator on a voyage of discovery*. The more I engaged with the case teaching process, the more I started to appreciate that the notion of *voyage of discovery* applies as much to the tutor as to the learner. Every case class is different and provides a unique opportunity for learning through *input, discovery and reflection*. The tutor's role is therefore something of a *voyage* or *journey*, as it differs with each case and is dependent on how the material is to be presented to the learners and how engagement with the case is best facilitated. There are tried and tested methods, from which some generalisations of good practice can be considered – these are each explored later in this section. However, the nature and character of the case tutor also plays a key role in the learning process, and so the first lesson of good practice is to BE YOURSELF. There are plenty of examples on the internet of case class sessions being delivered by experienced tutors, but ultimately it is YOU in YOUR classroom, and YOUR learners will learn best when you play to your own strengths and facilitate the group session in your own style. Naturally our styles need to change and adapt according to the developmental level of our learners; for example, we might find that we need to adopt a more directive (rather than facilitatory) style with those students who are less experienced users of the case method compared with those learners who have already been predisposed to the methodology or who have spent more time in the world experiencing the types of challenges that you will bring into the case classroom. Here are some general suggestions about when and when not to adopt directive styles of delivery:

**TABLE 4.1** Use of Directive Approaches to Case Teaching

|  | *More Directive* | *Non-Directive* |
| --- | --- | --- |
| Pedagogical Objective | To illustrate a concept | To encourage students to develop their own concepts |
| Nature of the Case | Unstructured | Clearly structured |
| Timing in the Course | At the start | Later-on |
| Learner Preparation | Low | High |
| Learner's Experience | Inexperienced | Advanced or experienced |

One common issue raised by tutors is why some case classes work well with, for example, a Master's group, in one year and then not so well in the same Master's programme in the following year. This clearly highlights the collective secret histories of each individual learner in the classroom and the contribution that these make to class group culture, ensuring that every class is a unique experience. Your approach to delivering the case might remain the same, but its impact could be entirely different and elicit a completely different response when used with different groups on the same programme. This demonstrates two key *needs*: firstly, the need for the tutor to gather as much information about their learners as is reasonably possible to inform their adopted style of case delivery; and secondly, to be ready to adapt their style for each individual learner group depending on their level of engagement with the case discussion.

One other factor that can have an impact on the success of the case is the timing of its delivery. Assuming that one of the roles of the tutor is *case selection* for the class, then if the tutor selects the same case for multiple use over a given period of time, it is worth considering how perceptions about the case situation might change over time.

## LESSONS LEARNT

A case tutor from Australia once shared a problem that he encountered when selecting a case focusing on Qantas: the Australian flag-carrier airline. He had selected the same case on previous occasions, and it had been well received by his learners, but more recently Qantas had been hitting the headlines and a shadow was cast over its likely survival (this was following the 9/11 period when many airlines were struggling with downturns in demand). The tutor was aware that his next group of students were unlikely to respond as positively to his Qantas case and that some might consider it to be 'old news', given the current situation facing the company. So rather than share the original case, he adopted a different approach and collated all the current media coverage on the most recent challenges facing Qantas to produce a Qantas B case study, complete with different learning outcomes that could be achieved through a new learning journey. He reported, with relief, that on completing the class discussion, students were so engaged with his new Qantas B case that, when asked if they would like to know where Qantas had come from to get to the position they now found themselves facing, the students responded with a resounding "yes, you bet we do!" Following this response, he handed out the original Qantas case, to an enthusiastic and engaged student group. A typical example of a 'chicken and egg' approach to case selection.

Once a good case has been selected, which seems to work well in the classroom, it is difficult to let it go. But every case has its shelf life, and students will soon provide the clues you need if your favourite case requires a dignified closure, and new materials need to be sought. If *case selection* represents the first responsibility of the tutor, then here are a few more key generalisations, when considering the roles of the case tutor.

## 4.1 Empowerer of learners

It might seem counter-intuitive for professors, lecturers or scholars to consider relinquishing so-called classroom *power* to the learner group, but if the case study is truly to engage the learner, then they need to get involved. I often use the analogy of learning to drive. Your student can read all the car manuals in the world, but until they get into the driving seat they are not going to learn to drive. Remember the saying by Confucius in Chapter 2:

> Tell me and I will forget;
> Show me and I may remember;
> Involve me and I will understand.

Getting learners involved in the driving seat of a case journey encourages participation, motivation, problem-solving and critical thinking as part of the case learning process. Occasionally, it can be a real challenge to encourage our learners into the driving seat, but sometimes the greater challenge is for us to get out of the seat to let them in.

## 4.2 Manager of group learning

Just because the student is now in the driving seat, they still need a driving instructor to be able to ensure that they are following correct practice and procedures to navigate a healthy learning journey. Without the driving instructor, the learner has the potential to make some very dangerous mistakes that can leave others in peril too. In the same way, the case tutor plays a key role in managing the group learning process, whether we are engaging in directive guidance or providing more hands-off facilitation. Ultimately, we still have to answer for the progress of our learners, so, on that basis, we need to retain the role of manager of group learning.

## 4.3 Good listener

As lecturers, we naturally have the capacity to communicate knowledge in an input-driven context. We most probably find speaking very easy, and yet listening can be a greater challenge. I am often reminded that we were born with only one mouth but two ears, so listening must be important. We can listen without really hearing, but active listening is a far more challenging responsibility for the case tutor, as we need to consider what we are hearing, what we are not hearing, and what might be meant by what is being spoken. We might have already mapped out our own journey through the case data, but if a student begins a line of enquiry that takes the group along a different route (possibly into unchartered or unplanned territory), then our inclination might be to speak over this individual to redirect the group back onto our planned pathway, but to do so has several risks. Firstly, if we do not appear to be listening and valuing the point that our learner is trying to make, then they might feel undermined and less inclined to offer a response in future. Secondly, it might just be that the learner has discovered a new aspect to the situation which the tutor had not considered before, and to prematurely recapture control of the conversation might steer the learners away from a valid new visiting point in the case journey. Poor listening risks disempowering our learners and can lead to disengagement or confusion.

## 4.4 Discussion Director

Asking the right question at the right time in the right manner is a key function of the case tutor for effective engagement with the learners. Types of questions and approaches to developing the right questions are discussed further in Chapter 6. In most other learning contexts, it is reasonable for learners to expect the tutor to answer questions, but key to effective engagement with the case process is the class agreement that the tutor is the question-master and the learners' responsibility is to consider responses to these questions as the tutor facilitates the journey. Selecting the right type of question ensures that the learners' journey through the case data continues to progress in a meaningful manner to achieve planned key learning objectives.

It is very important that the learner is aware of these different responsibilities if they are to engage effectively with the case learning process. It might require some form of student induction into case learning to ensure that the 'rules of the game' are clearly established, agreed and understood, before the class commences. There are resources available to support student inductions with the case method and these are explored further in the final section of this book.

## 4.5 Stimulator of student interest

Choosing the right case is just one of the responsibilities for the tutor that serves to maintain learner engagement and interest. Knowing your student is key, and knowing what types of approaches are most likely to stimulate and maintain their interest will pay dividends for student learning in the long run. As the case method involves a journey of discovery towards a clearer picture of a particular situation or sequence of events, then undoubtedly part of the challenge is to ensure that engagement with the data promotes the building of that picture. If the so-called *curtains are pulled back too quickly* to reveal this picture, then this could undermine the discovery process, leaving the learner with little to do for themselves. While managing this 'expository' component of the case process, the tutor needs to ensure that they neither underestimate their learner's intelligence nor overestimate their knowledge and capacity for active learning.

Our job as case tutors is not to entertain our learners, but it helps to ensure the subject matter and the way that we choose to treat the data piques the learner's interest, leaving them curious and hungry to pursue more.

## 4.6 Developer of critical learning points

The case is no more than a well-told story if it fails to take the student to a point at which learning can take place. *Key learning objectives* and *interesting visiting points* are key to effective journeying through the case data. The student might imagine that the goal of the case is to get to journey's end, but it is often the journey itself that is key to effective learning. Sometimes, rather than rush through issues to move towards the end of the journey, the tutor might prefer to pause and linger around certain themes to enable learners to reflect more on the prevailing issue. Students might prefer to move the conversation forwards, but deeper reflection and analysis can help to promote critical thinking as the group discussion delves deeper into a specific point; which subsequently helps to lock in learning. This practice of managing breadth and depth when planning a case journey is explored further in Chapter 6.

## 4.7 Specialist knowledge provider

The tutor is often respected by the class as the specialist knowledge provider, and rightly so. Not only are you in your position by virtue of your knowledge and experience, but you are also more than likely able to incorporate information in support of case preparation that the learner is unable to access. The *case teaching note* would normally be expected to provide additional information about the organisation and the issues and situations that it is facing. More often than not, recommended 'model' answers or examples of how the author has used the case in the past are also included in this note. If you are the author of the case itself, then undoubtedly you will have had exposure and access to organisational data which will put you at an advantage to the rest of the learner group, but this position comes with two stark warnings:

Warning No. 1: your students might feel undermined if you appear to have access to data that they cannot access. It is important to ensure that you manage data, knowledge, access and expository learning issues with care to keep the learners 'on track' with the case journey, without expecting too much or undermining them with what might ultimately feel like a parlour game if handled carelessly.

Warning No. 2: you might not be the only specialist knowledge provider in the room. No amount of intelligence on your learner group will unearth all their secret histories, family networks and other associations. Just occasionally you might be surprised to find that someone in the room knows more about the company in the case study than you do:

---

### LESSONS LEARNT

It was this latter point that caught me by surprise some years ago when delivering a case study on the marketing of whiskey from a Scottish distillery. I had used the case with undergraduates before and so was reasonably confident with the data and the likely journey that the discussion might take. However, on this occasion there was one student in the room who seemed more confident about tackling this data than everyone else (including me)! I was perplexed as both the name of the company and the key character's name had been changed to disguise its origin. Nonetheless, this student persisted with confident challenges to each question and issue that was raised. Eventually, we reached a tipping point as the student made a comment about the organisation that I was confident could not be found from the data within the case. Uncharacteristically, I paused the discussion journey and asked the student where she had found such information, feeling confident that she would be unable to answer given the disguises that had been built into the case. She put her case notes down and smiled at me, then to my surprise, she confidently announced the real name of both the company and its marketing manager, before declaring that, after all, she should know, up until six months previously, she had been a buyer for this distillery!

---

## 4.8 Timekeeper

Unavoidably, most case sessions will run overtime if we allow them too. One sign of a really successful case session will be the level of positive and critical engagement in the discussion process, but it is important to ensure movement through the case data, so that all the interesting visiting points have been captured and the key learning objectives have been met. To this end, we add to our list of roles the timekeeper. It might be helpful to work through a schedule of the discussion in advance, mapping out the likely amount of time needed to complete each section of the case discussion and analysis.

We can easily become overoptimistic when we come to plotting our case class sessions, so I took some advice from a Harvard professor, who had several decades more experience than I, when he advised me to 'always build redundancy into case class planning'. At first, I had no idea what he was talking about, but then he started to map out a teaching schedule to help me to understand. Imagine you have a ten-week module, with three hours of in-class delivery each week. As part of the planning for the module, you are looking to incorporate ten case studies to ensure that students can utilise their investigative skills to fully explore all the key learning outcomes of the module. If we plan out the sessions in advance, then it is highly likely that each case we select will enable us to capture, for example, three areas of learning theory or good practice. By *building redundancy into course planning*, you ensure that there is always a second occasion to revisit each of these key areas of learning theory. This is illustrated in the following table.

Let's suggest that each aspect of learning theory and best practice is denoted by a letter, so in week 1, the three areas covered are A, B and C. You will note that in the following schedule, these three areas are revisited in weeks 5, 7 and 9, respectively. In this way, every aspect of learning has a second outing, and some might event warrant three or four outings.

**TABLE 4.2** Illustration of Teaching Schedule

| Week of teaching | Key learning theory | Key learning theory | Key learning theory |
|---|---|---|---|
| 1 | A | B | C |
| 2 | D | E | F |
| 3 | G | H | I |
| 4 | J | K | L |
| 5 | A | M | N |
| 6 | D | E | H |
| 7 | G | B | G |
| 8 | E | J | K |
| 9 | N | I | C |
| 10 | F | M | L |

## 4.9 Recorder of discussion

Traditionally, the case tutor would also be the blackboard planner. The blackboard was then replaced for many by the white board and then more recently by interactive digiboards. And today there are any number of different recording tools that we can use to capture the learning progress of a case discussion. Some tutors prefer to use a third party, such as a classroom assistant, to populate content onto the whiteboard (or equivalent), others promote opportunities for student participants to capture the data for everyone in the group, while others prefer to maintain control of the recordings. Either way, it is our responsibility to ensure that our learners have some form of means to capture the learning from what can otherwise be mistakenly considered little more than an interesting discussion. We have heard it said often that a picture can paint a thousand words, so the tutor should ensure that the discussion is captured in such a manner that can maximise the level of engagement, participation and ultimately in a manner that locks in learning.

## 4.10 Establisher of group consensus

Harvard Professor Kasturi Rangan once proposed that one of the key roles of the instructor was to manage the 'choreography' of the class, suggesting that 'an instructor teaching by this method leads students through the key conceptual and decision issues in the class without necessarily prejudging the correctness of their students' contributions'. He argued that the class therefore becomes an 'instrument for inductive frameworking'.[3]

Learning is often, although not always, a democratic process. And management education can be a challenging subject for those learners who have origins in more systematic tenets of thinking, presenting possible scenarios and solutions where there is rarely an absolute right or wrong answer to a given situation. This is one area where the case methods excel at providing a slice of reality, as they emulates the workplace well when requiring decisions to be made where there are inadequate or incomplete data sets (evidence), leading to individuals having to handle assumptions, co-operate and often to compromise. The need to establish group consensus is commonly the only means possible by which the tutor can advance the discussion beyond specific sticking points and, as such, is a well-established practice.

## 4.11 Approachable and articulate

Arguably all tutors ought to be approachable and articulate, but the case tutor particularly so. If the case tutor's role is to provide the types of guidance that have already been listed in this section, they are most likely to achieve this if the case is conducted in an approachable and articulate manner, without which the capacity for inductive learning through the case method would be seriously compromised.

PAUSE FOR A MOMENT: take another look at the 11 different attributes of the case tutor, while reflecting on your own approaches to teaching and learning. Rank them in order of your perceived capacity to achieve each attribute. Undoubtedly some areas will be better developed than others. The key reflection should not so much be concerned about further development of your areas of strength, but rather to consider what interventions you could undertake to build on the areas of present weakness?

Now that you have completed this chapter, you should know that:

1.  The function of the case tutor is a critical part of the case learning strategy. The tutor's ability to guide the learner through a voyage of discovery is paramount to effective inductive learning.
2.  The approach undertaken by the tutor will differ with each learner context, from a more directive role for the inexperienced learner and for those learners exploring a complex new area of management theory, to a far less directive role adopted by tutors when teaching more experienced or executive learners.
3.  There are many different functions that a case tutor might need to undertake at any given moment. The skill of the instructor is not so much to demonstrate mastery in any one of these attributes, but rather to be able to manage the multi-functional delivery of these roles at any one given time, throughout the case discussion.

## Notes

1  Quoted in Gragg, 1940, p. 1
2  Schmenner, 2002, p. 3
3  Rangan, 1996, p. 2

# 5

# PRE-CLASS CASE PREPARATION

'It all begins with a commitment to set-up time and effort. The layout of the class-room must encourage participation. Secondly.... There is no room for anonymity in the case classroom. Lastly, materials must be available'.

*Canada*[1]

This section explores the following questions:

- What are the essential tasks that you, as the case tutor, need to do to ensure you are properly prepared to deliver the case?
- What does the student need to do to prepare for the case session?
- What creative thinking can be invested into learning environment, to ensure that it is most conducive to case study learning?

One of the most common complaints that I hear when discussing the use of the case method with other tutors is that students are insufficiently prepared to make the most of the case session, leaving tutors to make quick decisions to shift their delivery approach to Plan B. Scratch far enough below the surface, and it soon becomes clear that tutors too are often under-prepared for the case session. We have already discussed that the learning journey is based on the premise of the 'willing suspension of disbelief', (see Chapter 2). Therefore, any adaptation to the physical learning environment could well enhance the lear-ner's capacity to connect better with the situation and issues that arise from the case discussion.

It is all about preparation; therefore, this chapter explores what steps could be taken to ensure that, firstly, you as the tutor are fully prepared; secondly, that your students are fully prepared; and, thirdly, that their learning environment has been managed (wherever possible) to maximise the learning opportunity.

## 5.1 The Tutor's Preparation

Odd as it might at first seem, the first task that a case tutor should consider is their own preparation, before thinking about supporting the learner's preparation. The importance of knowing your learners has been explored in previous chapters, but it is worth remembering that any intelligence that can be gathered to identify learner behaviour will help the tutor to anticipate the learner's probable response to specific scenarios.

---

### LESSONS LEARNT

I decided to try out a new case study on a group of young learners, who were inexperienced with the case method of learning. I chose a topic that I felt confident they would have strong feelings about and decided to separate the group according to whether they supported or opposed a certain course of action that was central to the case. I then proceeded to group all those that were 'opposed' into a group that were to present arguments 'for' the proposal, and all those who had voted 'in favour,' to take the perspective of group members arguing 'against' it. I had not researched my group and under-estimated the strength of feeling that group members held towards this provocative subject. The discussion soon became highly emotionally charged and I ended up having to dismiss one group five minutes ahead of the second group, mindful that spirits were high with a toxic mixture of anger and frustration. It took a few days before the group gathered together once again and a different strategy was adopted to diffuse any lingering tensions, but the memory of this event still lingers (of more than 20 years ago), as it taught me the importance of knowing my learner group and, in particular, their emotional capacity to manage certain subjects and approaches.

---

So, getting to know the 'class profile' is at the very top of my list of 'first priorities' to consider when preparing and selecting the right case for the class session. This is then accompanied by:

1. Determining clear learning objectives for the case session, which are in line with the programme's learning objectives, and then ensuring the session is realistically resourced to fulfil them.
2. Identifying the available case resources/materials, including consideration for what formats are available and how/when you will enable the student to access this material. Will all case data be released in one batch or as phased release?
3. What links can be bridged between the case content and subject theories, good management practices and to other subject areas?
4. In what ways will the different case sessions be sequenced, to ensure the right balance of breadth and depth of learning, within the timeframe?

5.   Does this case session link to any assessment criteria?

6.   What instructions will be needed to encourage effective student preparation?

Once these top seven priorities have been established, you are ready to get started on your session planning by asking the *how* questions. Remember, all seven factors listed above should inform the way that you think about the following:

*How* do you master the facts of the case, to ensure that you are really clear about the themes, issues, actions, motives and context that frame the case? Students will soon notice if you have not fully familiarised yourself with all the content of the case.

*How* will you draft your own case delivery plan (often referred to as a map or teaching plan), ensuring that you also cross-reference your personal plan to the author's teaching note? It is only too tempting to simply adopt the author's approach from the published teaching note, but remember that the author wrote this case neither for you nor for your students. You know your students far better than the author, so make sure that you develop your own plan and then cross-reference to the author's note to add value to your own insights.

*How* will you manage the discussion? Knowing your students, what is the probable direction of their discussions? And having considered this, what would therefore be the best structure of a teaching plan to support learning through the discussion? How much time is necessary for the various blocks of the discussion to ensure a balance of breadth and depth of analysis and critical engagement?

*How* do you guard against any hidden case traps? Cases often provide a limited data set, which could lead students to make inadequate assumptions that can lead to traps or ambiguities in the case discussion. It will benefit the case tutor to have a practice run through these types of scenarios in advance of the class session, in order to work out the likely implications.

*How* do you determine the right questions to ask? As the next chapter will demonstrate, asking the right questions is a critical element of an effective case discussion that promotes learning and development. Having established the facts of the case and determined the purpose of the class session, the next step is to prepare the most effective 'lead' or 'primary' questions that will help the class to make progress.

*How* do you tackle the gaps in knowledge? While working through these questions, it is worth considering if there are any intermediate issues that must be tackled before the class can progress to the end of the case journey? This could involve the inclusion of a 'mini-lecture' or other form of input session that bridges any gaps in knowledge to promote ongoing engagement with the situation and themes at the centre of the case.

*How* do you provoke engagement? Knowing your learners, what would be the best springboards to provoke thought and controversy? It is often this approach to class facilitation that develops the mastery of the case tutor. The case master will look to establish the best connection points, provoking learners to engage with the case content, not simply by stimulating logical reasoning but also with emotional intelligence and each individual's personal perspectives, in order to foster a collective response.

*How* will you best deal with the *analysis* of case data? Cases often come complete with a range of different types of data sets, presenting opportunities for analysis and interpretation. Some management students will be reluctant to engage with numerical data, and so the tutor will need to find the most engaging approach to foster curiosity and intrigue, enough to stimulate engagement with the data and, where necessary, the task of number crunching. The timing of this is often critical too.

*How* can you connect issues raised in the case to earlier lectures/future topics/ other themes to ensure that the case is fully integrated into the course and does not present itself as an abstract stand-alone component? Carefully crafted 'supportive' or 'secondary' questions will help to achieve this.

*How* will you establish a clear case opening and a robust conclusion to the case discussion? Strong and clear case openings promote early engagement, which is critical to effective empowering of students into the case journey. The case should conclude in a manner that ensures that the learners are clear of its purpose, its 'takeaways' and how this links to the key learning objectives of the programme.

*How* will the key elements of the discussion be captured to develop critical learning points and to enable thoughts and suggestions to be rationalised? This is often achieved by the use of white-/blackboards, but it pays to ensure that you have already thought through a structure for the board in advance of the class session. Teaching notes often include exhibits with the author's suggestions for board plans and layouts, including key headings and sample responses.

Many of these *how* functions will inform a case teaching plan or map, which is considered further in the next chapter. Having considered your own preparations, it is time to then consider those of your learners.

## 5.2 The Learner's Preparation

> 'Case method learning should be seen as an exercise that moves through stages. Individual preparation serves two purposes. First, it prepares each participant to contribute in discussion group meetings. Most important it prepares participants to learn from what others say'
>
> *Harvard, US[2]*

The concept of the case study has become an increasingly familiar part of the student diet in most post-compulsory educational management programmes these days, but different institutions form different views about what constitutes a case study and how the student ought to participate in the case process. As Harvard Professor Kasturi Rangan once described: 'case teaching is not a tactical pedagogical tool but rather the very heart of a teaching strategy'.[3] However, in the same paper, he went on to describe four different approaches to delivering the case study. So, as a case tutor, one of your seven key priorities (as listed in the previous section) is the preparation of the learner. In most situations this will be enhanced by some form of induction process at the beginning of the programme, where the students can be introduced to the case concept and gain an understanding of what is often referred to as the educational contract between tutor and learner.[4] In these discussions, both sides agree a set of expectations of one another. In doing so, this creates an opportunity to address the art of learning and the learner's part in that process. Although cases studies can often be tied to assessment plans, it might help to offer an introductory case study at the beginning of the programme so that students can test and learn what is required without the undue pressure of grades and assessment benchmarks. This 'trial case' or 'warm-up' case provides an opportunity for initial feedback to ensure that all parties are agreed on future expectations. This approach to establishing the ground rules can also be an opportunity to convey what the course is trying to achieve and how engagement with the process will develop key employability skills. The Case Centre has developed a very helpful online interactive study guide for students to support this induction process.[5] In the British context, these types of metrics are becoming increasingly valuable for the University Teaching Excellence Framework. Further discussion might also include how future cases will be delivered and discussions facilitated, how performance will be measured, and how this might contribute to their assessment plans.

Here are a few suggestions that might be worth considering as part of a typical early discussion about the case method:

- Cases will always be provided xx days in advance and students are expected to have read and analysed the case in preparation for a class discussion.
- Key questions linked to the main themes of a class discussion will be issued with the case in advance of the class, for consideration in readiness for the discussion.
- Students are required to bring a one-page note/synopsis with them to the case class, outlining their responses to the xx questions set with the case.
- Students will be allocated to tutorial/syndicate groups which will be scheduled before each case class, to discuss the key issues for analysis and discussion in preparation for the main case class.
- Case tutors will not answer any questions during the case discussion, except for clarification of any technical details.
- Participants are expected to contribute to the case discussion and might choose to agree or disagree with other comments made by their tutor or by their peers and should be expected to defend their views.
- Where appropriate and where it is possible, students are expected to undertake further preparatory research into the company/industry/sector before the case class to use as further evidence in support of their contribution to the discussion.

## 5.3 Preparing the Environment

We are all stimulated to a greater or lesser degree by our external environment. Work environments matter, and so too do learning environments. If you were to take a journey into an organisation, you would not have to step too far across the threshold of its reception at the operational base to get a *feel* for the organisation: its culture, its workforce priorities, its values and its operational practices. The visual cues tell a story and enable us to take a measure of the type of organisation that we are engaging with. The case study journey can be enhanced when the context can be somehow captured in the physical learning environment.

---

## LESSONS LEARNT

I recall from my early days of lecturing having an equal measure of admiration and horror when hearing of one of my colleague's antics with his 'Organisational Studies' group. It seemed that the University's lecture halls were never good enough for this group and at the beginning of every class session students would be whisked off to another mystery destination: the boardroom of a local business, the warehouse of a distribution centre, the shop floor of a retail group to name but a few. On one occasion I even heard of students being found in the centre of a large roundabout at an intersection of two major roads. I was assured that this roundabout was big enough to accommodate the student group (it was so large that it incorporated three very mature trees in the centre). I later discovered that the learners were exploring the challenges of operational decision making in a fast-moving consumer goods (FMCG) environment – the noise and bustle of vehicles making their way around the roundabout were apparently simulating the challenges of the noises and distractions for the operational managers in their FMCG environment.

While I am not too sure of the legalities of this approach, it nonetheless struck a chord for the learners who were caught-up in their stimulating environments which both provoked and challenged them in their thinking and learning.

---

Environments matter, and anything – large or small – that we can do to stimulate the senses will also play its part in supporting the learning process. I recently heard of a professor from Bentley University who was explored the challenges of online case delivery. While noting that it was therefore difficult to envisage how the physical learning environment could be enhanced to promote a more favourable e-learning experience, it was agreed that, as the learners were exploring issues related to executive strategy formation, they would all be encouraged to dress formally for their remote case class, so that each person that addressed the class discussion would immediately be noticed by their executive dress code, which was perceived to imply a particular message about the nature of the tasks that the group was exploring.

If you are running a case with a small group, which is shaped around the theme of management decision-making, then is it possible to utilise a space that can be adapted to emulate a board room for the business? Other visual cues might include use of the organisation's logo for the door on entry or for visual displays on screens in the classroom. While it might be impossible to take the learner to the organisation, it might be possible to bring the organisation to the learner through video technology. Similarly, visiting speakers from an organisation (or even actors pretending to be visiting speakers from an organisation) and logo-emblazed packs with extra information (exhibits) about the organisation could all help as scene-setters, providing visual cues by introducing something of the culture of the case organisation.

PAUSE FOR A MOMENT: think about a case that you have enjoyed delivering, and ask yourself whether there are other ways of organising the external environment that could enhance the visual cues that accompany the learner as he or she participates in the case discussion.

Anything that can be done to affect the environment within which the case is experienced is likely to support the learning process and in doing so will fulfil McNair's proposal of delivering a 'slice of reality'.

Now that you have completed this chapter, you should know that:

1. As a case tutor, your preparation will make all the difference for the student learning journey. This preparation begins with your understanding of the student profile of your case class.
2. Students should be invited to think through the implications of the case programme and to discern how their engagement in the learning process will enable development and challenge of both their knowledge base and of key future employability skills.
3. Broader consideration should be given to the physical learning environment and how visual cues during the case group discussion can positively affect the learner journey.

## Notes

1  Erskine, Leenders and Mauffette-Leenders, 2003, p. 17
2  Corey, 1998
3  Rangan, 1996, p. 2
4  Heath, 2015
5  See www.thecasecentre.org/guide

# 6

# APPROACHES TO CASE TEACHING

'We believe that when educational objectives focus on qualities of mind (curiosity, judgement, wisdom), qualities of person (character, sensitivity, integrity, responsibility), and the ability to apply general concepts and knowledge to specific situations, discussion pedagogy may well be very effective'.

*USA[1]*

This section explores the following themes:

- How to create the case map to effectively plan a journey through the case data.
- How to decide on viewpoint in the case, while determining different roles for the student within the case narrative.
- Effective ways of opening and guiding the case discussion.
- Getting students engaged and involved.
- Hints for bringing the case to a closure.
- How to get case feedback and follow-up.
- Adapting cases for undergraduate, graduate, executive and work-based learners.

If you have already read the preceding chapters, you will understand by now that there is no silver bullet when it comes to case teaching. There are as many approaches as there are different types of case study, but the key to effective learning is to marry the right type of case data with the specific learner group by adopting the correct delivery plan or teaching approach:

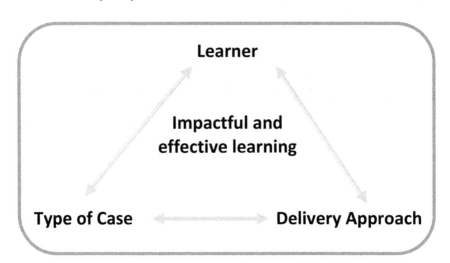

**FIGURE 6.1** The threefold relationship for impactful case learning

This chapter explores this threefold relationship and considers useful generalisations when preparing a teaching and delivery approach for your learner group. The starting point for this focuses on mapping the student journey through the case.

## 6.1 The case map

Every time I take a journey, there are three things that I essentially need to know:

- Where is my starting point – A?
- Where is my destination point – B – in relation to my starting point?
- What route options are available to me to migrate from A to B?

Armed with answers to these three questions I can pretty much migrate my way from anywhere to anywhere, and these days this is made even simpler with the advent of satnav and online maps that do most of the thinking for us. Nonetheless, in order for the satnav to work, the three same basic questions are raised. Once the satnav has determined where your starting point is, you can punch in the details of your preferred destination point, and then it will quickly identify the best options for your journey. Although it is easy to become dependent on the device to determine your route, over time and repeated use of the journey, you will start to become familiar with the routes, the interesting visiting points along the way and even some alternative routes, should you wish to divert from the original route.

Let's say that I want to make a trip from my home city of Worcester, UK, to visit Harvard University in Cambridge, Massachusetts. I know I can take a flight from London Heathrow or from Birmingham International Airport, which will take me to the US. To get to Birmingham Airport I could take a train to Birmingham and from there a connecting train to the airport. For Heathrow, I would need to take a train that would take me through Oxford and Reading to central London, before taking a connecting train to Heathrow. My Birmingham flight could get me to New York, from where I could take a connecting flight to Boston, but my Heathrow flight would take me direct to Boston. Once at Boston Logan International Airport, a connecting train would take me to the city from where a taxi would take me the short journey across to Harvard in Cambridge. If I was in a hurry, upon arriving at Boston Logan International Airport I could take a taxi direct to Harvard. I could chart my journey options on the following simple map:

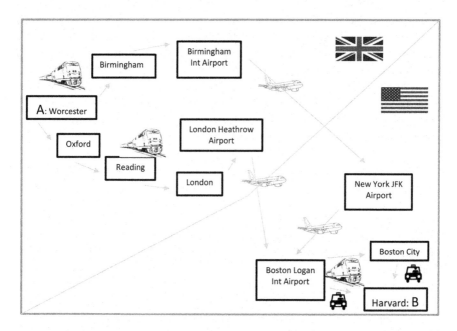

**FIGURE 6.2** Planning a journey

In much the same way as a satnav or old-fashioned paper map would allow you to plan and track your route, the development of a case map will enable you to plan your journey through case data, taking in interesting visiting points en route and perhaps even enabling you to migrate off the well-trodden path to explore new areas. The case map begins with the same three questions: Where is your starting point? Where is your destination point? And what route options are available to you? Once these have been considered, the case mapping process can begin.

Sometimes it is easier to start the mapping with the end in mind. The destination point should represent the key learning objectives for the group session. Once these have been determined, the next step will be to consider your starting point. This requires some knowledge or awareness of the learner group – their prior experiences, backgrounds and the learning that they have undertaken before the case session. All these factors serve as pre-requisites to the case class and therefore influence the most effective learning approach. Without this information, it would be easy to prepare a session that either underestimates the learners' intelligence or overestimates their capacity to manage the journey through the case.

Once these two points have been adequately captured, then the journey planning can begin. Remember, the journey that was planned from Worcester to Harvard offered travellers the opportunity to take in some *interesting visiting points* along the way, and it is these points that play a crucial role in enabling the learner to remain motivated and engaged throughout the journey. For example, when passing through Oxford or London on the way to the airport, these locations provide a great opportunity to pause the journey and linger while the traveller delves deeper into the interesting locations that can be found in these cities. In the same way, the case student can use the interesting visiting points of the case journey as 'resting points' or 'pause-points' along the journey, and while the students linger in these places they can also serve to promote more in-depth analysis. For example, take a strategy class where you are trying to assess the performance of a company. Oxford becomes a SWOT analysis, and London can become a PESTLE analysis, where students can take time out to consider each part of the analysis, based on what information they have captured so far on their journey. In this way, the map does not just serve as a two-dimensional route planner, but it also enables the case tutor to manage both breadth and depth within the learning journey. As the Worcester-Harvard map illustrates, there are different routes that the learner could take across the map, and different visiting points could be explored when an alternative route is planned (e.g. from Birmingham to New York JFK airport). It is therefore easy to imagine how the same case study could be used for different student groups, taking different journeys, with different visiting points, achieving different learning objectives. Although the map could be populated with many different visiting points, the tutor should limit each journey to cover no more than between three and five interesting points of analysis, or else the capacity for student learning and recall is likely to diminish.

There are three further components to the map that help to pinpoint the approach that the tutor might wish to take. Firstly, the arrows. Each visiting point of the map is connected to the next with arrows, with which the tutor can navigate a journey from A to B. Each arrow represents a carefully crafted question. Crafting the question will enable the tutor to determine the direction to which the learners will be encouraged to migrate. Careless questions can therefore lead the group in circles or potentially towards a cul-de-sac with no obvious place left to progress towards.

The map should also provide consideration for *orientation* and *mode of treatment*. When considering *orientation*, the tutor might wish to explore the viewpoint or perspective that the student is inclined to take in relation to the characters in the case. For example, the student might be invited to metaphorically step into the shoes of one of the key characters of the case study or be a hypothetical character who is not included within the existing narrative (such as a management consultant advising the case protagonist). Where a case includes multiple characters then different students could be invited to assume different roles, which could support a role-play approach to the case data.

Finally, when considering mode of treatment, the pre-requisites (prior learning experiences) of the students will determine which learning approach the case should adopt. There are four principle approaches: inductive (developing theory), deductive (applying known theory), divergent (creative and explorative thinking) and convergent (data analytical).

Each of the factors considered so far are explored in greater depth in the sections below and summarised in a template for a case map, which is proposed in the figure below:

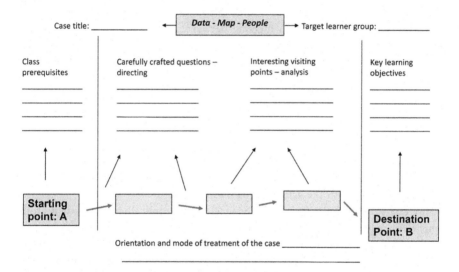

**FIGURE 6.3** A Template for the Case Teaching Map

A note of caution:

'There is a danger in attempting to manage a case method class so that the students arrive at a particular conclusion or theoretical construct. If the instructor controls the discussion so carefully that he or she can plan each step and makes certain that the class takes each step, the experience becomes a thinly-veiled lecture with the case as an illustration'.

*Darden School, USA[2]*

This cautionary note serves as a reminder that, although it is helpful to map out the potential routes for a journey of discovery, the planning process should then leave the case tutor confident enough to release control to the learners, ensuring wherever possible that the case discussion is student-driven, thus providing a genuine process of discovery and reflection, rather than a contrived and rigid set of processes towards a goal.

## 6.2 Deciding on viewpoint

There are many different roles that the student could be given when invited to participate in a case discussion. Prior knowledge of the student group will help to determine the most appropriate role. Role play is a common practice when conducting a case session, but some student groups might feel condescended to when invited to participate, so it is important to pitch or frame the opportunity in the correct manner to ensure buy-in from the participants. This works particularly well when characters from the case have significantly different attributes or contrasting orientations to the main problem outlined in the case narrative. For example, I often use a case that includes a meeting between an organisation's newly arrived *leader* and its workforce. The *leader* had previously spent 100 days reviewing different sections of this large and complex organisation and was now ready to make his first all-staff presentation outlining what he saw as the three future priorities for the organisation. The case study provides a thorough breakdown of the findings of his 100-day *walkabout*. When presented to the class, students are invited to imagine they are representatives of various different sections of the organisation drawn together to advise the new leader on how he should 'pitch' future priorities. A video of the *what happened next* all-staff presentation provides a fitting conclusion to the group discussion, accompanied by an opportunity to compare and contrast the group's proposals with the actual points presented.

If a case study includes a single individual or protagonist, then the student group might either be invited to consider the case from the perspective of this character or as an 'external consultant' who has been drafted into the organisation to advise the key character. In this latter scenario, the student playing the role of the consultant needs not only to take into consideration the facts of the case, but also the personality, opinions and motives of the character within the organisation. In each scenario the learner will be guided by carefully crafted questions to analyse the situation in the case and to make recommendations or propose possible solutions to the problem.

Each perspective or viewpoint draws different management skills from the learner, which might include:

- decision-making
- problem-solving
- problem-identification
- data analysis
- negotiator/persuader
- discussion-handler
- judgement of different courses of action

- balancing intuition and analysis
- risk management
- sensitive listening

## 6.3 Asking the right questions

One of the key responsibilities of the case tutor is to be the *question-raiser*. Choosing the right question and the correct timing for each question can make all the difference, potentially turning a dull Q&A session into a dynamic and engaging discussion. Different approaches to questioning can elicit different responses as indicated in the ten suggestions below:[3]

> Question 1: What is the problem here? (Orientation: Problem identification)
>
> Question 2: How do you feel about….? (Orientation: Attitude/opinion eliciting)
>
> Question 3: What do you notice about? (Orientation: Attention drawing)
>
> Question 4: What other examples are there? (Orientation: Thought-provoking/ generalising from the specific)
>
> Question 5: How do you think X felt in this situation? (Orientation: Sensitivity to others/empathy generation)
>
> Question 6: What might be done to? (Orientation: Problem solving/reducing)
>
> Question 7: What else might be done? (Orientation: Generation of alternatives)
>
> Question 8: Would you do that? (Orientation: Personal Preferences)
>
> Question 9: What would be the 'cost'? (Orientation: Proposal evaluation)
>
> Question 10: What would you do? (Orientation: Identification)

It is quite common practice to provide a few generalised questions when issuing the case study to the learners in advance of the class. This might help the participants to understand the probable focus of the case discussion. Students can be invited to consider their responses to these questions as part of their preparation for the class and, where appropriate, they might be advised to submit their responses in advance or to a syndicate group scheduled to meet in advance of the main case discussion.

The case tutor should begin preparations for the main case discussion with some primary questions, which will determine the orientation and direction of the journey through the case data. The tutor should also have in mind some secondary or ancillary questions that can pick up on the student responses and promote further progress through the case data, by supporting or reinforcing the *directing* nature of the primary questions. Examples of these types of secondary questions might include:

- Could you explain the reasoning behind your idea?
- What evidence did you use to determine that?
- Is there data to support ...............'s idea?
- Could you tell us what assumptions you made to proceed with your analysis?

- Can you see anything we have left out?
- I'm interested in knowing how you determined that?

Further clarifying questions might also be adopted where a particularly inexperienced group might use phrases that are inconsistent with normal management terminology. In these situations, it may be helpful to rephrase the student's contribution to ensure a more appropriate set of management terms are adopted and that these preferred phrases are clear and understood by the whole group. Such clarifying questions might include:

- Let's make sure we understand what you are saying…
- Are you saying that…?
- Could we say that…?
- Is this the essence of what you are saying…?

Remember, some questions tackle *breadth* (getting from A to B), and some will tackle *depth*, which are interesting visiting points where further analysis can be undertaken.

The number of questions and the frequency with which they need to be deployed will be determined by the developmental level of the learner, their degree of engagement and their familiarity with the topic under discussion.

## PAUSE FOR A MOMENT: CONSIDER THE FOLLOWING INCIDENT CASE STUDY: JAMES WALKER AND THE LINE MANAGER

James arrived at Johannesburg-based St Stephens Solutions, a project management firm, 18 months ago, having previously held roles at two rival organisations, also based in South Africa. He moved to South Africa from Australia five years ago and was keen to broaden his experiences as a project manager, having initially impressed the recruitment team at St Stephens with his recent portfolio of clients, with whom he had successfully been contracted to manage significant construction projects.

He reported to Bryan Pollard, who had been with the firm for more than ten years and who was responsible for a team of seven project managers, including James. At first, James seemed to get off to a good start, picking up new projects and working closely with Bryan and his team to develop project proposals in accordance with the client's demands. The clients seemed to take an immediate liking to James and his rapport seemed to be warm, friendly and positive. However, Bryan soon started to sense that something wasn't quite right as, one by one, the other members of his team began making comments about James's performance. James seemed to be very good at doing exactly what was requested and little more. He tended to find the simplest and most straight forward way to complete a task, rarely doing more than was asked of him, but always taking time to build his own networks and friendships with the clients. In some contexts, this would be fine, but often in Bryan's experience, projects would not go to plan and the team were frequently required to go the extra mile to complete additional work or manage other issues that had not initially been anticipated. One by one the team started to make comments back to Bryan suggesting James was avoiding these issues wherever possible, leaving other members of the team to pick up the extra workload. Bryan could sense that tensions were mounting among the team.

As James's line manager, Bryan knew that he would have to call James in for a conversation, but he was also aware that the clients had taken a real shine to him. He was unsure how to handle the conversation.

Think about the types of primary questions that could be developed to enable the students to form a meaningful discussion about the issues raised in this short incident case. What secondary or ancillary questions could add further support to these primary questions? Then, review the orientation of each question (using Figure 6.3: A Template for the Case Map earlier in this chapter), to consider how they could be sequenced to form a short journey with a key learning objective.

## 6.4 Opening and guiding the discussion

Anyone who has started a journey and taken a wrong turn at the first junction will be aware of the importance of getting off to a good start. The same applies when starting a case journey. If the opening of the case does not create an opportunity to grab the attention of the learner and begin a process of movement toward an initial scheduled visiting point, then the case experience is going to be a real challenge for the learners (and for tutors too). There are many approaches that can be taken when launching the case discussion, but selecting the right approach will, once again, depend on the nature of your student group and your existing relationship with them. A common and traditional approach adopted by long-standing case teaching institutions is to *cold-call* a student from the group to provide an initial synopsis of the issues raised in the case. This approach has its merits, because a cold-call ensures that all students arrive prepared, in case they are the one chosen to get started. It also serves as a checker for the tutor to ensure the student's synopsis of the issues in the case is consistent with the expectations from the teaching plan. The tutor might already have a board plan mapped out, to which the student's initial comments could provide content to begin populating the plan. However, this approach depends on the participants being committed to preparation in anticipation of a board plan. In some cases, a cold-call might be a step too far for an unwilling, anxious or inexperienced learner. In this case, eliciting responses from individuals might feel too intimidating and likely to put off students from engaging with the process, and other approaches might need to be considered.

There are three things that the tutor will want to achieve in order to get the case off to a good start: firstly, to engage the learners; secondly, to determine at least some of the key issues raised by the case; and thirdly, to agree a starting point from which students can be orientated to start the journey. *Voting* on a generalisation may be a helpful way of encouraging all the participants to get involved. For example, a tutor might wish to begin the case by asking: *would you agree that the company that is profiled in this case study has performed well so far?* The tutor could suggest students might vote 'yes,' 'no' or 'unsure'. By counting the votes and logging them on a white board, the tutor will immediately have a feel for the likely viewpoints of the students. It also provides an opportunity to identify one or two voters from the 'yes' camp and the 'no' camp to encourage them to consider explaining why they voted this way. The peril of this approach is that everyone might choose to vote in the 'unsure' camp (for fear of being seen to make a mistake), and if this is likely, then the question can be modified further to something like: *On a rating scale of 1–10, how well do you believe this company has performed to date (with 1=poor and 10=very good)?* Not only does this type of questioning get everyone involved quickly, it also signals that the conversation is starting at the interesting visiting point of '*performance.*'

Using *warm-calls* might encourage some learners who are less confident to ensure that they are prepared with a response when called upon, and the use of pre-discussion **syndicate groups,** which meet before the start of class with a list of prearranged questions to consider, can also alleviate resistance to participation. These are particularly useful approaches for online case participation. If, within the first five minutes of your case session, you are confident that everyone in the room has been engaged in some form, and the conversation is beginning to develop at a pace without ongoing reliance on the tutor's prompts, then it is reasonable to assume that the case opening has succeeded and the participants have been able to get started on their journey together.

## 6.5 Getting students involved

### LESSONS LEARNT

When I deliver case development workshops for case tutors, and I ask what are the greatest challenges with using the case method, the most frequently repeated response is 'student motivation'. Tutors frequently raise concerns about their students being unwilling to participate or get engaged in the case discussion. As a lifelong believer in the phrase: 'involve me and I will learn', it has therefore been a lifelong challenge to address these issues of student engagement. Every time I challenge a tutor about this, the discussion ultimately boils down to 'not wanting to get involved'. So before thinking about how to get students involved its worth asking why your student might not want to get involved. What are the resistance factors that need to be addressed before you get started?

'Cases are a jigsaw puzzle with the pieces arranged in a confusing pattern. You need to take the pieces and fit them into a pattern that helps you understand the main issue and think about the optimal ways to address it'.[4]

I have a petrol lawnmower, which I rely on to manage the grass lawns to the front and rear of my home. Sometimes the lawnmower takes time to get started, particularly if it has been left in a cold or damp environment for too long. I might need to use the choke key, check the oil and petrol levels or clean the spark plug from time to time. Having got the mower started, if I take my hand off the starting bar, the mower will grind to a halt, and sometimes I find myself needing to go through all these processes once again to get it started. Similarly, with the case discussion, getting started can be a problem, especially if the students are coming into the learning environment 'cold'. They might need warming up before the case discussion before getting started; and once started, it is important to maintain the pace of the discussion to avoid things grinding to a premature halt. Your familiarity with the learner group is key to determining the right approach to maintaining engagement through the case discussion. Normally, the following areas of consideration need to be managed:

- Level of tutor direction
- Pace of discussion
- Complexity of the case
- Balance between whole group and small group time
- Other tools to include which promote whole class engagement

The *level of direction* offered by the tutor will vary from class to class and is dependent on many factors. In general, a *more directive approach* is often required in the following circumstances:

- When the pedagogical objective is to illustrate a new concept.
- When the case narrative is largely unstructured or difficult to read.
- At the beginning of the course, where students might feel less inclined to freely engage.
- Where student preparation is not expected to be very high.
- Where the student group is largely inexperienced with the case method.

Getting the level of directive intervention right will enable the student to feel more comfortable and confident to participate in the discussion, without fear of failure or ridicule. Too much directive intervention can foster disengagement, as students might feel that their efforts are being repeatedly undermined. Insufficient directive engagement might leave students feeling too vulnerable to participate.

A good book is often characterised by the author's capacity to change the narrative pace from time to time, maintaining a constant level of reader engagement. Similarly, *the pace of the case discussion* plays a key role in maintaining engagement. If the pace is too slow students may become distracted, if too fast, they might miss critical learning points and lose their way on the journey. Pace should not be maintained as a constant. A change of pace is a useful approach to manage participation and guard against fatigue. As we have already discussed, the case journey is about both *breadth* and *depth*, so it is reasonable to agree that the pace will change when the direction of the journey moves from one to the other, with pauses for analysis and further in-depth exploration of an interesting visiting point signalling a necessary change in pace.

The *level of difficulty* of the case will influence student engagement. If the case is to address the application of a complex piece of management theory previously unfamiliar to the learners, then it might be necessary to even 'pause the journey' to allow a mini-lecture to unpack the details of the theory before proceeding to apply it in the context of the case journey. Case tutors have a long-established history of exploring how to manage case difficulty, the basic tenets of which are still relevant today.

The case difficulty cube originated from Leenders and Erskine, based at the Richard Ivey School of Business in Canada, and has subsequently been adapted by other case commentators. The model proposes that the level of difficulty of the case can be captured in any of three dimensions: according to (A), the concepts or techniques that need to be deployed; (B) the analytical tasks facing the learner; and (C) the manner in which the data and the details are presented within the case narrative, as illustrated in the following figure:

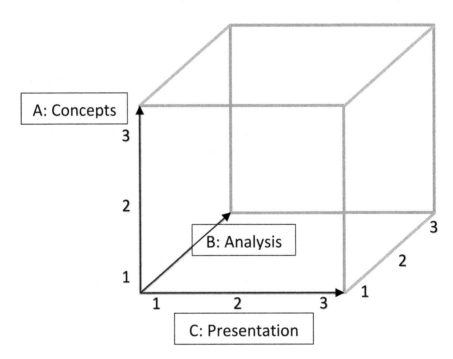

**FIGURE 6.4** Case difficulty cube
Source: Mauffette-Leenders, Erskine and Leenders, 2007, p. 17.[5]

If your learner group comprises relative newcomers to the case method, it is probably unwise to start with a case that is too complex across all three axes. The level of complexity ought to be matched to the student's competency and motivation, as well as to their stage of progress on the course. The number and complexity of concepts utilised will determine whether a mini-lecture is first required. The depth of analysis required to elicit the response needed to address the core objectives of the case will determine the complexity of the B (analysis) axis, and the manner in which data is hidden within the narrative will determined the complexity of the C (presentation) axis. Large cases with data that is dispersed across different pages of the text are likely to be more complex to manage compared with shorter cases where data is neatly captured in clearly presented tables. The choice of complexity will also be determined by the type(s) of learning skill that the tutor is seeking to develop with the learners.

Both the pace of the case journey and its complexity can be managed best when fostering a *balance between whole group and small group* times. These small group or break-out sessions provide a less imposing environment in which students can more confidently embrace the data and discuss different options and approaches without fear of embarrassment or ridicule from the larger group. If a mistake is made, the consequences are easily contained within the less formal environment of the small group. Small groups enable greater levels of individual participation and provide moments for individuals to pause, reflect and hypothesise before tackling the data head-on to address the issues raised by the tutor. Often, groups are then invited to return to the whole class setting, and individuals will be assigned roles to offer feedback and clarify the progress of their small group. If the case is tackling a particularly complex concept or dataset for analysis, then the time spent in small groups might need to increase.

---

### LESSONS LEARNT

How well do we know our learners, and how important is this when determining the breakout group members? It may seem simplistic to invite students to form groups of say between four and six for a breakout session, but further analysis undertaken by some institutions has demonstrated that a more strategically-driven group dynamic can be developed. For example, say the institute conducts a 'learning styles' test as part of the student induction to the programme. Knowledge of the results of this and the subsequent student profiles will enable the tutor to ensure an equal mix of pragmatists, activists, theorists and reflectors are assigned in each group. Or, by contrast, to place all the theorists together, the pragmatists together, and so on, to explore the implications of different learning styles on team dynamics.

---

If the tutor is confident with the use of *other tools* in the case classroom, especially with digital technologies, then these can be used to support the case discussion process. For example, there are many types of voting software that can be employed to support initial consensus-gathering questions. Some of these can be adapted to use with mobile phones. If mobile phone use is already a problematic distraction in class, then the tutor could turn the situation around by encouraging learners to explicitly make use of their phones for voting purposes. Similarly, there is evidence of case tutors who have encouraged mobile phone usage to tweet responses to themes discussed in the case, which can be synchronously displayed on a classroom screen. This has been particularly valuable when delivering cases to mixed ability groups or to international groups where some respondents, for which the class is not delivered in their mother tongue, might feel more confident to present a response by tweet rather than by oral discussion.[6] If you are working with multiple technologies as part of a case discussion, it might help to have a second facilitator present to manage the flow of responses, while the main tutor manages the pace of the discussion.

The case discussion is principally guided by carefully crafted questions, sensitive listening and constructive responses, each of which supports the ongoing movement through the case map towards achievement of the overall key learning objective(s). Having managed these processes, the final challenge of the case discussion is case closure.

## 6.6 Case closure

---

### LESSONS LEARNT

I recall running a case development session with an international group of experienced case tutors. One of the tutors made an honest confession, when asked about their greatest fears of delivering cases. He said that he always read the case in advance, made notes, considered interesting visiting points and the key opening questions, but once all the questions had surfaced and the key visiting points had been considered, the conversation seemed to go round and round in circles, and he would frequently find himself watching the clock and wishing the bell would ring to mark the end of the session. While admiring this professor's honesty with the group, I was left thinking about the importance of the case closure process. Ending a case well, ensures the students lock in the learning and can provide useful opportunities for broader reflection too. Without a clear closure, it can be so easy to find yourself stuck in a conversation that seems to be going nowhere.

---

Stephen Covey once famously stated that effective people should start with the end in mind.[7] Therefore, if you are to ensure that your principle objective of *learning* has been achieved, you need to manage the case closure process: ending well and allowing opportunities for learners to ensure that they have captured all the key points needed to 'lock in' their learnt experience.

One of the roles of the case tutor is the timekeeper. If it becomes clear that the journey is not going to be completed within the allotted timeframe, then the tutor needs to consider short-cuts in the map to ensure that the journey is brought to a natural end on time, in much the same way as the earlier Worcester-Harvard map provided the option of a train from Logan International Airport to the centre of Boston and then a taxi to Harvard, or a quicker route using a taxi direct from the airport to Harvard to shorten the journey. This latter approach means that the traveller misses the opportunity to experience the interesting visit to Boston and this might need to be compensated for later, but the journey needs to end well and end on time. Similarly, case tutors might need to omit an interesting visiting point and recapture the learning from this missed experience in a later session, while ensuring that the current case journey ends well. If the tutor tries to rush the ending to *tick off* one further interesting vising point, it is likely that the true learning from this experience might be missed by many from the group. By contrast, if the pace of the journey is managed carefully, this should allow time and space for more experienced participants to take occasional detours from the anticipated journey to capture other interesting learning points – for example, by relating a visiting point to a previous experience that they might have had in their own workplace. By providing this reasonable space in the group discussion, students can feel freer to make their own decisions and navigate their own journey, with the tutor's continued guidance and without feeling unduly controlled.

Wrapping up a case discussion allows for a moment of reflection whilst still in 'case mode'. While most of the case discussion is likely to have involved *discovery-type* learning approaches, a careful set of wrap-up questions provides opportunities for reflection even before the learner leaves the case discussion. For example, the tutor might ask: *if we were able to bring the main character from the case into this classroom now, what key generalisation would you like to share with him/her?* This type of question disguises the option of simply asking the students what they thought the key learning objectives were in the case today. By disguising the question in this way, the student can reflect on their learning while remaining in *case discussion-mode*, and the tutor can make a mental note of responses, effectively ticking off the intended learning outcomes as they are reflected in the students' feedback comments.

Other wrap-up techniques can be deployed to ensure that all students participate in the case closure process, such as:

- How else could we approach this?
- What else could we explore?
- On a single sheet of paper, make one recommendation....
- On a rating scale....

One very engaging way to end a case is to bring in one of the key characters from the case to discuss the closure themselves. This could either be done in person (if the relationship extends to this opportunity) or by pre-recorded video link. Such a closure often acts as a hook for learning and provides a real and credible dimension to the willing suspension of disbelief that the students have so far maintained in the discussion.

## 6.7 Case feedback and follow-up

In the first chapter of this book, the story of the high-performing student who challenged the lecturer with a *so what* question was discussed. If the case is presented in the module/programme without clear connections to other aspects of the programme, then the student can be forgiven for asking *so what?* And for feeling confused about how the experience might have contributed to their learning. In literature, each chapter of a book presents a consistently unfolding narrative. In a similar way, when the case study is used as part of a programme of learning activities, it should be clearly rooted and connected to the rest of the programme. Case feedback and follow-up play a key role in achieving this. It is common practice to provide some form of activity for students to undertake after the case discussion, with which they can connect all the 'takeaways' from the case class and identify key learning points that they can take back to their real world, once the discussions are over. If the case discussion has not fully resolved the issues raised in the case, then the learners might be assigned the task of following up from these discussions and making presentations or recommendations for the organisation under review. Alternatively, the students might be tasked with comparing and contrasting the issues raised in the case narrative to similar situations either in their own workplace, in other cases discussed as part of the programme or in another type or competitive organisation. These sorts of tasks evoke reflective practice after the case discussion and provide another critical component of the learning process.

> 'Reflective practice can enable (future) professionals to learn from experiences about: themselves; their studies, their work; the way they relate to home and work, significant others and wider society and culture; the way social and cultural structures are formed and control us'.[8]

Follow-up does not have to end with a reflective piece of assignment work. If the case is to be an integral part of the programme, which might include other cases, then it is important to consider where the critical reference points need to be captured in the programme plan. This is where students can be invited to reflect back on the case discussion as they consider a new component of the programme, or as they experience similar types of challenges in a future case. In this way, the development of a learning process by the integration of a number of cases can first *raise awareness* and then subsequently *reinforce* the key learning points through subsequent revisiting of the issues.

## 6.8 Adapting cases for different learning cultures

> 'Thinking out original answers to new problems or giving new interpretations to old problems is assumed in much undergraduate instruction to be an adult function and, as such, one properly denied to students'.[9]

Remember this telling statement from the introduction to this book? It is an extract from a 1940 Harvard paper which provides an indication of attitudes towards case use in those early years of the case method. The rapid development of the case method over subsequent decades, and particularly in the past 30 years, has led to significant expansion to engage many other types of learner besides the traditional MBA postgraduate. It has also migrated from its Harvard origins to all parts of the world, which provides different cultural challenges when considering the approach to case discussion and delivery.

---

## LESSONS LEARNT

I was delivering a case study to a group of students at a university in Turkey when it occurred to me that I had a very agreeable group of learners. I would frequently adopt an opposing viewpoint (or 'play Devil's advocate') in an attempt to evoke a contrasting response from the learners but, no matter what approach I took, my students seemed supportive and agreeable with everything I said. I discussed this dilemma with other Turkish scholars who were quick to point out that, while 'playing Devil's advocate' may work well in a British cultural context, in this particular Turkish context, students would normally agree with the tutor (as the perceived specialist knowledge provider) out of respect for the individual, even if (deep down) they knew the suggestion was wrong or impractical. So, faced with the fundamental choice of challenging this tutor's viewpoint and risking the tutor 'losing face' or simply agreeing with the tutor despite a deeper personal disagreement with the viewpoint, the student would normally favour the latter response. This cultural implication led me to revise my teaching approach to ensure that it was adapted to account for this cultural bias.

---

The case method has been adapted and adopted for use with undergraduates in the classroom,[10] with work-based learners and other diversified programmes, including part-time, degree apprenticeship, blended learning, online and distance learning contexts; and in many different countries and cultures across the world.[11] Its adaptability as a tool for participant centred learning has significant value for learners of all types because, as Professor John Hammond points out, 'case studies cut across a range of organizations and situations, they provide you with an exposure far greater than you are likely to experience in your day-to-day routine'.[12] However, for the case to be effective in such diverse learning contexts, different approaches must be adopted to best suit the learner group. In other words, you might be using the same data about the same story, but the journey might have to be quite different, and this could require significant revisions to a case map.

### Cases with undergraduates and international learners

For example, when adopting cases for undergraduate programmes of study, it is likely that the classroom size will typically be larger than that of the post-experience or postgraduate learning environment. Each of these contexts provides different types of challenges for the adaptation of the case method, not to mention the cultural challenges of using cases in a broader range of global contexts. Recent integration of the case method into undergraduate teaching in countries such as China, Indonesia, Turkey and South Africa have led to challenges of interpretation and approaches to learning which recognises the cultural distinctiveness of each classroom. Put another way, if the same case is taught the same way in the US, Spain, India and Kenya, it is likely that it will yield different responses in terms of learning effectiveness. It is therefore argued that it would be preferable to adopt a different teaching plan for each context, which has been adapted to the unique cultural in-class challenges facing each educational context. At the same time, cross-cultural awareness requires further enhancement to maximise learning opportunities by customizing the case study approach to the local context.

> 'Cases are the best way for undergraduates to gain an understanding of the real world in class. I often need to take my students into the mind of a protagonist and, as they usually lack the experience themselves, the right case can allow them to get right into the decision maker's shoes and to see scenarios through eyes other than their own'.
>
> *Singapore*[13]

Another challenge for working with undergraduates is the tendency towards engagement with social media and online communication possibilities. Teaching undergraduate learners through the case method has led to approaches that have evolved and adapted to a more remote concept of 'presence' for learning, making it far easier to contemplate a delivery method which encourages both face-to-face and remote discussion with interaction through social media platforms.[14] The use of short or limited-text communication tools, such as Snapchat, Instagram and Twitter, has changed the way that young people have adapted to online communication and is subsequently influencing undergraduate learning.[15] As a result, the evolution of shorter cases, with less text and a greater use of video imagery, adapted for use on social media platforms presents new opportunities for engagement and learning in under-graduate management contexts. The consequences could lead to a far more protracted learning approach, rather than an individual 60-minute classroom event. However, it could be argued that such an approach, while providing new complexities for managing debate and discussion, can nonetheless promote more space for reflection and the subsequent learning that can be captured from reflective practice.[16]

## Cases with work-based learners and apprentices

One of the most significant contributions of higher education to economic development and innovation in recent times in the Western world has been the development of work-based and apprenticeship learning.[17] In the context of knowledge economies, the role of knowledge or learning based on a binary distinction between creator and users has become blurred. The antecedents of the current push towards curricula that reflect employer, employee, and skills needs (in the idea of 'mode 2' knowledge)[18] which is produced and valued outside the university and is not discipline-based, and in the idea of experiential learning in which the learner is understood as 'skilful' – that is, with tacit knowledge and skill that can be theorised and applied through work based projects.[19] Such projects require the co-operation and collaboration of three key participants: the university, the employer and the employee.[20] Each is seen to contribute a distinctive perspective, and each is necessary to ensure up-to-date, work-relevant, and innovative outcomes that are practical and useful for the individual (by enhancing knowledge, skill and qualifications), the organisation (by contributing to a highly skilled workforce) and the academy (by satisfying the demands of the knowledge economy and remaining competitive).[21] The distinction between work-based learning and university education is further blurred in some contexts, such as in the UK, where recent developments have seen the emergence of higher and degree apprenticeships, providing new opportunities for level 5, 6 and 7 learning. These degree apprentices have enabled universities to play their part in delivering work-based learning/apprenticeship opportunities[22]. Into contexts such as these, the case method provides a clear opportunity for participant-centred learning, but such cases need to be crafted around the localised challenges of the workplace, in order to be perceived as tools that provide the value required by the employer, who is often the driving force and sponsor for the learning opportunity. This creates opportunities for localised case writers to produce new case resources that can adapt to local workplace contexts.

## Cases for entrepreneurship education

Evidence from certain parts of Europe and its neighbours points to a growth in entrepreneurial education, which reflects a rise in new and small business development.[23] Entrepreneurship degree programmes have grown in popularity in recent years and are likely to increase. New concepts in approaches to provision of entrepreneurial education have emerged which place the learner at the heart of the learning experience and often encourage a practitioner-oriented mindset to promote business development alongside the taught elements of their programme. In many contexts, such programmes are further supported by the alignment of university departments to local Technoparks, which enable entrepreneurs operating in hubs or incubators to develop their ideas.[24] Further integration of the case approach to learning in these contexts lends itself to the development of *live* cases, which showcase the real-time challenges facing the entrepreneur.

PAUSE FOR A MOMENT: Look back over the themes raised in this chapter and then revisit the case map template in section 6.1. Now think about a case study that you are currently using. It is very easy to be led by the author's plan in the teaching note, so think first about the type of student to whom you will deliver this case, and then start to populate the various sections of the template to sketch out your own case map, remembering to identify the key learning objective(s), the interesting visiting points (analysis) and the carefully crafted questions to enable the students to progress on the case journey. Then consider the perspective that you want the students to take in the case narrative and the mode of treatment of the case data, as you start to plan out the case journey for your next class.

Now that you have completed this chapter, you should know that:

1. The development of a case teaching map to accompany the case study provides the tutor with a tool to navigate a journey through case data with the learners, incorporating interesting visiting points and progressing towards planned key learning objectives.
2. Carefully crafted questions can promote learning through both discovery and reflective practice, presenting opportunities for analysis (depth) and progress (breadth) towards the key learning objective(s).
3. Cases can be used with a diverse group of participants with different learning capabilities and/or cultural contexts, but case delivery plans need to be adapted to best suit the specific target group of learners, taking on board their learning habits and cultural distinctions.

## Notes

1 Barnes, Christensen and Hansen, 1994, p.3
2 Clawson, 1995, p. 4
3 Heath, 2006, pp. 17–18
4 Ellet, 2018, p. 15
5 Reproduced by permission from Leenders and Associates Inc. and Erskine Associates Inc.
6 Jones and Balterzen, 2017
7 Habit no.2 in Covey, 1999
8 Bolton and Delderfield, 2018, p. 2
9 Gragg, 1940, p. 2
10 Velenchik, 1995; Kennedy et al., 2001
11 Raelin, 1997
12 Hammond, 2002, p. 1
13 Ohlsson-Corboz, 2017
14 Heckman and Annabi, 2005
15 Mollet, Moran and Dunleavy, 2011
16 Betts, 2004
17 Costley, Elliott and Gibbs, 2010
18 Gibbons et al., 1994
19 Elliott, 1999
20 Gibbs and Garnett, 2007
21 Boud and Soloman, 2001
22 Kirby, 2015
23 Kyro, 2015; Mwasalwiba, 2010
24 Lenger, 2008

# 7

# INTEGRATING MULTIMEDIA CASES

'Multimedia cases present a wonderful opportunity. They mirror the real world, where so much data can be included and students can engage in a more exploratory way to come up with endless new solutions'.

*Darden Business School, US*[1]

This section explores the following themes:

- The limitations of using paper-based cases
- Using video cases in class
- Web-based case studies

The traditional mode of development for the case study is paper-based, but over the past 30 years there has been growth in the use of video and digital technologies to present case data in a range of different formats, to improve engagement with learners. Video cases provide opportunities for students to see and hear the key characters within the case and to get a better sense of the culture of the organisation as they are invited to virtually step into the organisation and see the physical environment of the employees' workplace.

Albert Mehrabian, Professor Emeritus of Psychology at the University of California, Los Angeles conducted research on communication, which led to two conclusions: Firstly, that there are basically three elements in any face-to-face communication – words, intonation of voice and body language. Secondly, that these three elements account differently for the meaning of the message, with the proposal that:[2]

- Words account for 7%
- Intonation of voice accounts for 38%
- Body language accounts for 55%

However, when cases that are designed to bring a slice of reality to the class-room are presented in text-only formats, then it is reasonable to assume that this places limits on the learner's capacity to fully deduce the true impact of the messages that the characters within the case are communicating.

## 7.1 Using video cases

> 'Video based cases provide a rich environment for providing a descriptive story of the situation under account. Video cases offer immediacy not possible in text cases. Videos offer more graphic and persuasive form of the shared situation'.
>
> *Middle East Technical University, Turkey*[3]

The integration of video into cases provides opportunities for learners to not only analyse the words that are used, but also to appraise the intonation and body language that research suggests contributes so much to the meaning behind their words. The intonation of voice, facial expressions, body language and hand gestures of the characters can provide multiple messages that can be interpreted in different ways by the case class, as part of their analysis of a management situation. This can evoke responses about the trustworthiness, openness and persuasiveness of characters facing a certain situation in the workplace. Participants will immediately be drawn to similar experiences of such visual and oral signals in their own contexts, enabling them to form opinions about the individuals, which might subsequently shape how decisions are made within the case class.

Utilising video in education is widely researched and has been adopted as a valuable tool for learning in many disciplines and genres. Research from the University of Queensland, Australia draws attention to a range of pedagogical benefits of using video in education, including its capacity to inspire and engage students:[4]

- Increased student motivation
- Enhanced learning experience
- Higher marks
- Development potential for deeper learning of the subject development potential for deeper learning of the subject development potential for deeper learning of the subject
- Development of learner autonomy
- Enhanced team-working and communication skills

Videos cases present new opportunities for the tutor to consider how to 'treat the data'. Viewing video on a screen is often associated with passive behaviour rather than active participation, and yet if the video case is to fulfil the objective of learner engagement then it is important to consider how video might be incorporated in a class discussion, in a manner which promotes engagement and participation. I often find that this is best achieved by encouraging the learner, where appropriate, to view the whole video before class and then to target small bite-sized chunks of video around which discussion points can be raised. These bite-sized components should be no longer than 2–3 minutes to ensure that the learner has not disengaged from the process. Where the video contains multiple characters, I often tend to find that this raises the scope for role play, recreating a 'what happens next?' scenario.

If the technological resources are available, then students can be encouraged to develop their own videos as responses to the case video. This *video reporting* approach further enhances learner engagement.

## 7.2 Web-based cases

Since the introduction of web-based technologies and CD-ROMs, scholars have explored the benefits of developing cases in web-based or multimedia formats. This reformatting of data permits a very different approach to presenting and analysing case data, which would normally be formatted with a linear narrative form. As multimedia and web-based cases became more popular, so too did the complexity of formatting, allowing the gamification of the case study, to create possibilities for learners to curate their own journey through multiple layers of case data. One such multimedia case author from Darden University compared the experience to arriving at a buffet table and selecting whichever parts of the meal seemed most appealing, and then returning again and again to try more. Such cases were no longer formatted with narrative prose that followed a chronological sequence, but rather resembled a multi-storey department store which had different 'levels' and different 'aisles' from which students can pick and choose what to take from the 'shelves' in order to test where the data best suits the objectives of the case investigation. These often complex case studies permit multiple journeys through the data to discover different areas of interest and achieve different learning outcomes on each visit.

The difference between the text-based case and the multimedia case can be compared to the difference between a train journey and a car journey. Train journeys require everyone to enter the journey at predetermined locations and to travel together along a singular route before departing at predetermined points, in much the same way that text-based cases that are often led by a tutor at the front of class can draw the class together to make a single journey through the data. By contrast, multimedia cases can place the participant in the driving seat, and in doing so present opportunities for much greater autonomy when determining the routes of the journey to be taken. This is particularly useful for asynchronous online learning. This by no means removes the need for the tutor, as case facilitation remains a key function of the learning journey.

Although these types of cases can appear to be very attractive to tutors and students, one of the challenges with multimedia cases is the fast-paced changes in digital technology which may lead to learning platforms being supported for a limited period before newer platforms emerge to offer even greater levels of complexity. As a result, many of the early multimedia cases are no longer supported on most popular platforms today. As most multimedia cases switch from CD to online, web-based platforms these compatibility issues can be managed better to extend the longevity of the case.

However, the use of web-based and multimedia cases continues to increase in both popularity and in complexity. These types of cases are particularly effective at delivering simulation-type learning opportunities, promoting a greater reflection of reality. Research from Leeds Becket University exploring the benefits of using multimedia case studies in management education determined that *engagement, realism* and *handling complexity* were themes better achieved with multimedia than with more traditional paper-based cases. The research went further to propose that this level of enhanced engagement improved learning outcomes by facilitating greater student interest, understanding and skills.[5]

The UK-based Case Centre compiles regularly updated lists of bestselling global cases, and of those within the 'bestselling' categories, at least 20% incorporate some form of video or multimedia technology. Some case development organisations have particularly invested in digital media cases. For example, IE University in Madrid boasts a growing case collection of which more than 20% is multimedia in format. One of the largest developers of multimedia cases is Darden School, with its own dedicated case writing research group. Similarly, ESSEC Business School, with bases in France, Singapore and Morocco, has developed a growing reputation for providing a substantial case collection with many multimedia case studies. For many years, Harvard has been hosting workshops and webinars in using multimedia cases resources, and this is reflected in the growing number of Harvard cases which incorporate some form of digital media content. There are similar ventures being developed in Asia with significant investments in multimedia cases from IBS, Hyderabad in India and at Hong Kong's Asia Case Research Centre.

## 7.3 Virtual reality

Pioneering new research is beginning to explore the scope for integrating virtual reality (VR) into case learning. A team at INSEAD's Singapore campus has been developing trials of integrated case learning with VR as part of their *experimental, immersive, innovative learning* initiative.[6] Participants are handed a VR headset device as they arrive in the lecture room, and the professor facilitates the immersive audio-visual learning journey. It is proposed that these experimental approaches enhance the individual's capacity to capture data and to assimilate information at a much faster rate than when reading. The 360-degree viewing capacity brings the user much closer to that simulated *slice of reality,* to develop the illusion that they really are present in the context of the case environment. VR is yet another example of how the boundaries for case development are continuing to expand.

PAUSE FOR A MOMENT: Reflect on how digital and video technology is currently incorporated in your own teaching and learning programmes. In what ways do they appear to stimulate and engage the learners to participate in their class sessions? How has this been reflected in course surveys and participant feedback? And in what ways could multimedia be better integrated into future course planning in a manner that stimulates higher levels of participation and engagement?

Now that you have completed this chapter, you should know that:

1.  There has been a significant growth in multimedia, digital and video content in case development across the globe.
2.  The adoption of multimedia resources requires technological support to ensure that platforms remain viable for the learners to access the relevant data in the right format.
3.  The challenge for case tutors is to ensure that such gamification of learning resources does not simply serve to entertain the students, but, by contrast, is utilised in a planned and strategic manner to ensure greater engagement and participation in the learning process.

## Notes

1  Asst Prof. Gregory B. Fairchild, speaking to The Case Centre, 2008
2  Mehrabian, 1981
3  Bayram, 2012
4  See www.uq.edu.au/teach/video-teach-learn/ped-benefits.html
5  Jones and Kerr, 2012
6  INSEAD, 2020b

# 8

# LIVE CASES

'Students are tackling and solving real-world problems. There are no teaching notes and no solutions. Students are tasked with coming up with the solution on their own'.

*Ohio University, US*[1]

This section explores the following themes:

- The benefits of a live case
- How to prepare the class, the actor and yourself for the live case
- The potential benefits of introducing co-opetition into live cases
- The challenges of using a live case

A natural extension of the case method from text-based resources to digital and multimedia platforms leads to the potential for greater engagement in what many have referred to as *live* cases. In many ways, these cases provide the ultimate slice of reality by bringing real people with their real-time problems and work-based challenges into direct contact with the learners, to enable them to engage directly with the challenges that these live contributors present. For some this might be conceived as a blurring of the boundaries between case study analysis and management consultancy, as students are required to engage, quiz and challenge the live *actors* to provide real-time data to inform creative problem-solving opportunities.

## 8.1 The benefits of the live case

One of the obvious advantages of this approach to case delivery is the presence of real people with real business challenges, which immerses the learner into the complexity of the organisational issues and challenges, from where they can tackle not only the 'above the line' issues with objectivity, but also experience the more nuanced challenges of operating within specific cultural contexts, considering the opinions and backgrounds of individuals and the power dynamics in certain organisational structures. The live case has very blurred boundaries, as it is no longer limited to the data contained within the text, but rather its boundaries can be extended to the degree to which the live actor is willing and able to respond to the questions raised by the learners. While the more traditional approach to case delivery limits the questioning to the case tutor, in live cases students are often permitted to be the question-raisers, to elicit as much information as they might need from the live actor to enable them to address the key issues facing the organisation. Although students might be encouraged to apply abstract theories, models and approaches in more traditional case settings, during the live case, students are immersed into the organisation and work with genuine complex data that require real strategies and solutions to support improved performance for the organisation. By bringing the learners much closer to the real workplace, they can improve their critical thinking skills and develop much stronger employability skills for the future.

Evidence suggests that students who have to report back to the organisation with recommendations based on their deliberations from the live case tend to think more about how to articulate their responses to the live actors, compared with how they might respond in a more traditional case class with their peers and a tutor.

> "'When students know they have to defend their choices to a real client, there is a level of ownership and involvement with the process that I've never seen students express otherwise'.
>
> *Marquette University, USA*[2]

The additional presence of a live actor from a real organisation somehow heightens the level of expectation, which subsequently motivates the learner to think more carefully about how they might present and then defend their arguments. There is also a suggestion that such experiences tend to 'lock in' learning for the students, as the heightened reality and level of expectation tend to cause the learner to dig deeper for their carefully considered responses and to allow the learning from the experience to cement itself deeper into their cognitive processing. This experiential learning process tends to be much easier to subsequently revisit and apply to other case contexts.

Live case studies have been widely adopted as an approach to case study methodology for more than 30 years, as they contain all the critical components required for experiential learning.[3] In addition, they often provide unpredictability, greater ambiguity and deeper complexity that can create a heightened sense of challenge to the learner.[4]

New Zealand-based research explores the main differences between traditional case studies and live case studies, pointing to the emphasis on the process of discussion and evolution of the case itself. Live case studies present real-life situations which, it is argued, are much more complex as the more traditional decision-focused case underplays social, political and economic influences which most often shape real managerial outcomes. This therefore allows the learning process in live cases to become more alive and dynamic.[5]

## 8.2 Live case preparation

'The use of live case studies in business education is growing. Mixing realism entices students to think critically in an unpredictable environment. Live cases are often deemed appropriate for international business and strategy cases'.

*University of Guelph, Canada*[6]

The key to a successful live case is the relationship with the actor(s) and the organisation that they represent. It is important to ensure the actor is fully prepared for the case class and that the problems/issues/challenges that are to be presented to the learners are clearly understood by the tutor and articulated as part of the live case's introduction to the participants. Just as in more traditional cases, the participants will need to ensure that they can access enough data (normally through questions to the actor) to be able to determine the issues, opportunities and options facing the organisation, and to be able to make informed choices. The success therefore hinges on the willingness of the actor to effectively communicate a 'good story' with some 'interesting visiting points' that enable the learners to engage and journey with the actor towards 'key learning objectives'. The advantage of the live case is that a win-win situation can be achieved, provided that the session is well managed, which enables both learning attainment for the participants and potential new solutions to problems for the organisation.

Live cases are less impactful if the preparation is lacking between the case tutor and the actor. Just as the writing of a traditional case requires careful investment and planning, so too does a live case, to ensure it is more than just an enjoyable chat with a visiting business leader. A case writer might normally spend considerable time in the organisation, researching its history, culture and how is tackled similar issues in the past, as well as evaluating the motives, drives and opinions of current protagonists engaged in the issue which will be the focus of the case. A similar level of scrutiny and planning is required as part of the preparation of the live case to ensure that it has meaning, impact and meets the learning expectations of the programme.

Research on live cases undertaken at the University of Guelph, Canada, has explored the potential benefits of establishing students into teams to both co-operate and compete for the preferred response to the challenges set in a live case scenario. They have termed this approach *co-opetition* with live cases.[7] One example of a live case scenario involved students being presented with an ethical dilemma facing an organisation, where students were required to co-operate in the first instance to elicit as much data as possible from the live presenter (in this case, the company CEO) as the classroom became what the tutors referred to as a 'laboratory of knowledge and sharing'. Students were invited to design a strategy for the Canadian company to enter the Chinese market. It is worth noting that before commencing on the live case, all participants were required to sign a confidentiality agreement in order to safeguard the sensitive information that the company would be sharing. The team that provided the most favourable response to the competition was then sponsored to travel to China to develop its ideas further and offered internships with the company. Final presentations were made to the organisation three months after the initial CEO visit, to allow students time to gather data and consider options. Having reflected on the impact of these live cases, the tutors noted the benefits that co-opetition provided to the live case, as students were required to provide regular updates on their own research of the industry and the country relevant to their project. This pooling of knowledge also served to keep the students engaged with the process over the period allotted between the initial live case launch and the final presentations.

## 8.3 The challenges of using live cases

The disadvantage of using *live* cases is that in many circumstances the opportunity can only be captured once, and therefore, unlike other case studies, cannot be repeated for use in other classes. It is therefore time-consuming, and costly in terms of core staff time, with a limited return on investment. *Live* cases also require a high level of agility on the part of the case tutor, which might not suit all scholars, given the balancing needs of the *live* organisation and competing academic commitments. *Live* cases are also dependent on university departments developing strong professional relationships with external organisations who are willing to engage and entrust learners with key responsibilities for handling often-sensitive internal data.

Early research on *live* cases conducted by Derbyshire College, in the UK, identified a number of challenging areas for those looking to develop live cases. These provide useful hints for anyone looking to develop *live* cases today. Following trials of a live case, conducted with undergraduates, it was noted that its preparation and delivery was both time-consuming and resource-intensive, the participants were insufficiently prepared to fully engage, schedules were difficult to maintain, students needed to be skilled in questioning techniques prior to commencement, and certain business-specific strategic issues were too complex for students to identify. Despite this, the students were highly motivated because of the *live* experience, and the organisation involved believed that it was a useful internal developmental opportunity.

By contrast, similar research from the USA provides a strong, positive argument for *live* cases, proposing that they enable student participants to apply their learning across all stages of an experiential learning cycle, with a high level of engagement, positive student feedback and improved grades in assessments.[8]

In summary, research into *live* cases demonstrates that, in general, they are of most benefit to participants who already have a clear understanding of management cases and level of expertise in the case development process, as well as sound knowledge of their respective subject discipline. Cleary organised parameters for engagement between the case tutor and the respective *live* case organisation increase the likelihood of impactful and effective learning.

> PAUSE FOR A MOMENT: Think about the organisations with which your department has developed significant relationships, and ask yourself what is the potential scope for inviting an organisation to present a live case scenario with your students. Think about the likely resource implications and how you might present such a pitch to the organisation in a way that could promote the potential 'win-win' argument for further engagement.

Now that you have completed this chapter, you should know that:

1. For more than 30 years, there has been widespread global adoption of live case scenarios to foster strong engagement between learners and the real-time challenges facing organisations.
2. The development of a live case requires significant planning and preparation with a co-operating organisation.
3. When live cases are introduced with a co-opetition approach, this could lead to enhanced engagement with the learning process.

## Notes

1 Adam Rapp, quoted from Rapp and Ogilvie, 2019,
2 Jessica Ogilvie, quoted from Rapp and Ogilvie, 2019
3 McKenna, 1999
4 Elam and Spotts, 2004
5 Bridgman, 2010
6 Charlebois and Foti, 2017
7 Ibid.
8 Green and Erdem, 2016

# 9

# USING CASES FOR ONLINE LEARNING

'The essential question needs to be how you can develop online learning well. High quality presentation and impactful pedagogy are best achieved by working together across multi-disciplinary and multi-level teams, while pulling in the expertise of external resources and drawing on the experience of colleagues at other schools'.

*Imperial College Business School, UK[1]*

Initially, this chapter was due to form part of the previous chapter, but given more recent global changes in education and classroom delivery imposed by social-distancing measures, the role of the case study as a learning strategy for remote teaching sessions and distance learning has propelled itself to become a major feature of new ways of thinking about management education.

This represents some relatively new challenges and has forced new ways of thinking about using cases with distance learners, many of which I have attempted to captured in this chapter, which explores the following themes[2]:

- To consider the merits of both synchronous and asynchronous approaches to online delivery.
- Revision of expectations in terms of quantity of content, pace of delivery and frequency of breakout groups to maintain engagement
- Management of the functionality of online case delivery platforms.
- Capitalising on the extra benefits of remote and online delivery, as well as mitigating against the challenges presented.

Demand for online learning opportunities has been growing for some time, and new universities and learning institutes continue to emerge that specialise in the delivery of online and hybrid learning programmes. In light of the coronavirus (Covid-19) epidemic, most universities and higher education institutes across the world needed to quickly adapt their delivery patterns to switch to managing pro-grammes remotely, and this has produced interesting consequences, causing many to question what a 'new norm' in case class delivery might look like, as the benefits of remote learning have prompted a rethink for future programme-makers.

Given that 'online case teaching is an area that evolves rapidly (mostly because the software tools and learning environments do)',[3] this chapter has avoided focussing on specific online platforms or tools, as there will undoubtedly be more in the marketplace as global engagement with online learning is developed. Instead, the focus is on approaches and techniques to using cases for online learning.

Earlier studies identified a number of factors that can inhibit engagement with online learning, with typical student barriers including administrative issues, lack of social interaction, inadequate academic or technical skills, poor learner motivation, inadequate time and support for studies, cost, access to the internet and technical problems.[4] Further inhibitors, such as boredom, working with silence, lecturing (rather than participating), distractions and feelings of being invisible, have also been observed.[5] If the case method is to be used for online delivery, then these typical inhibitors need to be addressed as part of the online case strategy. The next two sections explore potential responses to these factors for both synchronous and asynchronous delivery approaches.

## 9.1 Synchronous remote case delivery

> 'The biggest mistake you can make is just to do online what you do face-to-face without establishing the needs of the target students'.
>
> *Open University, UK*[6]

Real-time remote learning does come with challenges, particularly as the *technology platforms* required to support engagement are commonly inconsistent and unreliable in different contexts. This can lead to students being logged out, freezing or at best communicating with a constant time lag between participants, which creates a space, which is often then filled by several respondents attempting to share at the same time. Too many unmuted participants can lead to echoing effects or feedback received over the headphones. Students can be encouraged to mute when not commenting and use the *hand-raise* option to facilitate group chat, but this una-voidably affects the natural rhythm and flow of a discussion, especially when a participant is midway through the delivery of their response before realising that they have forgotten to unmute themselves.

Ultimately, this draws attention to the emotional energy that is expended in a case class context and which is unavoidably affected by the challenges of remote delivery. Some tutors have described the detachment issues as an ongoing struggle leading to greater cognitive overloading, with so much more for both the learners and tutors to keep track of.

This is further hampered by the numerous external challenges facing the remote learning environment. In face-to-face (F2F) classroom scenarios, there are little or no distractions, but in remote contexts participants are commonly facing the distractions of other devices, emails and multiple screens, as well as other noises from the household, generally making this hard for classroom management.

With these challenges in mind, it helps to set realistic expectations for both yourself and your students. Working remotely can easily tire people, and what you think you should be able to cover in a F2F context is unlikely to be achievable with remote delivery. It is therefore helpful to plan by considering the tension between what you can realistically cover in contrast to what you might ideally want to cover. Some experienced online case tutors have commented that somewhere between 75% and 90% of the content that you might expect to deliver in a F2F classroom is a more realistic target for remote delivery.[7]

In fact, although much of this chapter compares online and remote delivery with F2F delivery, in practice some argue that it might be more favourable to let go of the tendency for comparison with F2F delivery altogether to allow remote delivery to be accepted as its own type of learning strategy, without constant contrasts and comparisons.

One of the starting points for online case teaching is *case selection*. In much the same way as you would with F2F teaching, selecting the right type of case is essential. Some cases work better when delivered online, and others might require some tweaking first to ensure that content is available in the right format and released in appropriate portions to support the online approach. Multimedia cases, such as those discussed in the previous chapter, which have been devised with online delivery in mind, might prove to be most beneficial for this; but it will be necessary to keep checking the digital platforms to ensure that the content is accessible by all learners, regardless of their remote context. Search engines, such as those used by Harvard, Ivey and The Case Centre all incorporate terms such as *multimedia* and *online* as part of their case search criteria.

Having selected the right case, it is time to turn attention towards the *delivery plan or map*. In contrast to F2F delivery, it might be worth segmenting your planning into three components:

- The 'must haves'
- The 'nice to haves'
- And the 'bonus content'[8]

Some established practitioners of remote and distance learning case sessions believe that it is helpful to think more modularly in terms of delivery, to consider how long each segment of altogether-time should last before moving people into breakout groups or individual time-out sessions. Where previous F2F plans might have been established to foster a journey with three, four or five different visiting points, online modular segments ought to focus on a single 'takeaway' at a time.

For remote classes, it is even more important to ensure that you have a well-developed teaching map with really carefully crafted questions to make sure that they foster creativity and curiosity, which in turn provokes clear responses from the group, critical thinking and greater depth of analysis.

Having selected the right case, prepared the map, the next step is to determine how to *manage the discussion*. We all tend to use three fundamental resources for communication: our *words*, our *intonation* and our *body language*. Working remotely can limit the degree to which we are able to interact with our learners, but careful attention to all three factors should still be considered. A friendly smile or a knowing look can provide useful prompts for participant engagement, as will the intonation of our voice and the clarity with which we stress key points. These traditionally help with F2F teaching and therefore should also be encouraged for online delivery. Consider pace carefully, and monitor the quality of the spoken word throughout the class session. Students will value a more sensitive approach when working remotely, at least until they have effectively warmed up; and cold-calls should probably be replaced by gentler warm-calls to allow the student to prepare a response rather than be put on the spot. It might be helpful to build space or redundancy into the classroom planning to allow for students to catch up or take a break where engagement through remote technologies could become burdensome or lead to fatigue and burn-out.[9]

In larger classes, fewer participants can fit onto one screen, and so it is easier for individuals to be lost in the shadows, which could subsequently lead to fewer active participants. Many have noted that where online discussion involves more than around 40 participants, then the nature of the discussion changes. One of the benefits to online case discussions is that you can incorporate different approaches to the participants' responses, as research from Ivey has identified: 'in addition to live discussion via video, asking for written responses or comments on posts encourages all participants to think about their responses and show that they are actively engaging'.[10]

Every case tutor has encountered quieter students who avoid participation unless called upon. However, oddly enough, those who are the quieter ones in remote classes might not be the same as those who would be quiet in F2F scenarios. Some students manage the remote context better than others, in much the same way as some manage F2F discussion more confidently than others. If you have shifted your F2F class group to online learning, take care to observe the change in dynamic between the participants.

It is even more important for online case tutors to be fully engaged with the learning process, managing everything that is happening around the group and being ever more responsive to all the cues that the group provides. Where technology and size of class permits, then the tutor's camera, as well as students' cameras, should always be switched on, as this enhances the sense of community, as well as fostering accountability. If bandwidth does not support this, then at least the tutor's camera should be switched on. While body language might be difficult to interpret, often just a slight change in tone or facial expression can provide a useful stimulus for a follow-up question or enquiry, to provoke issues to surface in the conversation.

In order to maintain engagement, it might help to encourage greater screen-sharing from your participants, particularly when they return from breakout groups, to support the summaries of their discussions or group investigations.

Working with digital technologies has its advantages, such as polls, voting software and hand-raising tools that can be used to promote and monitor engagement. Chat boxes, running alongside the main discussion enable others, who might be less confident to initially engage with the vocal discussion, to provide a secondary commentary. Although it might be difficult for tutors to engage with text-chat alongside the synchronous discussion, each time that you send students out into their small group sessions, this gives you time to review the text comments and identify those key points that you might wish to comment back to when all groups return. If additional classroom support is available, then you could deploy a classroom assistant or colleague to manage the chat-box discussion in parallel with the main group discussion. This is particularly valuable when conducting remote learning case studies with larger groups. In addition, online delivery provides new challenges for participants with hearing impairment and similar accessibility issues, for which mitigation will also need to be considered.

Having completed the discussion sections, it is time to start thinking about how to manage the *summing-up* process. It is common practice to invite participants to suggest some generalisations or 'takeaways' from the class session. While F2F cases probably permit only a handful of these suggestions to be captured, synchronous use of the chat-box creates opportunities for all participants to leave a comment; and the advantage of working with many remote group software packages is that you get to record the session, so both you and the learners can revisit the experience to capture any missing elements from the discussion.

*Recording* remote sessions provides other invaluable opportunities with online learning. Research from MIT has identified five common benefits to recorded online learning, which can be summarised as:

- It enables students to review the class afterwards.
- Provides access for different learning styles.
- Allows absent students to see what they missed.
- Allows students in different time zones to watch the session afterwards.
- Tutors can review to take attendance and review group chat afterwards.[11]

If you are planning to record the class, you will need to consider the legal implications and compliance with data protection legislation. Normally, it is good practice to ensure that you have all participants' consent before recording and that the recorded video is located in a safe password-protected or encrypted environment.

With online cases, it is more important than ever to ensure that you get to *know your students* better when managing a remote class. Once you have captured the data needed to generate a clear understanding of the profile of your learner group, here are a few more questions that you should ask as you prepare to deliver your class:

- How do you agree the boundaries of professional practice/team etiquette when delivering classes remotely?
- What advice would you give on dress code (both to your students and to yourself)?

- How do you manage late arrivals to the group?
- What extra factors will maintain interest and foster curiosity during the case journey?
- How do you determine the organisation of breakout groups? How frequently do they meet throughout the case session? How do they capture the content of their discussion in such a way that enables effective feedback when returning to the main session?
- Can all participants access the content using the same digital platform?

In conclusion, many of the *hygiene factors* that need to be considered for effective online case delivery are summarised by research from Columbia Business School, which segments the essentials into three categories as summarised below:[12]

1. Clarity

   a  Establish clear rules of engagement
   b  Provide clear and precise instructions
   c  Practice being a participant (viewing proceedings from the other side)
   d  Test the set-up
   e  Create a checklist for the learners and for yourself
   f  Ask for feedback

2. Engagement

   a  Draw from students in examples
   b  Cold call participants
   c  Utilise lots of polls
   d  Incorporate sparks (something different) to re-engage every 10minutes or so
   e  Vary the style of questions asked

3. Accountability

   a  Set clear expectations beforehand
   b  Nudge the less engaged learners from time to time
   c  Develop multiple grading components
   d  Consider peer assessments
   e  Use reports from the software to identify content for grading/attendance

## 9.2 Asynchronous remote case delivery

'Getting case learning online in an asynchronous format is not easy….. Just preparing for those all-important 'aha' moments requires thinking through and preparing for how participants are likely to react to content'.

*Harvard, USA*[13]

Online case delivery can be considered in both synchronous (all at the same time in real time) and asynchronous modes (facilitating information sharing outside the constraints of time and place with a remote class group). Similar questions to those in the previous section should be considered if using cases for online programmes in asynchronous contexts. In addition, using cases for asynchronous delivery provides opportunities for the case tutor to prepare pre-planned recorded content in advance for students to visit at a later period (or periods) to formulate a response. Asynchronous learning relies far more on peer-to-peer engagement, initial cold-calling of students online, sending them specific invites, and encouraging them to send answers into the online text-chat (forums or discussion boards are often located on screen to the side of the participants), so that other participants can see their comments and respond. Once again, recordings of all comments can then be captured by the whole group, from which conclusions can be drawn and learning outcomes can be developed.

Carefully scheduled small group work is even more important for asynchronous delivery, as is the slow release of case content to facilitate the opportunity for discovery by enhancing the expository nature of the case, (so that the end is not clear from the beginning). In addition to monitoring individual and group participation, as well as content in the text chat, students could be encouraged to record their experiences in a journal as a reflective exercise, which would enable tutors to further engage with the learning process on a one-to-one basis, while monitoring student engagement and performance. This could serve as a formative assessment or contribute to a final summative assessment.

Case content might need to be further segmented into smaller sections for asynchronous online learning. The case data and the tutor's case map invariably need to change, as the journey through the data will differ for asynchronous learners, and the map will need to be revised to reflect this.

Research on the adoption of online asynchronous case learning methods conducted by IE Business School[14] supports extensive use of discussion forums integrated with videos, simulations and online exercises. The research also draws attention to the importance of clear communication of expectations with students to avoid confusion or ambiguity. By setting clear ground rules, students should feel able to conduct activities asynchronously in a supported and co-operative manner. To support this process and ensure effectiveness, it is vital that technical details have been well managed and communicated, learning goals are clear, students are informed to prepare in advance of the case, and those that are disadvantaged are clearly signposted to additional support. There are non-engagement risks to work through, particularly if participants are not undertaking the tasks required of them within the allotted timeframe.

One of the major benefits of asynchronous case programmes is that it overcomes the limitations of time-zones and broadens the potential geographic reach of the programme, given that participants from across the world are able to access resources in their own time, rather than be tied to a delivery schedule which might otherwise mean logging into synchronous programmes with scheduling that spans across inconvenient hours of the day or night. Asynchronous learning has the added benefit of enabling participants to work at their own pace rather than be governed by the pace of the case tutor and class participants, which is particularly helpful when working with international learners where some will be learning through a language medium that is not their mother tongue.

## 9.3 Combining synchronous and asynchronous with blended learning

As synchronous cases tend to work best when case material is limited in size and scope, it is feasible to consider how some of this content could be made available through asynchronous access. In this way, synchronous and asynchronous case delivery can occur independently or as a complementary approach to online learning.[15]

It might be helpful to use asynchronous approaches to capture data about your learners that can better inform how you deliver your synchronous case programmes. Observing asynchronous responses can help identify the areas of a case that provide greatest engagement and the approaches to learning that the students apply to the case data, which they can then bring to future synchronous classes. In this way, asynchronous engagement with a case, could be conducted as a forerunner for a synchronous case event.

On the one hand, it can be argued that synchronous delivery is a preferred approach for student exchange and shared experiential learning, to support the development of a community. On the other, asynchronous learning can better support student assessment, as well as opportunities for students to either go and explore other content to bring back to the case forum, or develop longer periods of time for case reflection and evaluation.

Many of the established case-based learning institutes have developed a portfolio of learning opportunities, which not only distinguish between synchronous and asynchronous online learning but also incorporate F2F sessions (often as day schools or weekend residentials), to provide a more blended approach to learning. Arguably, if these three approaches are combined and managed carefully, then it is possible to draw out the specific benefits of all three, while using each approach to mitigate against the weaknesses of the other approaches.

> 'Spending time lecturing synchronously in an online course is wasteful. If you have lecture material you feel is best delivered that way, then record the lecture, post it online, require the students to watch it, and spend the synchronous meetings fostering interaction'.[16]

By combining these three approaches of synchronous, asynchronous and F2F you might find that you are able to make better use of impactful approaches to learning and teaching in a more time-efficient manner. For more than ten years the *hyflex* mode of delivery has been growing in popularity in management

**TABLE 9.1** Moving from F2F to online using synchronous and asynchronous styles

| Synchronous | Asynchronous |
| --- | --- |
| Consider pace of discussion carefully | Students work at own pace |
| Fixed scheduling | Students work at a time to suit themselves |
| Warm call participants | Cold call participants |
| Revise case map, with fewer takeaways | Revise case map |
| Allow more breaks, to mitigate against online fatigues | Students choose when to engage with the case, within pre-determined parameters |
| Encourage greater use of text-chat box/Discussion forum | Schedule greater use of text-chat box/Discussion forum, with prompts to individuals to invite responses |
| Make frequent use of breakout groups | Carefully scheduled small groups |
| Record session for later playback and review | Prepare pre-planned recorded material for students to view |
| Draw from students in examples | Encourage students to journal their experiences |
| Expect less coverage in the discussion time | Similar coverage over a longer period of reflective time |
| Encourage screen sharing | Consider slower/phased release of case content |
| Utilise lots of polls | Utilise lots of polls |

education. This approach essentially uses all three of these online and F2F modes simultaneously and often involves livestreaming. This model normally allows participants to choose which mode of delivery they wish to select, promoting student choice, a more active approach to learning and yielding higher levels of student satisfaction.[17]

## 9.4 Examples of online case delivery

A growing number of established case-based learning institutes are making significant investments in technological and plant resource to promote further anticipated growth in online delivery. As Harvard Business School was the original pioneer of the management case study, it is perhaps not surprising to see that in 2014 it launched its dedicated HBX CORe online teaching programme with its synchronous digital learning platform HBX live (now rebranded as HBS Online), where you can 'immerse yourself in real challenges faced by seasoned leaders across a variety of industries, develop business intuition through interactive learning exercises, and join a global community of peers'.[18] Since then many thousands of students have participated in the entry level online programme, using Harvard's online platform. These programmes have subsequently become an access route for entry onto Harvard's MBA.

Similarly, INSEAD Graduate Business School, which has bases in France, Singapore, Abu Dhabi and San Francisco, has a long-established record of case teaching and writing. In 2020 INSEAD launched its Go Live series of online programmes, enabling learners to log into synchronous online training across a range of different business, leadership and management and entrepreneurship disciplines. The series, which was launched as an extension to INSEAD's executive education suite of programmes, promises a 'real-time, immersive, virtual learning' experience for all participants.[19]

Across the world, similar online programmes are being developed, including case-based initiatives at IMD in Switzerland, Boston University in the USA, Ivey Business School in Canada, the Lee Kong Chian School of Business at Singapore Management University and Imperial College Business School, London. Further details of organisations supporting such programmes can be found in the final section of this book.

Whichever distance learning approach is adopted, commonly held views on building community have proven to be invaluable to case practitioners, ensuring that the group remain 'sticky' and 'connected'; often supported by tertiary software such as Whatsapp, Instagram, Twitter or Facebook. It might seem obvious, but the more interesting, creative and compelling the case material, and the more creative the delivery approach, the greater the level of student curiosity and engagement. One final consideration is the technological burden of remote delivery. If you are to sustain an online or remote delivery approach to your case programme, you will need to ensure that you have full institutional infrastructure and ICT support for the ever-changing platforms and other digital functional challenges of remote delivery. As a case tutor from Singapore noted:

> 'A typical team developing an online course may include specialist learning designers and editors, a video producer, an IT expert and a project manager, all working in close collaboration with the faculty'.[20]

PAUSE FOR A MOMENT: While considering the development of a remote delivery or online programme, make a list of all the pros and cons, given your own experiences of working with such digital technologies, and consider the actions you might need to undertake to mitigate against any identified risks.

Now that you have completed this chapter, you should know that:

1. Online or remote delivery case sessions are achievable both in synchronous and asynchronous contexts.
2. Sensitivity is required when inducting students to online case modes of learning, with a realistic measure of expectation of learner thresholds and capacities in contrast to face-to-face delivery contexts.

3.   While there are unavoidable challenges to online and remote delivery, there are also new benefits to be pursued when these opportunities are approached in a planned and integrative manner.

4.   Remote and online case learning works best (in much the same way as it does in F2F contexts) when there is a healthy marriage of (i) the right type of case data with (ii) a clearly profiled specific learner group by adopting (iii) the correct delivery plan or teaching approach. However, both the format of the case data and the teaching approach will need to be adapted for remote delivery, as it is unlikely that they would work as effectively if unchanged from those used for F2F delivery.

## Notes

1  David Lefevre, 2019
2  This book was completed shortly after the outbreak of the global coronavirus (Covid-19) pandemic, and much of the thinking around the theme of remote and online delivery was still at an early stage and so is widely expected to continue to evolve.
3  Shiano and Andersen, 2017
4  Muilenburga and Bergeb, 2015
5  Kupp and Mueller, 2020
6  Fenton-O'Creevy, 2019
7  Narayanan and Schiano, 2020
8  ibid
9  Sklar, 2020
10  Ivey Publishing, 2020
11  Liu, Socrate and Pacheco, 2020
12  Lee, 2020
13  Mullane, 2019
14  Gabaldón, 2020
15  Levy, 2000
16  Shiano and Andersen, 2017
17  Kyei-Blankson, Godwyll and Nur-Awaleh, 2014
18  Harvard Business School, 2020
19  INSEAD, 2020b
20  Sridharan, 2019

# SECTION SUMMARY

This brings us to the end of the first section of this Handbook, which has focussed exclusively on teaching and learning methods with case studies. By now you should be aware that there is no single, unique right or wrong approach to effective case teaching, but there are some commonly held principles of good practice which continue to guide thinking as the case study approach to management education expands geographically, technologically and across a broader range of different learner groups. Ultimately it is for you to determine which approach is going to be most effective with your specific participants, with all the secret histories, cultural nuances and personal motivations that they bring to the class sessions.

However, this by no means concludes our thinking and learning about case teaching. The following section moves this exploration of the case study towards principles and good practices related to case writing. It is perhaps inevitable that the more that you invest in the case teaching process, the more attractive case writing becomes, enabling the facilitator to develop their own teaching and learning resources for in-class case sessions. The following section unpacks key principles and practices in case writing, but does so in the continuing context of good practice for case teaching. So, even if you are not planning to be a case writer yourself, do read on, as the following section continues to provide helpful hints for effective case teaching.

This next section focuses on all aspects of case writing, including formatting, writing styles, presentational options, classical writing theory and more contemporary adaptions to traditional practice, drawing insights once again from practitioners across the globe.

# SECTION II
# Case Writing

# 10

# SOURCES OF CASE DATA

Around the world, case authors are adapting their writing techniques to develop new cases. Here is what scholars have had to say about their approaches to writing a case study:

> 'A case must be written in a simple, narrative absorbing style to keep the class engaged. .... At the end of the day, a case should have learning value for the students'.
>
> *ICFAI, India*[1]

> 'Writing a teaching case is more similar to writing a spy novel than a research article. To begin with, a case has to have a hook: an overriding issue that pulls various parts together, a managerial issue or decision that requires urgent action'.
>
> *University of Hong Kong*[2]

> 'Apart from a sharp focus, a good teaching case should also have an engaging story. A case story is more than a business history: It has a setting, actors with their perspectives, and dramatic elements such as a dilemma or a conflict'.
>
> *Case Development Centre, The Netherlands*[3]

> 'The information in the case provides the context for the problem - the setting or circumstances in which the problem is occurring. The details of this context are crucial for understanding the problem and how it can be resolved'.
>
> *Massey University, New Zealand*[4]

This section explores the following:

- How to source the right types of data to inform case writing.
- The merits of classic field research case studies.
- The pros and cons of desk-based case research.
- The argument for the armchair case study.

'Content is king', as the founder of Microsoft once famously claimed; this phrase could also be reasonably applied to effective case writing. Similarly, the popular computer programming quote: GIGO ('garbage in, garbage out') might also apply to case writing. Sourcing the right data and formatting it in a manner that enables the learner to journey through the case narrative on a 'voyage of discovery' is both an art and a science, which requires creative thinking as well as careful planning and preparation. This opening section on case writing explores the merits of different sources of case data that could be adopted to inform the case writing process.

Principally there are three different approaches to sourcing data to create a case: field research, desk research and personal experience. Traditionally, the case study would have been based on field research conducted within an organisation, where the general expectation would be that everything that you need to address the issues raised in the case study can be found in the data contained within the case. When cases were first created for management education in the 1920s, this would seem to have been a sensible approach. After all, the search for further information would have been a long, costly and complex ordeal that would have almost certainly undermined the learning process. In those early days, postgraduate learners did not have the benefits of online and digital services providing huge search engines and responses to queries within seconds. As a result, it made sense initially to ensure that the case contained all the data needed to address the issues that required a response. Consequently, these cases tended to be very long and complex, demanding a high level of intensive pre-class preparation. We live in a very different world today. Information is at our fingertips. Decisions and policy are made on the whims of no more than 280 characters of a tweet, and our world contains an abundance of easily accessible data, and yet this often leads to a paralysis of analysis. It is therefore no surprise that the average length of a case study has decreased significantly over the past three decades. According to The Case Centre, which holds the world's largest collection of management case studies, the average length of its cases has halved in 30 years, from 28 pages to 14 pages (including exhibits and appendices), with 77% of its best-selling cases containing no more than 20 pages.

Size matters, and so too do structure and format (which will be captured in greater detail in the next chapter). Given that our students have access to management information at their digital fingertips, cases can afford to contain fewer data, as students are then left with the challenge to conduct their own research around the themes raised in the case, to build a bigger picture of these issues.

The impartiality of the case writer will benefit the case writing process, and this is often captured in a sub-note on the opening page of the case, which reads: 'this case is derived from XXX data and is intended to be used for group discussion rather than to illustrate either effective or ineffective handling of a management situation'. The next three parts of this chapter consider each type of data source and their merits for case writers.

## 10.1 Field research

Field research continues to be the most popular approach to case writing, with more than 50% of The Case Centre's best-selling cases being attributed to field data, captured from within an organisation. There are obvious benefits for case writers who are able to enter the organisation as a case writer to capture the 'inside feel' of the business and its cultural nuances. Individual contributors can say a lot about their organisation not only with the words they use but also with the approaches that they take to supporting the research, the eliciting of opinions and the intonation and body language that accompanies their verbal responses. However, a counterargument might suggest that a contributor to field research is only going to share the story that they *want* to share and so, untested, these stories are likely to contain unavoidable biases and limiting boundaries to the full picture of the situation. Nonetheless, it has often been demonstrated that opinions can be more important than facts, and it is difficult to elicit opinions of key stakeholders from an organisation without conducting field research within the organisation.

Field research case studies have fallen in popularity proportionate to the number of desk-based case studies, for a number of reasons. The development of a field-based case is a costly process and requires a significant investment in time and relationship building to ensure the right contributors are agreeable to providing the required responses to enable the case the be developed with credibility and with adequate scope for a learning journey. One of the first hurdles that a case author must overcome is approval from the organisation to use such data for case development. This could be harder than it initially seems, as evidence has demonstrated that not all case contributors have the power to authorise release of their own data to the case writer.

## LESSONS LEARNT

I remember the face of the kind professor from a highly reputable university in India who shared with me the pain of withdrawing his case after months of time spent within the organisation to capture the necessary case data. He thought that he had honoured all the right principles and practices to develop his field research case, but the eventual outcome left him bereft and emotional as he shared his insights with me. He had contacted a friend from within the participating organisation and, together, they had agreed the parameters of the case that would be developed in time for the professor's new programme starting later that year. Mindful of the sensitive nature of some of the issues and data that would be required, the professor offered assurances that certain data would be disguised to safeguard the integrity of the organisation. He even sought additional verbal reassurances from the organisation's legal team to ensure his visits to the business to conduct the necessary interviews would not be in vain. Once these interviews were completed, the professor started curating the narrative structure to produce the case study, occasionally making use of secondary data about the organisation. On completion of the case he contacted the legal team for a statement to provide release authorisation and to enable the case to be used in class. However, during the time that had elapsed since he started his enquiries a new head of the legal team had been appointed and, with no prior formal documentation from the team to back-up the professor's claims, this new head of team was unwilling to support a formal release authorisation for the case data, citing reputational concerns. The professor was unsure what to do next.

We live in an increasingly litigious world, and so it is perhaps not surprising that these days field-based case studies require formal release authorisation from the organisation, and my recommendation is always to get this *in writing* before starting the research process. An agreed outline of the research, identifying its purpose, scope, the required contributors, the boundaries (what will and what will not be included) and any other caveats around how data might need to be disguised should be approved with the organisation and then compiled in a letter to which the organisation's legal team should be able to provide a written response, authorising the research to be undertaken. Having completed the work and assembled the data into a case study, this should then be sent back to the organisation (together with a copy of the original signed approval letter), to seek final written formal release authorisation, to enable the completed case to be used, and where appropriate published for wider circulation.

In certain situations, organisations might initially be reluctant to agree to participate, for fear that key commercially sensitive data might be compromised, or that individuals might feel undermined. In such scenarios it might help to offer in advance to disguise key elements of data in order to alleviate the concern. This might include changing the names of key individuals or products, adjusting key location details or amending financial figures by multiplying all data by a certain factor to ensure the data remains intact, but conceals the true financial figures.

Here is a suggested summary of the proposed steps that you might consider taking when developing your field-based case study:

1. Identify the key focus of the case study within the specific organisation.
2. Seek out appropriate opportunities with potential contributors.
3. Make initial contact with the organisation and determine who, from within the organisation, is responsible for providing formal release authorisation.
4. Agree the parameters for the case research.

5. Decide the boundaries of the research, and compile a letter for initial organisational sign-off in principle before undertaking research.
6. Undertake the desk research.
7. Complete initial field research within organisation.
8. Write up first draft.
9. Compile supporting material.
10. Check draft against original objectives.
11. Further field/desk research, where needed.
12. Formal release authorisation from the organisation.

During this planning process, it is helpful to think about the likely structure and format of the case. For example, if the technology is available, is it worth capturing some of the content from interviews on video to provide multimedia content as part of the final case format?

> 'At the end of the interview, "keep a foot in the door", with a comment such as, "May I get back to you if I have any questions?" or "I'd like to send you a copy of my notes and then call you to get any suggestions you might have for corrections or added information" '.
>
> *Harvard, US*[5]

One of the key attributes of successful case writing is determining the case *focus* and then sticking to it. It is easy to become distracted by secondary issues, which might arise during the interview process, which could also be of useful learning value. The peril is that these can often lead to confusion for the reader if they draw attention away from the focus of the case. As one popular case writer once stated: 'Always keep the main thing, the plain thing!' All the case interviews conducted within the organisation should reflect this primary focus to ensure that the narrative remains on-message when you come to construct the case itself.

When planning and preparing to conduct interviews, it is important to consider how to avoid interview bias wherever possible and to elicit a clear, honest and unambiguous response from the interviewee. As has already been highlighted, one of the weaknesses of the field case is its potential for a biased viewpoint that reflects what the organisation wants you to know rather than a full statement of the facts about the situation under review. Similarly, field-based data must be constrained to remain within the boundaries agreed with the host organisation. In some cases, this can mean that the writer will experience limited editorial control, from which to establish the facts around key themes in the research. To this end, some writers are starting to prefer the option of developing desk-based research, to alleviate such bias and limitations.

The 'Trimming the FAT' case in Chapter 20 is an example of a field research case using data derived by the author from a government ministry.

## 10.2 Desk research

Cases developed entirely through desk-based research do not normally require formal release authorisation from the organisation under review, provided that the case writer can clearly demonstrate the secondary sources that have informed the research. These types of cases do not therefore normally involve any field research and, as a result, can be developed without the time-consuming requirement of securing interviews with contributors within the organisation under investigation. They are therefore considered to be a lower-cost solution to resourcing the case class, as all the content used to inform the case is derived from already published resources. This also removes any restrictions or bias that would normally be imposed by a contributing organisation and provides the case writer with autonomy to make editorial choices around the focus of the case and the parameters of the data that is captured.

This effectively permits anyone to research and write a case about the organisation regardless of their relationship and/or geographical proximity to the business. However, although this might seem like a win–win solution for case writers, there are some notable drawbacks.

The first and perhaps most obvious limitation of desk research is that the writer is unable to fully experience the culture and 'feel' of the organisation, which can so often provide additional cues to enhance the case narrative. Given that we have already considered that 'opinions can be more important than facts', desk cases tend to rely more on facts and are less able to get 'under the skin' of key protagonists to capture opinions. The desk case is largely dependent on the authenticity and validity of the sources that the writer is able to capture to inform the case data. One notable case author compared this to his view of accounting practices by stating: 'as much as the difference between financial accounting and management accounting is that one is there to provide information and the other is there to hide information, so too can case study research require detective work to discern what data is true and what is hidden'. In a world of fake news, it is easy to consider how an over-reliance on a limited data set might lead to the creation of an entirely distorted picture of the organisation, if left unchecked. This can be offset, somewhat, by ensuring that the desk-based research draws evidence from a wide range of sources from different reference points to alleviate any extremes and biases. This prospect might seem unlikely or unimportant to the case writer, until such point as the case is delivered in class and one of the participants appears to have greater insider-knowledge about the organisation than that of the writer. This can unavoidably lead to challenge about the authenticity and credibility of the case, which could undermine the entire learning process.

Another challenge facing desk-based case writers is the dynamic and interplay between individual actors, which often contributes to the plot structure of the case. If missing, then the desk-based case might feel rather dry and read more like a report rather than the unfolding of an interesting story. The writer should ensure that the narrative includes plenty of quotes from key characters within the story of the organisation, in order to provide a level of vitality and depth to the case which fosters the illusion of a willing suspension of disbelief.

Despite such drawbacks, desk-based cases are increasing in popularity, and some have more recently become significant award-winners. From a recent study of The Case Centre's bestselling cases from across the world, just over 40% were desk-based.

The Monarch Airlines case in Chapter 20 is an example of a desk-based research case using data derived by the author from published resources.

## 10.3 Armchair cases

Fewer than 10% of cases in The Case Centre's global collection are based on what is often referred to as the author's *personal experience*. While many of these cases are biographical in nature, they also include *armchair cases*, which are largely fictional, but represent true-to-life scenarios in similar organisations, which enable the user to focus on key themes which might otherwise be unavailable from current literature. These armchair cases are therefore a projection of the imagination of the experienced case author and often reflect the writer's real experiences, but which the author is unable to publish as real data.

There are both benefits and pitfalls to using armchair cases, but they do serve an important purpose as examination and assessment cases. It is often difficult (if not impossible) to find the required case that addresses the specific learning objectives within a certain word count, delivered in such a manner that might achieve all the requirements of a module assessment. In such situations the armchair case provides a helpful solution. They allow the case writer to determine their own boundaries and parameters, to shape the scenario, themes, viewpoints and context around their own knowledge of the specific leaner group and can ensure that the assessment objectives meet the desired criteria for the module. The limitations of such cases are that, in a normal classroom discussion context, they tend to lack credibility, and, given that the fictitious company is unknown to the learner, this might serve to demotivate the group and inhibit engagement and participation. As the organisation is fictitious, there are no real boundaries that would normally hem in the discussion, and this porous context can also negatively affect the perceived credibility of the case. Therefore, novice writers should be cautioned against armchair cases until having developed some field or desk research cases.

There are hybrids adaptations to the armchair case that overcome these credibility issues to a certain degree. Where a writer is unable to write explicitly about a real company situation, an armchair version might be conceived in such a manner as to conceal any direct link to the organisation in question, with changes to business names, stakeholders, locations and other data, while ensuring that the general themes of the situation remain visible for the class to explore.

Having determined which source of data best suits your case research, the next step in the case writing process is to consider the structuring of the data, which is covered in the next chapter. The Ereuna Research case in Chapter 20 is an example of an armchair case derived from the author's personal experiences.

PAUSE FOR A MOMENT: Think about some of the cases that you have most enjoyed – either as a tutor or as a participant. Are they principally derived from field research or desk-based or are they armchair cases? Was any of the data disguised to the best of your knowledge? How did the construction of the case influence your engagement with the in-class experience? What does this imply for you in terms of your preferred choice of case data?

Now that you have completed this chapter, you should know that:

1. Cases can be derived from a range of different data sources, albeit traditionally the case study was the product of field research.
2. When engaging in field research, it is vital that you establish support for release authorisation from the contributing organisation at the earliest opportunity.
3. There are a growing number of award-winning, desk-based case studies.
4. Armchair cases can provide helpful solutions to case selection for exam and assessment purposes.

## Notes

1 Vedpuriswar, 2003b, p. 3
2 Farhoomand, 2004
3 Yue, 2016a
4 Van der Ham, 2016
5 Corey, 1998, p. 6

# 11

# CASE STRUCTURES

'The restructuring involves the telling of a story within which there are discoveries to be made and things to be learned. In some ways a case study is like a detective story'.

*The Case Centre, UK[1]*

This section explores the following:

- How to develop different frameworks for case data.
- Traditional best practices for developing case structure.
- Getting the case opening and closure right.
- The pros and cons of different case formats.

Long-established case writing institutes and centres have adapted their own best practices over time for structuring the case study. This chapter does not seek to support any single practice or format, but rather presents a broad range of different perspectives to inform your own choices for case design, structure and formatting.

The Case Development Centre, based in the Netherlands, has a long track record for supporting case writing. It proposes that the starting point for case writing is determining the *focus* of the case.[2] Subsequent case structuring should ensure that the focus is maintained and not lost within complex narratives. Another long established producer of case studies is IMD, which is based in Switzerland, which proposes that the first responsibility in case writing is to tell a good story, and to tell it well, to enable participants to place themselves into the shoes of some of the key characters in the story.[3] Similarly, Harvard Professor Malcom McNair spoke of the significance of developing a *willing suspension of disbelief* by presenting a case that immerses the reader into the very heart of the situation within the organisation.[4] And evidence from China and across Asia point to a greater demand for shorter, more practical cases based on the local economy.[5]

The case should be written in parallel with the creation of the *map* or *teaching note*. If you look to develop the case without a map or teaching note, you are more likely to create no more than an interesting illustration or a readable story, rather than a case study for learning and teaching. Some case writers advocate completing a full map or teaching note before even beginning to start to structure the text and data of the case study. From my own experience and having talked to many case writers from around the world, cases are normally developed in tandem with the teaching note or map, and often with the map evolving just slightly ahead of the case data. This evolutionary ebb-and-flow of map- and case-writing enables both parts to form in sync and in harmony, informing each other as the structuring evolves.

The Case Development Centre, based at the Rotterdam School of Management, works closely with case writers to support the development of their own cases. They have created a helpful checklist when preparing to write your own case.

## Ten questions to ask yourself before writing a teaching case

You can only write clearly if you think clearly. Before you begin writing a teaching case, it is advisable to ask yourself 10 sets of questions that can better prepare you for the writing:

1.  How does the case fit into my teaching? What are my teaching objectives? What key discussion questions do I want to bring into the classroom?
2.  Who will my audience be? How difficult should my case be?
3.  How fresh is my case topic? Do similar cases already exist? Have I done an internet search (e.g. on www.thecasecentre.org)?
4.  What type of case do I want to write? A field case, a 'library' case or an 'armchair' case? A full-length case, a mini-case, a case series, or a multi-media case?
5.  What is the decision focus of my case? Who will be my protagonist? Why is his or her decision urgent?
6.  Does the case include controversy, contrast, conflict, dilemma or other dramatic elements?
7.  What are the standard components of a case? How shall I open the case? What sections shall I create thereafter? How shall I close the case?
8.  What data do I need to complete a case? Do I need interviews, and if so, with whom, and how many? How can I get an organization to co-operate on allowing interviews?
9.  Within what time frame do I want to finish the case? What if I experience a writing block?
10. In what style shall I write a case? Which writing rules I should follow? Do I have any tips for editing the draft?

*Authorised permission for use by Tao Yue from the RSM Case Development Centre, (Erasmus University) who prepared this document as the basis for training and teaching*

While views about structures, formats and styles continue to evolve, there are four fundamental structures that are normally found in most cases used for teaching and learning. These form the fundamental skeleton of the case and enable it to be adapted and developed to meet all the functional demands of the local case writer. Each of these four structures is captured in this chapter.

## 11.1 Narrative structure

Every case has some form of narrative structure which determines the order and manner in which the story is told. The structure can vary in formality and ought to reflect the style that is most likely to be appealing to the target learner group. The structure can tell a story from different viewpoints, using descriptive or conversational styles, but the key responsibility of the narrative structure is to tell a story, to achieve a clear and unambiguous unpacking of information (data) for the reader, to enable critical enquiry, evaluation and, where appropriate, decision-making.

For example, the typical structure of a Harvard case, as unpacked by Professor Jane Linder, is structured as follows: 'Cases almost always start with a description of the setting – the problem or situation at hand-then go to company and industry background…. three general frameworks are used frequently: chronology, organisational structure and problem structure'.[6]

The author's approach to the narrative structure will determine whether the learner can enter into the shoes of the characters, to capture a realistic picture of the situation in the case and the unfolding events which require addressing. For example, I often tend to find that my undergraduate students prefer clear details about the events within the case and the opportunity to unpack statements or conversations between the characters within the organisation, which can often be used to support opportunities for role play. Here is an interesting style adopted in the opening section by a London-based case writer of an award-winning and one-time bestselling Amazon.com case study:

> 'The debate in the executive classroom had raged for over an hour, despite the end-of-term Christmas party in full swing just down the corridor. All the other classrooms in the London-based business school had emptied out long ago, as the participants rushed to the party, or to do their last minute Christmas shopping. But not the class debating the strategy Jeff Bezos, founder and CEO of Amazon.com one of the flag bearers and icons of the e-commerce era, had used to achieve success so fast since he had created the company in 1995'.
>
> *'Amazon.com: Marketing a New Electronic Go-between Service Provider –*
> *Taishoff & Vandermerwe'. Reproduced with permission*[7]

From this short introductory paragraph, it is easy to see how the case author was creating a picture of a scenario that would be very easy for students from other business schools to step into and explore from their own perspective. It is also worth noting that this case was derived entirely from published resources.

Here is a very different approach to a case opener from another award-winning, field research case from INSEAD:

'After three successful years in the Personal Care division of Unilever in Pakistan, Laercio Cardoso was contemplating an attractive leadership position in China when he received a phone call from the head of Unilever's Home Care division in Brazil, his native country. Robert Davidson was looking for someone to explore growth opportunities in the marketing of detergents to low-income consumers living in the Northeast of Brazil. An alumnus of INSEAD's Advanced Management Programme, Laercio had joined Unilever in 1986 after graduating in business administration from Fundação Getulio Vargas in São Paulo. He thus had the seniority and marketing skills that were necessary for the project. More importantly, he had never been involved in the traditional approach to marketing detergents and, having witnessed the success of Nirma in India, he was acutely aware of the threat posed by local brands targeted at low-income consumers'.

*'Unilever in Brazil (1997–2007): Marketing Strategies for Low-income Consumers – Chandon & Guimaraes'. Reproduced with permission*[8]

This opening paragraph is somewhat different from the previous case in that it immediately reveals a high level of content to establish key factors including the location, the industry and the product/competition-related theme of the case.

This next case opener is from another desk-based, award-winning case from the China Europe International Business School (CEIBS), this time based on China's retailer Best Buy:

'In late February 2011, major Chinese business journals and newspapers published a piece of astonishing news:

On February 22nd, 2011, Best Buy announced the closure of eight Best Buy branded stores in China and its retail headquarters in Shanghai. However, Five Star Appliances, a brand acquired by Best Buy in 2006, would continue its business. Many suppliers and customers were surprised to read the news and came to Best Buy-branded stores to find out what happened. Best Buy staff, who felt deserted when Best Buy announced the closure of the stores without any prior notice, protested by requesting Best Buy to "give me a job and compensate for my lost youth." On February 24th, Best Buy decided to reopen four stores, with two in Shanghai and another two in Suzhou and Henzhon respectively, to deal with follow-up issues for a month. Nonetheless, the stores were flooded with customers and scuffles broke out between customers and staff. Therefore the reopening of the four stores had to be postponed'.

*'Hard Choices: Best Buy and Five Star in China (A) – Tsai, Zhu & Xu'. Reproduced with permission*[9]

Unlike the previous two case openers, the approach adopted in this third case immediately draws the student's attention to the tensions and drama within the case, which will no doubt stimulate debate among local Chinese audiences, who are more familiar with the brand and its history. The format of the fourth case opener is quite different:

### Phone call, November 2010

TO: Sankar Krishnan, Managing Director at the global professional services firm Alvarez & Marsal (A&M)

FROM: Steve Cohen, Managing Director of Alvarez & Marsal's North American Commercial Restructuring practice

STEVE COHEN: Sankar, I've just received some worrying news from Sapphire Capital (SC). You know the firm? It's one of our large US-based distress private equity fund clients. We have advised them on several engagements. One of their Indian portfolio companies has some serious issues. It seems the top management may have been involved in some irregular activities and the company is in a crisis. That's all the information I have at the moment, but they seem very nervous.

SANKAR KRISHNAN: Yes, I know SC. This sounds serious. We need to organize a call with the fund and with Nikhil to discuss what steps we should take next. Nikhil is on vacation with his family, but from the sound of it we can't wait. Let's speak tomorrow at 8.30am. I'll call Nikhil if you can organize getting the SC people together?"

'Crisis at the Mill: Weaving an Indian Turnaround - Alvarez & Marsal'.[10]
*Reproduced with permission*

The narrative style adopted in the opening section of this EFMD award-winning INSEAD field research case is distinctly different from the others, introducing two key characters and immediately setting the tone for what is clearly a serious issue of concern. Although short on details, the case author uses terms like *serious* and *crisis* to develop the sense of urgency first before introducing content and context in the following paragraphs.

> PAUSE FOR A MOMENT: Look back over the four case openers and ask yourself which is your favourite? And which is your least favourite? And why? All these openers have strengths and weaknesses and, having conducted this exercise with many case scholars from across the globe, it has become clear that different attributes appeal to different writers who teach in different contexts. What is important for you to determine is why do certain attributes appeal to you? And how does this inform your own personalised approach to case writing?

It's worth pausing to note that all these case openers were selected from award winning cases, which therefore demonstrates that there is no single silver bullet when it comes to defining a winning narrative style. (Details of how to access these cases can be found in Chapter 19 in the last section of this book).

There are some common editorial points of good practice worth considering when developing your narrative structure. Always remember that your starting point is to tell a story that is readable, intriguing and engaging for the reader. Allow the opportunity for curiosity to force the reader to remain engaged with the text. The types of words you use should reflect this, and you should avoid using unnecessarily complex or jargonistic terms. For those case writers, who are used to writing academic journal articles, the challenge is to unlearn some of these common journal writing practices to ensure that the style adopted for the case presents an easy-to-read, captivating story. Think carefully about the sequencing of events, what leads to what, to maintain the flow of an unfolding story. Avoid unduly long and complex sentences and guard against information-dumping, in favour of a gradual releasing of easy-to-digest data, with a steady unveiling of the key issues and themes.

It is standard convention to address the characters in the case by their last names, after their initial introduction. Avoid sexist, racist or inflammatory language. Use headings where appropriate as they help to maintain engagement throughout the text. If the case is being developed by more than one author, ensure that you have identified one person who will retain editorial control to manage the internal consistency of the narrative structure, otherwise the case might feel more like an unappetising sandwich of many different fillings.

Remember, you should be developing the teaching note or map at the same time as you are structuring the case study. At this point it is worth reflecting on how you intend for the participants to *treat* the data? For example, will they apply a *deductive* (theory applying) approach or an *inductive* (theory developing) method? This might help to determine how you set out the narrative structure. Similarly, will the data be provided in a *convergent* format (information released across the whole case to allow for data to be captured and reformatted, before analysis can be undertaken), or will there be significant gaps in the data enabling the adoption of a more *divergent* or creative learning approach?

By this stage you will also need to determine how difficult the case should be. This will inform how many tables and diagrams to use and where you are going to locate them, how many concepts will be introduced in the themes, what methods of analysis will be adopted, and what additional materials or exhibits will be required.

Finally, as you are writing, it can be easy to get carried away with descriptive content and meta-narratives, but remember that the most popular cases are short cases, so only include the information you need to include, avoiding ambiguity, over-complexity and repetition. Keep yourself out of the text, unless you are writing your own biographical story. And of course, always *keep the main thing the plain thing.*

## 11.2 Chronology structure

Every case has some form of chronology or time structure that determines the sequence of events and the order within which things are reported. Although it might at first appear obvious that the case narrative should begin at the beginning of a story and work through the sequence of events in a logical and chronological order from beginning to end, a closer look at most cases demonstrates that this is rarely the approach.

A common chronology structure in case writing, begins by introducing the issue that needs to be addressed by the readers, or the situation that has occurred in the organisation. It often then introduces the context and the characters within which the issue is set. After this point, it is quite common to go back in time to an earlier period in the organisation to provide some of the history and build-up to the current situation. For example, the case might focus on a key character and step back to the point at which this character first arrived at the company and then unpack the key milestones that have been achieved since the arrival, working back to the present situation. Alternatively, the case might reflect back on how the company faced similar issues or situations which occurred in the past, before returning to the current situation. It is quite common for the opening and closing sections of the case to mirror each other chronologically, as the writer closes the case by reinforcing the key issues that now need to be addressed in light of the emerging situation.

There are some common editorial points of good practice worth considering when developing your chronology structure. Always write in the past tense, unless using reported speech. The use of actual dates can be really helpful to maintain structural consistency, and you should avoid terms like *currently, recently, lately, last year* and *this year*, as they create contexts that are vulnerable to misinterpretation.

Finally, make it very clear when events actually took place, guarding against moving backwards and forwards in time too frequently as this can lead to confusion for the reader:

## LESSONS LEARNT

As I prepared to write my first case study, I had the opportunity to attend a three-day residential intensive case writing workshop, working alongside other novice case writers and being supported by two case writing experts. It was a wonderful opportunity to close the doors on all other distractions and, with a single minded focus, bring all my data together (along with my case map) to develop the structures of my case study. During the three days I was inspired by the creativity of the other novice case writers on the workshop and regularly guided by the thoughtful advice of the two case experts. On the final day I presented my case draft to the rest of the group including the two experts and then left the workshop to await their feedback. The case presentation was also videoed so I could look back on my own behaviour and mannerisms from the front of the class (that was an eye-opener!) Two weeks later I received a copy of the video and two reports, one from each of the case experts. A week prior to the workshop I had watched a movie that included regular flash-backs as an unfolding drama emerged. I thought this would be a useful approach to adopt for my own case writing. However, the perils of over-indulging this approach was made only-too-clear to me when I read the two reports, both of which drew attention to my chronology structure. One report read: "I think this could be a really interesting story with some challenging ideas, but I wasn't too sure because I soon lost sight of when each of the events in the case actually took place". It concluded: "Your time structure was all over the place!" More than 25 years later, and this message has stayed with me: keep the time structure clear and uncomplicated.

## 11.3 Expository structure

This structure needs careful attention and should be guided by your knowledge of your target learner group. The expository structure determines the degree to which your participants need to work at the data in order to elicit relevant outcomes in response to the questions raised by the case. In other words, it is where the *discovery* learning process starts. To get this structure right, the case writer determines what issues and facts should be made explicit to the learners and which information should be more covert or hidden. If the case is to be a reflection of reality, then it is reasonable to assume that not all information should be immediately visible or presented in an obviously accessible format. This structure enables opportunities for detective work as the participant probes the data and gathers additional informal to supplement their discoveries before making decisions regarding what to do next with their findings.

Your knowledge of the target reader group enables you to pitch the expository structure within the fine balance required to ensure it neither overestimates the reader's knowledge, nor underestimates their intelligence. Sequential cases provide a perfect context for a focused, phased-release, expository structure. These types of cases are commonly referred to as A-B-C cases, as the whole story tends to be broken into smaller bite-sized mini-cases (or caselets), that enables a slow release of data to the learner, with which they are then able to make certain enquiries and deductions before progressing to the next mini-case. These types of sequential cases are also helpful for keeping all participants within a study group focused on the same part of the narrative, rather than some progressing ahead of others.

## 11.4 Plot structure

The plot structure incorporates drama into the case and commonly involves the actions of key characters internal and external to the organisation. Often this structure is the essential glue that engages the learner and allows then to step into the shoes of one of the characters that are experiencing the situation described in the case, in order to make measured decisions on the basis of this character's perspective. Plots (and sub-plots) generate interest and intrigue for learners and clearly separate the case, as a literary form, from a more traditional journal article. It is within the plot structure that you might also wish to think about the 'pace' of the case. To maintain reader engagement, it helps to change the pace from time to time.

Again, your knowledge of the target learner group will determine the degree to which you need to indulge them with the plot structure, in order to ensure engagement. Some argue that more experienced and mature learners are less enamoured by an over-indulgent plot structure, as they would prefer to get straight to the heart of the problem and begin their analysis, without the need to be caught up in drama. You know your own students best, so you should be led by this when considering the plot structure. The case tutor's questions are often drawn from the plot structure.

## 11.5 Constructing the first draft

'Case headings…. provide a scaffolding or framework by which the reader can organise the data presented. The framework should make it easier for the reader to remember and relocate particular data points'.[11]

If you are entirely new to case writing, then here is a suggested classic format for a case structure:

1. In the first paragraph you make the statements about the key issue(s) that need to be addressed within the organisation.
2. In the second paragraph you introduce the context, giving a little background about the organisation and how it is located within its sector.
3. In the third paragraph you explain how the situation that now requires some form of action initially developed.
4. Then, in the subsequent paragraphs you include the necessary history of the organisation, how it handled similar situations in the past, and details of the roles of the key characters in the story.
5. At the end of the case you remind the reader of the key issue(s) that now require addressing, the questions that need to be considered, the analysis that needs to be undertaken and the problems that require recommendations or potential solutions.
6. Add all necessary exhibits to ensure there is enough data to tackle the issues raised in the case.
7. Avoid including any of your own opinions and evaluation in the case. (These should be captured in the teaching note. If they are left in the case, it will undermine the expository structure and create a bias leaving little scope for *discovery* learning).

Case openers have already been discussed, but it is also important to consider how to close the case. The closure should normally reinforce the main focus of the case. There may be some key questions that still need to be addressed (which could therefore stimulate the potential start of a class discussion). There might be decisions that need to be made and further considerations that need to be explored. All these can be added to build up the tension in the closing section. However, be careful not to introduce any bias into this section that might detract from the learner's freedom to draw their own evaluations and conclusions.

Once you have compiled all your data and restructured the case, reflect on all four structures listed in this chapter and then consider the target audience once again. By this point you should also have a reasonably well developed map to accompany the case draft, which sets out:

- The starting point and end point for the class discussion
- The key learning objective(s)
- Interesting visiting points (including opportunities for analysis)
- Carefully crafted questions to navigate the conversation from beginning to end
- The orientation (learner viewpoint or perspective) of the case and mode of treatment of the case data

Now it is time to face the harsh reality of sharing your creation to gather peer feedback. I tend to recommend three initial forms of feedback before you trial the case in class:

1. Ask someone known to you, who is an expert in English grammar and literature, for feedback on style of presentation.
2. Ask someone with the knowledge of the subject discipline covered within the case, for feedback on its appropriateness to elicit the key learning objectives.
3. Ask someone known to you with experience of using the case method in class, to determine the degree to which the map provides a suitable approach to tackling the case data.

The ultimate test of the effectiveness of your case will be your learner group who, from my experience, are only too willing to find the faults and shortcomings in your creative masterpiece if you ask them. Sometimes, student feedback can be brutal, which is why I recommend the three steps above first.

Having trialled your case with your learners, it is worth considering what elements worked well and which had less effect. Were there sections where the participants appeared to lack sufficient data to adequately address the discussion points? Were there any noticeable errors, confusing statements or areas that seemed to lack clarity? This is the chance to address these before completing the final version of the case.

There is no reason why cases cannot be living documents that continue to be finessed by the case author, as different experiences draw out new opportunities for the case over time. However, if the case is to have transferable value to a wider audience, there will need to be a point where you, as the case writer, have to draw a final editorial line under your masterpiece.

PAUSE FOR A MOMENT: Three cases are presented as examples at the end of this book in Chapter 20. One, commissioned by The Case Centre, was derived from desk-based research and is based on an airline facing administration. The second is an armchair case from Turkey, derived from personal experiences of the author and focusing on ethics with big data analysis. The third case is from New Zealand, based on field research from within the Ministry of Foreign Affairs and Trade. As you look through all three cases see if you can identify how the four key structures are integrated into the design of each case. An annotated version of the airline case is also is available in the Support Material, which can be found at www.routledge. com/9780367426965, where you will find comments identifying how the chronology structure was developed. These notes also contain further ideas which shaped the other three case structures as well as identifying points for analysis.

## 11.6 Case formats

Traditionally, the case study was one single paper-based item, which would have a cover page, an opening section, the main body of text and a closing section, followed by a collection of supportive exhibits. The cover page would normally indicate a title for the case, the authors and their institutions, the year of production and a statement identifying whether the case is field research or based on published resources. This normally also includes a disclaimer stating that it is only intended for use for classroom discussion rather than as an illustration of good or poor management practice. The choosing of the case title is significant, especially if you are anticipating your case could be made available to other users. Normal protocol dictates that the title should reflect little more than the name of the company, however more recently authors have transgressed from traditional protocol, with titles that have included a few words to indicate the nature or general theme of the case. Occasionally the theme can be captured as a subtitle, for example: *Smith and Jones PLC – Launching a new product into the Asian market.*

Here is a list of titles of some of the most popular and widely used cases from 2018:

- *Zara: The World's Largest Fashion Retailer*
- *Cola Wars Continue: Coke and Pepsi in 2010*
- *Healthy Life Group*
- *Wolfgang Keller at Konigsbrau-TAK (A)*
- *Michelin Fleet Solutions: From Selling Tires to Selling Kilometers*
- *Corporate Entrepreneurship and Innovation at Google, Inc*
- *Uber: Changing the Way the World Moves*
- *Mountainarious Sporting Co*
- *HP at a Strategic Crossroad: 2005*
- *Tony Hsieh at Zappos: Structure, Culture and Change*[12]

This short sample of best-selling cases illustrates the range of different approaches to using (or not) the titles to introduce the theme of the case. One thing that all these titles do at least have in common is that they all reveal the name of the organisation at the centre of the case study.

As this chapter has already revealed, it has become increasingly common for case writers to segment case data into smaller bite-sized chunks. This creates the opportunity to reveal content to the readers in a phased approach, rather than placing the whole story into their hands in one sitting. This *sequential case* approach is particularly valuable where later mini-cases from the sequence contain revealing information that would have otherwise undermined an initial investigation, had it been revealed sooner; or where a larger full case would potentially demotivate the learners by virtue of its size.

Cases can be developed to form part of a group or series. These often centre around a specific theme, genre or sector. These series of cases provide the opportunity for learners to repeatedly visit themes or key learning points from different cases to compare and contrast findings and eventually to reinforce the overall learning experience. The potential peril with these cases is that students might complain that the series can drag on too long if too many cases are included without sufficient distinctions between each case. Mixing up the structure and form of the cases within the series can ensure that the students still have a variety of different experiences.

Occasionally cases can tell two stories – a *before* and an *after* story. These types of chicken-and-egg cases can be valuable tools to expose significant learning opportunities from events that have unfolded in the distant past. Often students tend to be put off by what at first appears to be outdated stories (I remember one student once chastising my case choice, pointing out that the copyright date listed at the bottom of the case was from before he was born). Where there is still valuable learning to be derived from a case that has a historical context, it might help to provide a case with an up-to-date narrative about the same organisation. The effective unpacking of this case in a class discussion might legitimise the proposal to then explore the history of the organisation, as illustrated below:

**LESSONS LEARNT**

During a Case Writing workshop that I was running some years ago in Australia, one young associate professor discussed the challenges that he had faced with outdated cases in the classroom. He had planned to use a long-established and much-loved Qantas Airlines case study with his Strategy students, having successfully used the case study in previous years and receiving very positive feedback from his students. He ordered copies of the case, scheduled the timetable to include the case for the sixth week of his programme and then launched the course. Shortly after the course had started, Qantas began hitting the news headlines – the airline was in trouble. Like many national airlines in that season, (which was shortly after the events of 9/11), demand for flights was floundering and Australians were in danger of losing their flag carrier. The young professor was immediately aware that his Qantas case study was likely to be poorly reviewed by his students, given that the current situation facing the airline was far different to the one in his somewhat aging case. To remedy this problem, he quickly collated many of the current TV news clippings and newspaper coverage of the current situation facing Qantas and produced his own Qantas B case study, which provided useful insights that were still of relevance to the learning objectives of his Strategy module. With relief, he reported that the Qantas B case study had been a hit, with one student even claiming he must be "one of the trendiest professors in the Uni" with such up-to-date, relevant case material. At the conclusion to the class, he summarised the discussion and ended with the question: "Do you want to know where this organisation came from to get to where it is today?" Of course, every student cheered a resounding "Yes we do!" To which the professor produced his original Qantas case – a typical example of a chicken-and-egg case situation.

Finally, it is worth considering if there is value in providing a different language version of your case to broaden its appeal. I have recently discovered for myself the value added by developing some of my own cases in more than one language, when I have been working with Turkish authors to develop new material. Despite the cases being initially intended for use only at English-led classes at Turkish universities, the benefits of a Turkish translation to the native Turkish-speaking learner are obvious. Recent trends analysis from The Case Centre suggests that more than 40% of their best-selling cases from around the world included at least one additional language version.

## 11.7 Adapting data for multimedia and online cases formats

The arguments for developing multimedia and online cases have already been made (see Chapters 7 and 9). The four key structures listed above should still be considered when structuring a non-paper-based case study, but the formatting style offers much greater scope for creativity. The flow of information is often presented differently in multimedia cases, as students are given the responsibility for determining which part of the case they wish to explore first and in which order to then progress through the case's various data sources. These cases might incorporate text files, diagrams, statistical tables or video and audio content. Information might be captured through interviews, adverts, news clippings and company reports. Although these can be captured and presented in a non-linear chronology, there still needs to be well-defined chronological structuring, as the learner will need to be clear about the dates that are represented by each piece of data. All of these can be creatively set out in a structure that invites the learner to carve their own unique journey through the data. In some cases, the structure has been so significantly developed as to encourage a gamification approach to the data. When developing any of these different approaches, it is important to ensure that the final format is the best fit to encourage maximum participant engagement with the case data. Over-enhancement of case formats can distract from the core learning objectives or lead to confusion, as the main focus of the text might be less easy to identify.

Traditionally, a view was held suggesting that all of the information required to tackle the issues raised in the case should be found from the data within the case. As we have already suggested, the invention of the internet and the advancement of available data search engines mean that this is no longer always necessary. As a result, multimedia case studies can sometime serve as signposts to direct learners to sources of information with which they will be left responsible to capture the relevant data and evaluate its significance in preparation for a group discussion. Although proving increasingly popular, the obvious peril of this approach is that internet sources can change over time, and thus the tutor (and the author) should regularly check these hyperlinks to ensure that they continue to link effectively to the desired external data sources. When managed appropriately, this approach to case development can significantly reduce the editorial time required to structure the core text of the case, as much of this is relegated to signposting the learner to external (unedited) data sources. This approach should not entirely remove the need for some form of narrative content, as a case bereft of everything except hyperlinked signposts might prove to be somewhat unattractive and lacking in creative tension.

Some case writers tend to produce a written case in the first instance, to which multimedia resources are added afterwards, often by means of a hyperlink to a webpage that contains all the linked resources. Irrespective of which approach you choose to take, if you are looking to develop your case using multimedia resources, in addition to the three individuals outlined earlier in this chapter who provide editorial support for your first draft, a fourth group of technical supporters are required to ensure that the content is appropriately accessible on a platform that stands the test of time and affords maximum accessibility to learners, irrespective of which desk-based or portable device they choose to use to open the case. (Note: as I write this concluding section, I have just used four different devices to attempt to open one of my favourite, but now ageing, multimedia cases. All four attempts failed as the platform is no longer supported.)

Now that you have completed this chapter, you should know that:

1.  Cases should first draw from the right sources of data, which then need to be restructured to provide a learning journey.

2.  Although many different approaches and formats exist, four key structures – the narrative, chronology, expository and plot structures – should normally be found in each case; and together these four structures provide the internal consistency to ensure that a *voyage of discovery* can be initiated with some interesting learning surprises along the way.

3.  Like all good pieces of literature, cases require a beginning, a middle and an end. Attention to all three will ensure that the learner remains engaged by the text, directed to consider key issues and themes and informed to participate in subsequent discussions.

4.  Cases often include all the data needed to tackle the issues in the case, whereas by contrast some provide hyperlinked signposting to locations where students can complete their own detective work to capture and evaluate sources of data in relation to the themes of the case.

5.  You should not try to go it alone. Draw insights and feedback from colleagues and friends who can help you to refine your style, approach and narrative practice to add that final polish to the case writing process.

## Notes

1  Heath, 2015
2  Yue, 2016a
3  Abell, 1997
4  McNair, 1971
5  Jack, 2018
6  Linder, 1990, p. 4
7  Authored by M. Taishoff and S. Vandermerwe, 1998 © Imperial College London. www.thecasecentre.org/educators/products/view?id=22628
8  Authored by P. Chandon and P. P. Guimaraes, 2007 © INSEAD. https://publishing.insead.edu/case/unilever-brazil
9  Authored by T. Tsai, J. Zhu and L Xu, 2014 © China Europe International Business School. Case ref: 318-0302-1 available at: www.thecasecentre.org/educators/products/view?id=157674
10  Authored by C. Zeisberger & A.M. Carrick, © INSEAD. https://publishing.insead.edu/case/alvarez-marsal
11  Gentile, 1990
12  Source: The Case Centre

# 12

# CASE ENHANCEMENT

'Cases with visuals are always stronger than those with only words, which is why figures, tables, pictures and videos are useful'.

*Case Development Centre, The Netherlands*[1]

This section explores the following:

- How to provide the finishing touches to your case study.
- Providing additional resources to supplement the case.
- Considering wider circulation to other users.
- Developing the case brand.

Having captured the relevant data for your case and worked on all the structures and formatting to produce your draft copy, this chapter explores how to add the final polish that ensures that your case has the greatest impact in the classroom, locks in learning for the participant and provides scope for use across multiple student groups.

## 12.1 Final editorial check

Most case writers begin with delivery to their own class in mind. But many aspire to see their case attracting broader appeal. If you are looking to develop your case for other classes, whether internal to your organisation or further afield, you might wish to take another look at the editorial content, typeset and style to ensure that it conforms to a standard that is likely to be well received by other tutors. If your case is being used alongside cases from other authors as part of a series or programme, then put on your *case editor glasses* and take a good look at the styles adopted by the other cases to ensure that there are sufficient consistencies in your approach, such that your case appears to fit well, or at least does not stand out for the wrong reasons. Disclaimers on the home page, use of questions for the reader embedded in the text, font size and style and page lay-outs can all leave an impression with the reader, and so attention to these smaller details can make a big difference.

Furthermore, you should have a clear understanding of how the case is intended to be used in the class discussion, but your peers will be less clear. So, be sure to check that your case map provides clear guidance to your colleagues, making clear the intended approach to treating the case data; which is of particular importance for internal consistency and standardisation when you are working with other tutors to deliver the same programme across multiple groups. You might choose to formalise your map into a teaching note for broader appeal, (see next chapter), but if not, then at least ensure that your map accompanies the case and that it is ade-quately annotated to enable tutors to have a clear understanding of how the case is intended to be used.

## 12.2 Developing the case brand

You might wish to take this process one step further by exploring how your institution presents its formal outputs. There might by a communications, public relations or publications office which manages the release of such reports and out-puts on behalf of the institution, ensuring that a consistent 'house brand' is main-tained with all outputs for external use. Many of the major case writing institutions have their own publishing office which manages the final branding of these out-puts, ensuring that the correct use of logos, symmetry of typeface, etc., is main-tained for all published cases. Adopting a house brand for your case writing can provide a distinctiveness that sets your material apart from other cases, and that immediately enables the reader to build an association between you, your case and your institution.

## 12.3 Incorporating supportive human resources

The crafting of the 'live' case has already been captured in chapter 8, and the contributors to your case data might well be able to offer additional time and resources to add further value to the case, by supporting its presentation in class or by producing some form of pre-recorded endorsement or introduction to the case, which you can use as a scene-setter for your learners to further reinforce the *slice of reality* within the case narrative. I have often found that if an individual, from a contributing business of organisation, has invested a significant amount of time supporting my case writing process, then he or she is often flattered to be invited to endorse his or her own case story by some form of participation. Sometimes, with an injection of some carefully planned creativity, this can induce some inter-esting results:

## LESSONS LEARNT

Having completed a case that explored a particular difficult situation facing a pharmaceutical company, I invited the main protagonist from the case to join me to assist in its delivery. I knew that the case was scheduled to be delivered to a mixed group of students and that not all members of the group would be familiar with each other. After talking through different options, we decided to have a little fun, and the protagonist agreed to simply join the students in the classroom for this mixed cohort and 'blend in' with the group. Throughout the class discussion students shared lots of opinions about the company (not all of which were complimentary) and at the end of the class, I suggested that 'if we could bring in the protagonist today, what one generalisation or recommendation might each student offer?' Once almost all the students had offered their responses, I invited the 'very quiet student towards the back of the room,' to come to the front and join me. This unusual request caught everyone's attention and there was silence in the room as, to the astonishment of my group, I introduced the very protagonist that they had been discussing. The room was totally silent as I invited the protagonist to share what really did happen next and what the company could have done differently. This prompted lots of further questions from the students, many of whom commented after the programme had finished just how impactful the introduction of the protagonist had been to their learning experience. When I have shared this story with other case writers, some have asked why a protagonist would even be willing to undertake such a task, especially considering such negative opinion-sharing during the discussion. When I put this to the protagonist, she shared two important reflections. Firstly, this was no altruistic venture for the contributor as she believed this opportunity gave her the chance to listen and capture insights from the next generation of leaders in her field – market intel. And secondly, she then gets ten minutes at the end to share her insights on how the company is operating, which in her view is of immense marketing value. So, we agreed we had struck a win-win deal.

## 12.4 Adding value with additional resources

The case can often be supported using additional resources that are used either to set the scene, reinforce key messages of the case, or authenticate the reality of the story contained within the case. These might include resources provided by the contributing organisation – for example, company reports, marketing and promotional material or advertising videos. Sometimes these resources can be used to develop the physical learning environment and support that *willing suspension of disbelief* that the students are indeed in class, as the lecture room is transformed to the board room of the organisation under investigation, with company reports, handouts, posters and logos helping to create the illusion of the boardroom meeting.

Similarly, I once adopted a BBC case study for an undergraduate class and decided to use BBC logos included with the case to temporarily transform the lecture room into Studio 16 of BBC Broadcasting House, to support the illusion of the facility where the case study was actually located.

Once when I was finishing the final draft of a case about a Formula 1 motor racing sponsorship deal, I wrote to the organisation for final release authorisation for the primary field data that had contributed to the case. The respondent replied, confirming support, and added a further report that had only just been published and was so far available only internally which, he added, I would be welcome to duplicate for my student group when I came to deliver the case.

Each of these additional resources can play their part in providing that final polish to the case, endorsing and validating the content while providing additional insights and sources of information as takeaways for the learners.

## 12.5 Submitting your case to a global repository

There are many different routes that a case writer can take to ensure their case has broader impact and appeal. Cases can be redeveloped for publication into learned journals and into some practitioner journals for teaching and learning purposes. Cases can also contribute to *special collections* which further enhance their global appeal. There are open-access repositories for case studies to which you can submit your own work. Case study organisations that host such repositories often serve to provide a platform for you to showcase your resources to the wider academic and professional development community. These organisations normally require specific details about the case – for example, whether conducted using field or desk-based research. If it is a field case, they would normally require evidence of formal release authorisation from the contributing business. Irrespective of the type of case, they normally look for evidence that it has been tested in class at least once, and therefore has been checked for its rigour as a learning resource. Many also require a teaching note to accompany the case. Further details of these types of organisations can be found in the final section of this book.

Now that you have completed this chapter, you should know that:

1. Cases can be enhanced further with careful consideration for final typesetting and editorial design.
2. Branding your cases either as an author or at an institutional level can provide a distinctiveness that establishes your case as part of a collection.
3. Introducing other resources – whether human resources or additional content resource – can extend the credibility of the case when received by its readers.
4. Case repositories exist where authors can lodge their work for circulation to the wider academic community.

## Note

1  Yue, 2016a, p. 3

# 13

# THE CASE TEACHING NOTE

'Teaching notes don't give you the only way to teach a case or even the best way, but they do give you ideas about how other people have taught the case and what worked for them. They often have tips, supplemental anecdotes or data, a fairly rigorous analysis and often an epilogue'.

*University of Virginia, USA*[1]

This section explores the following:

- Arguments for and against developing your own teaching notes.
- How to formalise the content in your map to produce a teaching note
- Essential ingredients of the teaching note
- Additional adaptations of teaching notes.

While a case *map* principally exists for the benefit of the case author, to provide an informal reminder of the scope for using the case to navigate a pre-planned journey through the case data, the teaching note is an extension of this function and is more widely regarded as being of principal benefit to other tutors looking to use the case. So, the teaching note takes the map to its formalised conclusion to make it a separate publishable document – the student gets the case and the tutor gets the teaching note with the case.

## 13.1 Why produce a teaching note?

'A teaching note is a document that accompanies a teaching case to help potential instructors gain insight into the case and achieve better usage of the case. Although it is not a rule for every case to have a teaching note, cases with a teaching note are proven more popular than those without'.

*Case Development Centre, The Netherlands*[2]

Not all case writers produce teaching notes. So long as the author has a map that gives clear guidance to learners about how to navigate through their case, then this could be fine. But, if the case is to be delivered by other colleagues or other external users then, while a map contains some details, there are still many assumptions that underlie the detail of the map which other users might not understand and should therefore be clarified in a teaching note.

There are some institutes that favour only publishing cases and not the teaching note, preferring to safeguard the note as the intellectual property of the institution, for internal use only. This trend is diminishing as more and more case studies are available for global circulation, forcing a growing demand for teaching notes to accompany cases as part of the case selection/programme planning process.

The teaching note represents only one viewpoint and the author's intended purpose for the case. Arguably another potential user might see the case and imagine a different journey with a different map, so to this end the teaching note has limitations.

However, the vast majority of cases that are available for global circulation to scholars tend to include teaching notes, which are often considered an essential *hygiene factor* for case adoption. Without the author's map, a case tells an interesting story but requires the potential future adopter to work harder to determine its value to a class session, whereas the teaching note can provide helpful insights, clues and examples of how the case can achieve key learning objectives, while also being clear about its limitations and boundaries.

Furthermore, the teaching note identifies how the case has already worked well in a class environment, and so future users can benefit from class feedback and the experiences of its original user. It is then up to the adopter to determine whether to follow all the advice in the teaching note or alternatively to take the learning derived from the teaching note and develop their own map.

More recently, some case distributors have started to insist that all new case submissions should include a teaching note, as their own market research demonstrates that the most in-demand cases always contain notes, so this indicates that the teaching note accompanying the case is the common preference of the 'marketplace'. For example, when looking at examples of the best-selling cases from The Case Centre, over a five-year period, more than 90% of all bestsellers had a teaching note.

## 13.2 Core components of the teaching note

Not all teaching notes are helpful or easy to read, so it is worth considering how to develop a structure for your teaching note to ensure that it is a genuinely supportive tool for tutors seeking to potentially use your case study. Almost all teaching notes include the following eight key ingredients: a summary, teaching objectives, target audience, teaching approach, analysis, additional resources, feedback and 'what happened next'.

## The case summary

This initial synopsis should present a very concise, unambiguous and easy-to-read account of the core elements of the case narrative. While efforts might have been made to disguise content in the case itself, the synopsis in the teaching note should be very open and clear, as it ensures that the true message of the story within the case is made clear to the tutor.

## Teaching objectives

The key learning objectives from the map should be included here to make clear to the potential tutor how the case was intended to be used. Some case authors also use this section to make alternative suggestions about how the case could be used, to broaden its potential appeal to a wider student audience. Writers often begin this section by identifying the key themes in the text – for example, *this case explores issues related to business ethics and change management*; before then identifying more specific issues and takeaways explored in the case.

## Target audience

This section makes clear the intended user-group for the case. Many writers tend to avoid focussing too specifically on one particular learner group to avoid alienating other potential adopters. This is sometimes achieved by offering a primary suggested group, followed by other groups that it could be used with. The pre-requisites required by the group to ensure that they can tackle the issues raised in the case should be included here. For example: 'This case was specifically intended for use with final year business strategy students and those in the early stages of their MBA studies. It can also be used with other undergraduate and postgraduate groups studying strategic issues related to business development, after having developed an understanding of the fundamentals of strategy'.

## Teaching approach

This is where the core content of the map is drafted into the note. The teaching approach tells the story of how to navigate a journey from A to B with the use of carefully crafted questions to enable progress through the case data. Authors often tend to include suggested examples of approaches to case opening and closure, as well as lists of likely questions that promote movement through the case. These questions might also be accompanied with explanatory notes to identify how they could be used and what types of responses might be anticipated. If a certain *red herring* or complex point has been presented in the case, it should be clearly explained here or in the original summary at the beginning of the teaching note.

## Analysis

Previous chapters have drawn attention to the purpose of the case discussion which involves both breadth and depth of exploration. A focus on *breadth* ensures that there is movement through the case towards the destination point, whereas the focus on *depth* explores the *interesting visiting points* of the case journey where different types of analysis can take place. This is often the part of the case discussion that involves either the forming of management theory (inductive) or the application of known theory (deductive). Teaching notes often include worked-out examples of responses to these areas for analysis. For example, the note might include a suggestion for a SWOT analysis and include some examples of responses that might be presented by students in response to this.

## Additional resources

This section provides an opportunity for the author to incorporate suggestions of other key areas of reading that might accompany the case discussion. If the case forms part of a series of cases or learning resources, then these are often referenced here too. While this section has historically contained details of journal articles and book references, more recently it tends to serve as a signpost for other internet-based resources available to the tutor or case participants.

## Feedback

One important prerequisite of publishing your case for access by the wider academy is that it should have been tested in class at least once or twice. This inevitably ensures that the author is armed with feedback from the experiences of class discussion and delivery. This feedback is summarised here to provide helpful tips and prompters for future case tutors. If a specific snag or repeated problem tend to be captured in class discussions, then it is particularly helpful to identify this here.

## 'What happened next?'

Many teaching notes provide an epilogue, which identifies what happened next in the continued unfolding of the narrative of the case. For example, if a case required a specific decision to be agreed, from a possible set of three or four options, then the actual choice taken by the organisation could be summarised here, together with any consequences of this decision. The *what happened next* element of the case discussion is a very common and popular way to end the group session, but it does come with certain caveats. Students often tend to assume that the actual course of action chosen by the organisation is *the right answer*, rather than just a choice that an individual character from the case might have made. Sometimes these choices can be ill-informed or subsequently proven to be unwise, so it is helpful to challenge the rational of the choice to ensure that students can think beyond the notion of a simple *right and wrong* answer.

## LESSONS LEARNT

One of my favourite cases was a decision making case for an international chocolate manufacturer, faced with three significant strategic options to break into a new market. Students are invited to consider the merits and pitfalls of all three options. I would start my class discussion with a vote for the favoured option and then I tend to use a role-play format inviting three groups to consider one from each of the three options and to imagine they are the 'project development team' for their specific strategic option, effectively pitching their option to the other groups towards the end of the session. I tend to adopt an approach in group selection where I ensure individuals are forced to pitch for an option that would not be their normal preferred choice, encouraging them to consider other viewpoints. At the end of the group presentations and discussions, I invite all the class to have a free vote once again on their favourite option, having now had the opportunity of looking at this from many different viewpoints and perspectives. It is surprising to see how many have changed their preference over the course of an hour's deliberations. Students are determined to discover what the company actually did choose to do next, and when I close by informing them of the option that was actually chosen, (from additional data in the teaching note), those students who also chose the same option as their preference were naturally pleased to discover that 'they got the right answer.' Or did they? I allowed the 'winning group' a moment to revel in their success before then drawing out some additional data (also from the teaching note), that identified the consequences of the company's strategic decision: Within less than 18 months the organisation had significantly lost market share. The smiles were soon removed from the faces of 'winning group' as all were left to contend with the question – was the 'what happened next' action the right answer after all?

## 13.3 Additional functions of the teaching note

Technically, there is no reason why a particular data-rich case might not have more than one map (and subsequent teaching note) to demonstrate how multiple journeys could be taken through the case data to achieve different learning objectives. In addition to providing new perspectives on the case, the teaching note can provide many other resources and details for the case tutor.

The author might wish to include discussion notes in the teaching note, which will be particularly useful if the case is being used internally across several tutors delivering to different cohorts within the same programme. These discussion notes will further support standardisation of approach to case delivery. Such notes might also contain questions used for case assignments/assessments.

The author might wish to include timeframes for case delivery,dividing class sessions into different periods of time, based on past experiences of using the case in class. Some teaching notes contain multiple suggestions for how the case could be used in different ways, depending on how much time the user is able to allot to class delivery.

Additional background materials, in-class slides and handouts can also be included in the teaching notes to be considered as optional learning resources at the discretion of the case tutor.

PAUSE FOR A MOMENT: Take a look at the teaching note in Chapter 20, which accompanies the Ereuna Research case study. Examine the degree to which the note provides all the essential attributes of a *map* with which a case tutor could then orientate the class for a journey through the data from the case study. Read through the various elements of the teaching note to evaluate how it could guide you as a tutor to prepare a class discussion.

Now that you have completed this chapter, you should know that:

1.   Teaching notes are the formal presentation of the author's case map, which have been enhanced for use by other tutors less familiar with the origins of the case.
2.   These notes should provide all the additional guidance needed for a tutor to deliver the case to achieve its intended key learning objectives.
3.   Many case distribution organisations insist on a teaching note accompanying a case. Therefore, case authors looking for wider circulation of their cases should ensure the note is developed on completion of the case map and the case study.
4.   Notes could be used to provide further resources or signposting for the learners to extend the learning potential from their case experience.

## Notes

1   Clawson and Weatherford, 1995, p. 1
2   Yue, 2016b

# SECTION SUMMARY

This brings us to the end of the second section of this Handbook, which has focussed primarily on writing case studies and their accompanying resources, including teaching notes.

Once tested in class, these completed cases can then be circulated for wider use among scholars in the global academy. If this is the aspiration of the case writer, then refer to the fourth section, which contains details of other organisations that exist to support the distribution of cases across the globe.

Now that we have considered case teaching and case writing, the next section looks at how we can deploy the skills learnt in the previous two sections to develop case studies for assessment purposes.

If you are looking to incorporate case studies as a significant learning process in your programmes, then it makes sense that where such programmes require some form of assessment, the case method should continue to be incorporated. This section looks at different considerations and approaches that could be adopted when using cases for assessment purposes.

# SECTION III

# Case Assessments

# 14

# APPROACHES TO CASE ASSESSMENT

For as long as there have been management case studies, tutors have been using cases as tools for assessment. The traditional Harvard approach was to ensure that all cases incorporated some form of assessment based largely around student contribution in the class discussion. This section focuses on the different approaches to using cases for assessment. Here are what scholars have had to say about their approaches to using case studies for assessment:

> 'Ideally, a case exam should cover similar analytical and decision making issues, conceptual knowledge and information management challenges as those raised in earlier classes, and allow the students an opportunity to demonstrate what they have learned'.
>
> *Canada*[1]

> 'A case study typically contains a wider range of issues. Its use as a vehicle for ongoing assessment or final examination must therefore be planned with care'.
>
> *UK*[2]

> 'Teachers must provide concrete instruction in peer and self-assessment and carefully manage interpersonal issues for successful implementation'.
>
> *Australia and New Zealand*[3]

This chapter explores the following:

- How to identify the right type of case for an assessment?
- What attributes of learning are assessed with cases?
- The arguments for and against assessing individual or group learning?
- The merits of peer assessment

Are you making an assessment *of* learning or an assessment *for* learning? Unlike many other forms of assignment and examination, case studies provide scope not only to make an assessment *of* learning, but also contribute to the learning process by enabling participants to engage with the issues in the case. As a result, they are commonly used for assessments, whether as written assignments or for examination purposes. This section is separated into two chapters which explore approaches to developing a case assessment, different types of cases that can best be utilised in different assessment contexts and the processes by which a student can be guided, when instructed to develop their own cases as an assessed exercise. This chapter will also consider how best to appraise the contribution for assessment (whether oral or written) and includes suggestions for approaches towards group work and peer assessment.

## 14.1 Case assignments

When developing the case assignment, the first question to ask is what exactly is being assessed? Is it about knowledge of the subject matter? Is it about how to apply theory to practice, to make sense of situations? Are you seeking to assess leadership and management skills or written reporting practice? Is it about how an individual can critically evaluate a situation? Or it is how a group has worked together to develop a deeper, richer picture of the same situation? The answer to any of these questions could be yes – it depends! So, you might ask, it depends on what? It depends on you, your learners, the culture of your programme, the institute and the context within which you are learning, and it depends on the nature of the programme design. Many management programmes in business schools across the world place a strong emphasis on professional accreditation, and so any approach to using cases for assessment needs to bear in mind not only the philosophical approaches to assessment held by the institute, but also by the professional body that dual-accredits the programme.

Most professional bodies require some form of written evidence or presentation to form the majority of the assessment criteria, but there is much to be said for assessing the quality of the contribution of individuals in a class discussion, as the verbal reasoning skills, capacity for negotiation and the manner with which individuals handle their peers in a discussion about a management situation are all employability skills that are highly sought by the workplace. Similarly, participants might be required to lead and manage teams and groups as part of their case exercise, as well as participating in role play (requiring agility and quick-thinking). Again, these skills will be important for future employability.

As the previous sections have already identified, cases can provide excellent opportunities to develop good practice in analysis and critical thinking, decision-making, judging between different courses of action, handling assumptions, presenting from different viewpoints and perspectives, active listening and relating theory to practice. All of these could therefore be subject to appraisal in a case assessment.

When appraising contributions in class, there needs to be consideration for both the quantity and quality of the contributions made to the group discussion. While participants could be rewarded for breaking the ice, providing positive and creative thinking, demonstrating sharpness or persuasive responses, they could be discredited for being verbose, restating issues already covered or making comments that are disconnected to the flow of the discussion, as well as a general reluctance to contribute. Metal agility, risk-taking and demonstrating a humility and sensitivity to others are also attributes that should be recognised and rewarded.

Once you have determined the types of assessment objectives that need to be covered by the assignment, the next task is to select the right case. What type of case is best suited to testing your assessment attributes and objectives? Case tutors might also want to consider the following:

- How large should the case be?
- In what format should the figures and data be made available – e.g. neatly tabulated or mixed within the narrative of the case?
- How soon in advance should the case be provided?
- How familiar are the learners with the intended assessment objectives and how these will be measured?
- What is the word-count for a written response?
- What essential criteria should be included in the written response?
- Should the case be considered in isolation or should it be related to issues raised in other cases or in comparable situations from other organisations?

As we explored in the second section, sometimes the right case needed to achieve all the assessment criteria simply does not exist; and on such occasions the tutor might then consider developing an armchair case.

## 14.2 Cases for examination

Setting a case for an examination brings new constraints to the learner experience and is normally undertaken as a solitary written exercise, absent of group discussion. Many of the considerations and criteria already discussed in the previous section of this chapter need to be considered when using cases for examinations. In addition, the length of the case and the opportunity to preview material also require thinking through.

While opinion is mixed on the value of examinations as an assessment tool in management education, the use of the case in an exam does present challenges. Not all people read and assimilate information at the same rate. Therefore, if a group of learners are required to appraise the content of a large and complex case study, some might be prejudiced by the constraints of completing the examination within a fixed timeframe. It might be feasible to offer some reading time (under examination conditions), before the exam starts, to allow participants to assimilate the data before completing a written response. This raises a further question – should students be permitted to take notes during this 'reading and preparation' time? It might be reasonable to permit this, especially if the questions related to the case are withheld during this period. It is increasingly common to permit students to view the case before the exam, by issuing it a week or two in advance, but not permitting students to see the questions until under examination conditions. Having established these rules, it might also be worth considering whether students are permitted to bring any other notes or resources into the examination. Are they allowed to access the internet to explore issues related to the company? Can they bring in notes that have been taken from previous case classes? Answers to all these questions will differ from group to group and should be clearly determined and approved before setting the examination.

While the examination case does not normally provide an opportunity for a group discussion, students can be invited to take the position and perspective of an individual character from the case, from which to provide a response to a series of questions, which might normally have formed the basis for the discussion process. In this way, the case examination becomes less of an exercise and goes some way to emulating the experience of the group discussion. The student will need some training in exam technique in order to understand how to address this approach appropriately. Normally students would benefit from being coached to consider three actions: identifying your position on the statements contained in the case, then developing the argument to support the position you have taken, and finally to detail a set of actions or recommendations that could be undertaken in response to this position. This approach supports an evidence-based, theory-informed response to the case issues, raised through exam questions and based on the situation and themes contained in the case.

## 14.3 Group learning and peer assessment

Having discussed case assessment with scholars and case tutors from across the world, one of the most contentious issues about case assessment is whether to offer paper assessment. In many ways this reflects society at large, where peer assessment could be more commonplace in certain parts of the world than in others and similarly more permissible in certain business sectors of types of organisations than in others. Some scholars argue that peer assessment prepares the learner for the real world, as this practice is widespread in both the business community and the public sector. However, the management of the approach to peer assessment can be time-consuming and subject to challenge by quality-control measures, given its potential lack of objectivity.

With clear attention to a grading matrix, it is feasible to provide a reasonably objective scorecard with which to support a peer assessment process. This enables groups to participate in a team to produce a piece of assessed work in response to questions raised in the case, from which a peer review process can be undertaken.

The figure below provides an example of how this peer review process could be undertaken:

| Student name | Harry | Lois | Esme | Martha | Marks allocated |
|---|---|---|---|---|---|
| Harry | | 120 | 120 | 60 | 300 |
| Lois | 100 | | 100 | 100 | 300 |
| Esme | 120 | 100 | | 80 | 300 |
| Martha | 120 | 100 | 80 | | 300 |
| Individual total | 340 | 320 | 300 | 240 | Group mark |
| Individual mark | (340/300 x 60) 68 | 64 | 60 | 48 | 60% |

FIGURE 14.1 Example of peer assessment

In the example in Figure 14.1, a group of four participants had to produce a case report, to which a collective mark of 60% was awarded by the tutor. As the tutor was unaware of which student provided the most effort to ensure the report's completion, the group were required to peer-review each other's response. To enable this, the tutor provided each individual with 300 marks to allocate across their three peers. Strict criteria were also included to ensure that the individuals were aware of what they were scoring against. In response, Harry provided an equal allocation of marks for Lois and Esme but fewer marks for Martha, whereas Lois allocated the 300 marks evenly across all three peers. Once all the marks are allocated, totals for each participant are added, then divided against the original allocation of 300 marks and multiplied by the 60% group mark to provide individual marks for each participant. In this way, the final individual grade is derived from a combination of an overall group mark and the responses to the peer review.

As one might imagine, this approach, together with many similar peer-review approaches, is riven with perils and dangers, but it does provide a relative approximation to the challenges often associated with real-life experiences of peer reviews in the workplace. In my experience, these approaches continue to be met with mixed reviews from case tutors in many different countries. Some have reported having tried the approach without success, others have reported success but have since withdrawn the approach on the basis of the amount of time consumed, while others refuse to consider such an approach, as it would contravene institutional guidelines.

> PAUSE FOR A MOMENT: Think about the case programme that you are currently delivering or looking to develop. How might the case method be utilised for the assessment of the programme? What type of assessment criteria might you be looking to appraise? Will the assessment be solely paper-based, or could student participation also be assessed? What scope is there in your current programme for peer assessment?

Now that you have completed this chapter, you should know that:

1.  Cases can be used in range of different ways for assessment and examination
2.  The tutor needs to determine exactly what is being assessed by the case study, which might include a combination of knowledge-input related to the subject discipline and many of the management development skills that often accompany the case analysis and discussion process. Clear assessment criteria need to be determined and communicated in advance.
3.  Peer review and group work assessments are both tried and tested approaches which have been adopted with mixed reviews, and which bring both time- and quality-related challenges to the assessment process.

## Notes

1  Erskine, Leenders and Mauffette-Leenders, 2003, p. 180
2  Heath, 2015, p. 47
3  Harris and Brown, 2013, p. 101

# 15

# GUIDING STUDENTS TO CONSTRUCT THEIR CASES

'I usually specify that the organisation chosen must be at least one year old and must employ a number of people so that the roles and functions covered in the course-work are represented. Students should look at organisations with easily accessible information so that they can quickly assess whether or not an analysis will be possible'.

*New Zealand*[1]

This chapter explores the following:

- How to prepare the student to develop a case as an assessment.
- What attributes of learning are assessed with case presentations?
- The pedagogical benefits of student-researched, student-led case discussions.

Having delivered case studies for group discussion as part of a programme of learning, it is not uncommon for participants to be invited to create their own case study by means of an assessment. There are various ways of pursuing this, but I favour ones where the learners prepare a case and are then invited to present it to the rest of the group for discussion, rather than to simply produce a written case report which showcases some form of practice in a particular organisation. This participative approach permits greater whole-class engagement and promotes the *discovery* element of the learning process.

To enable this approach to be effective, students will need to have experienced case delivery in class beforehand and will need some careful guidance on case writing approaches to ensure that they are able to facilitate their own journey of discovery. I have often found that when I introduce this assessment approach with students, it also motivates them to be more engaged as participants in future case classes, as they have a greater appreciation for the learning process.

I have found that developing a template for learners as the basis for case planning, alongside a copy of the 'map' template (from Chapter 6) will help to guide and steer the case development process and avoid it from becoming excessively onerous. Students are reminded that the case needs the following (I intentionally keep this short and simple):

1.  Title – related to the company
2.  Subtitle – related to the theme/subject matter
3.  Opening paragraph – identifies the problem
4.  Second paragraph – introduces the context/situation and the organisation
5.  Third paragraph – identifies the key characters in the case
6.  Core body of text: no more than three pages
7.  Conclusion – reinforcing the main focus of the case
8.  References
9.  Exhibits, tables or diagrams – no more than four

I normally stipulate that the 'map' should include at least one aspect of management theory and no more than three. Students are then given 30 minutes to facilitate a short journey around their case data. This works well in a relatively small group of students over the course of a semester, or if the group is larger, then small teams can be formed to develop and deliver their cases.

Given the level of investment that the participants have made to deliver their short case sessions, I ensure that each session receives feedback, not only about the appropriateness of subject matter and level of depth of the case content, but also about the manner with which it was facilitated in the class session. I am keen to point out the positive *communication* and *people* skills that were evident and draw attention to how important these will be for future employability.

Research from the Richard Ivey School of Business, Canada[2] draws attention to the positive reasons why such student-researched, student-facilitated case presentations can be an effective way to support learning, citing a range of purposes including those summarised below:

- Adds variety to the learning experience.
- Develops presentation skills.
- Develops communication skills.
- Experiences in line with making briefings to senior management.
- Emphasises action and implementation planning.
- Develops prioritising skills.
- Develops time management skills.
- Practice in using audio and visual supports.
- Forces participants to prepare.
- Develops practice in managing group dynamics
- Promotes active listening and evaluation skills.

These approaches to learning and assessment provide a time efficient manner with which to equip motivated students to draw insights from real-world examples, to prepare their own cases in an engaging and fulfilling experience. In my view, they should never replace the tutor-led, in-class case discussion and analysis, but rather complement these cases by providing a different supportive approach to participant-centred learning. Occasionally, I have found that such approaches also provide insights into opportunities that might be subsequently developed further for more extensive use as a teaching case for future classes.

Now that you have completed this chapter, you should know that:

1.   Cases can be researched and then delivered by learners to facilitate peer-led learning across a range of contexts.
2.   To ensure effective implementation of student-led case research and teaching, clear guidance and boundaries need to be agreed in advance.
3.   There are many pedagogical benefits to engaging the student in the research, writing and case delivery process, many of which are also highly prized employability skills that stretch and challenge learners for their future workplace.

## Notes

1   Van Der Ham, 2016
2   Erskine, Leenders and Mauffette-Leenders, 2003

# SECTION SUMMARY

This brings us to the end of the third section of this Handbook, which has focussed primarily on using case studies for assessment and examination.

The use of the case method for assessment purposes has grown significantly, in tandem with the growth of the case as class discussion tool.

The fourth and final section examines other resources that you might wish to explore to enhance case development and to potentially improve the circulation of case material to a wider audience. Details of all references cited in this book can be found in this section.

# SECTION IV

# Further Resources to Enhance Case Development

# 16

# CIRCULATING THE CASE TO A WIDER AUDIENCE

As the adoption of the case method has expanded across the globe, so too has the number of supportive agencies and distribution centres that have emerged to assist in bringing cases to a much wider academic and professional audience. This section explores how cases can be made more accessible for a wider audience and begins, in this chapter, with a review of the teaching case distribution process. This is followed by two chapters devoted to getting a case study published, including a repository of supportive agencies that are available to case users and writers.

This chapter explores the following:

* The arguments for and against case release to a wider external audience.
* How authors can develop approaches to make their case more attractive.
* Opportunities for wider case circulation.

So, you are writing a case study and you are planning to use it in your forthcoming programme. But is that the limit to what you could achieve with your case? For scholars and academics who are research-active there is a well-established creative tension between investing time in case writing for teaching purposes and investing time in research publications for research journals. If you are going to put the time and energy into case writing, then it pays to consider its capacity to reach a wider audience, and there are other reputational benefits to be gained too.

## 16.1 The pros and cons of case release to a wider external audience

Some scholars have insisted to me that they are satisfied, so long as their case can provide high-quality personalised teaching resources for their learners and that the positive feedback from student satisfaction surveys is a sufficient reward for their efforts. When challenged about releasing cases to a wider audience, some have suggested that they would prefer to avoid the public gaze. Still others have said that the corresponding organisation has provided release authorisation on the basis that the material is to be used only in the author's classes, and not elsewhere. Although this latter point is a compelling argument, there are plenty of examples of cases where some content has been disguised (by negotiation with the corresponding organisation) to support wider distribution for teaching and learning purposes. In my experience, organisations have been flattered and intrigued to discover that their 'story' is being adopted in different parts of the world to support education and learning in business and management studies. Some have even gone to some lengths to showcase these altruistic achievements in order to bolster their own public image.

You have written your case, and, as a case author, you can be proud of what you have achieved. Few things inspire and energise me more as a scholar, than to discover that someone else values my work enough to want to use it themselves to support learning and teaching in their own institution. Having delivered cases and worked with case writers in developing countries in Africa and Asia, I have discovered that our cases can have insights into management education that are otherwise inaccessible in certain parts of the world, and which we can make available to broaden the horizons of lifelong learners from across the globe.

Everyone has their own style of writing, and each writer's creativity develops a new perspective on the case development process. This book has sought to showcase developments in case study teaching and writing by drawing on examples from across the globe, rather than simply focus on two or three major case writing institutions and their preferred approaches and styles. After all, not everyone wants a Harvard case or an Ivey School case, despite being confident that if it bears such trademarks, then you are guaranteed a product of high quality. Diversity and creativity in case writing can serve only to broaden the popularity of cases and enhance learning opportunities from which the whole academy can benefit.

---

### LESSONS LEARNT

I spent a number of years in Turkey, speaking with scholars and academics from many Turkish universities. I ran numerous case workshops and introduced many different cases and insights from leading case writing institutions, but the most common response that I received during my many visits, was the need for Turkish scholars to be writing Turkish cases in a Turkish style about Turkish businesses and organisations, for students in Turkey. While valuing the resources that were available from lead institutions in other parts of the world, they made a strong argument for the need for localised cases. I've heard these similar arguments in almost every visit that I have made to deliver a case development workshop across many parts of the world.

So, if you are looking to provide a case to circulate to a wider external audience, the starting place could be within your own national or regional proximity. But before submitting your case, read on, because the next section offers a few hints about how to improve its appeal to other users.

## 16.2 How to make your case more attractive

Assuming that you are looking to have your case made available to a wider audience, there are a number of things that you should think about when planning your case writing process. Ideally these things should be considered before you even start your case research. It is worth starting by reflecting on why you need to write your case in the first place, and you might find it is likely that the gap you are trying to fill is the same gap that others are looking to fill in their own teaching programme.

The type of organisation, its public profile and the situations that it is having to face are a good starting point. Is this organisation the type that others are likely to want to read about? Is the organisation already in the public eye and catching the attention of a wider readership? Have they been recent headline-grabbers? And do you have an insider perspective that provides a unique angle on the situations and issues that the company is tackling?

As you explore the type of scenarios that could be captured in your case, you might wish to consider how many different approaches could be adopted to tackle these issues. Does the case fit into more than one subject discipline? Is there the capacity to buddy up with a colleague or peer from another discipline to co-create your case, to broaden its appeal across more than one subject matter, without diluting the richness of the narrative?

The argument for a powerful teaching note has already been made, but this is particularly important if you are looking to circulate your case externally to a wider audience. Within your teaching note, it might help to demonstrate multiple routes with which to journey through the data, to enable potential tutors to consider the case for more than one developmental level and across different periods of class discussion time. I have viewed many teaching notes that seek to demonstrate how their case could be of value for undergraduates and postgraduates alike (with slightly different approaches to the journey), and, likewise, I have seen notes that describe how you could deliver a journey over a 45-minute period or over a three-hour period using the same case data. This level of flexible thinking might broaden the case's perceived appeal by increasing its capacity to be a credible resource in a wider range of contexts.

The inclusion of other resources, especially video and multimedia resources, will no doubt broaden its appeal to other users too. As the statistics demonstrate, at least 20% of the global best-selling cases incorporate some form of video or multimedia technology. Some authors submit their multimedia content in a DVD or down-loadable format, while others provide a text-based case and a teaching note that includes password-protected links to the author's website which contains additional multimedia resources.

And finally, depending on your institute's location and the location of the case narrative, it might be worth considering if the case has broader appeal if it is translated into other languages. More than 40% of best-selling cases have at least one alternative language translation.[1]

## 16.3 Opportunities for wider case circulation

Having determined that you want to make your case available to a wider audience, the next step is to consider the profile of the case. This might initially be linked to your own profile and networks. If you keep your own webpage, blog, LinkedIn or Facebook profile, then these are ideal starting points to provide links to your own case teaching materials. Local case writers might consider pooling resources around a certain geography or subject discipline to produce a book of cases. There are many publishers that have supported these types of case book, as their appeal is captured in sales to both tutor and students.

It is worth checking whether your own organisation already has a case collection or a publications release and editorial team, which can provide further support for your publication options.

There are many different types of case study competitions that provide national and international profiling opportunities for your teaching case. A number of different organisations run annual case writing competitions, inviting entries from a global audience across a broad range of subject disciplines. The Case Centre hosts an annual case competition which has become renowned as the equivalent of the 'Case Oscars'. The Case Centre also provides insights into competitions hosted across the world, including events in China (CEIBS), Africa (Emerald Publishing), Dark Side Competition (Academy of Management) and other global case events (for example, EFMD). Some of these are subject-specific with awards for cases in Public Relations (Arthur W. Page Society), Cases for Women (Emerald Publishing), Public Sector (E-PARCC), Sustainability and Social Entrepreneurship (Oikos) and Corporate Social Responsibility (AEMBA, Montreal & IJCSM).

In some competitions, case award winners are invited to present a synopsis of their case in global or regional conference events. Other award winners are showcased on case awarding body websites.

There are also a wide range of case competitions for students, often hosted by large case writing institutions, which can provide tutors with opportunities to register student groups for submissions of student-led, student-researched case studies. These offer significant opportunities to profile institutions with aspirations for developing a case writing and teaching reputation.

By far the most common way of raising the profile and access to your case is through a case distribution centre. In the first instance, it is worth exploring if there are any local or regional case collections in your vicinity which you could seek to join. The Case Centre has established links with more than 70 regional case collections from countries spanning six continents, including in Argentina, Nigeria, India, Mexico, South Africa, Egypt, Singapore, Australia and Switzerland.

You might decide to submit your case directly to The Case Centre or to a similar global case distribution service. As the organisation providing access to the world's largest collection of management case studies for teaching and learning, The Case Centre accepts cases from individual authors and institutes, as well as larger case collections. Like many case distribution centres, the Case Centre requires a teaching note and evidence that the case has previously been delivered in a classroom environment (at least twice). If the case is based on field research, then the author will need to submit a copy of a formal release authorisation from the contributing company. Their online case submission process enables the author to select from a range of groups to identify which areas of management to use as the primary search criteria for the case. This enables the case to be more easily located in search engines for distribution to wider audiences. The Case Centre, like many other case distribution groups, sends regular case updates to its followers to assist in the profile-raising of your newly submitted case. When you submit your case into their global collection, you and your institution retain the copyright, and there are opportunities to claim royalties from other institutes that choose to adopt your case.

Details of many case development organisations can be found in Chapter 18.

Now that you have completed this chapter, you should know that:

1. There is wide demand for local and regional cases, which provide opportunities for you to showcase your case study.
2. There are a range of different approaches to making your case available to a wider audience.
3. Developing the content in your teaching note will maximise the likely appeal of your case, by broadening the different learning opportunities that could be taken with the case data.

## Note

1 The Case Centre, 2019

# 17

# GETTING YOUR CASE STUDY PUBLISHED

Many case-based journals have emerged in recent years, spanning the whole range of management disciplines, as well as others in fields outside of business and management. These are largely created to serve the research case study, rather than cases for class-based teaching and learning. But there is scope for adapting your teaching case in preparation for circulation through such journals. This chapter explores this possibility further.

This chapter explores the following:

- The arguments for developing the case for publication in case research journals.
- Tips on re-constructing the case to meet the required journal format.
- Examples of case research journals,

Presenting your case for publication in a case research journal is a popular way of showcasing your case study and building your own profile as a case writer. The research case differs significantly in structure in comparison to the case for teaching, and so more time will need to be invested to deconstruct the teaching case and to re-present it in a format consistent with the requirements of the case journal. This normally requires taking the analysis, evaluation and conclusions about the case situation (normally found in the teaching note) and adding them to the journal case to re-present it as one whole and complete report, often lacking any *expository* or *plot* structure.

## 17.1 Why develop a research case?

The research case can be a profile-raiser from which to draw an international audience's attention to your teaching case. Most universities encourage research and scholarly activity in addition to class-based teaching. Lecturers and professors are normally expected to maintain a research profile, often demonstrated through their research publications. In some research-led universities, the development of a teaching case could be seen as distracting from the greater priority to providing research outputs, based principally on conference presentations and journal articles. By adapting data for use as both a teaching case and a research case, writers have the potential to achieve two outputs with only a little additional investment of time, rather than focussing on either the teaching resource or the research output. Similarly, scholars based in teaching-led institutions may wish to take advantage of developing a research output from their teaching case to develop their own profiles and broaden future employability options.

The challenge of the teaching case versus the research case resembles a chicken-and-egg scenario. In some situations, the teaching case comes first and leads to a research case and vice versa, depending on the priority of the author.

## 17.2 Reconstructing the teaching case for research journals

Much of the content of the first two sections of this book has been devoted to using the case to tell a story in such a manner that the reader needs to exercise discovery learning skills to investigate issues and themes contained within the story, and to conduct analysis and make conclusions, recommendations or decisions based on the case situation. Little of this is required in the research case for journal publication, which means that a significant element of reassembly is required if you are going to adapt your case content for a research publication. The original data that was captured remains the critical element that forms the starting point for the journal article.

The four structures described in Chapter 11 are effectively deconstructed, and a new, often linear, *chronology* is adopted, and a more traditional research-reporting process is undertaken. The teaching case contains twists and turns as the *plot* structure is exposed, and the research case is faithful to a traditional reporting formula (normally prescribed in the case journal's notes to authors). The plot structure in the teaching case is often supported by drama and controversy, but this is usually absent from the research case.

The *narrative* style adopted in the teaching case often disguises information to support the discovery and *expository* processes. By contrast, data needs to be presented in a clear and unambiguous manner for the research case. The focus is less about telling a story and more about providing a full description of events. While key aspects of learning derived from the teaching case are embedded in the story, the research case requires a more explicit and critical explanation. The teaching case is often presented from the perspective of a particular protagonist, whereas the research case tends to avoid such perspectives and is normally delivered in the third person.

## 17.3 Examples of case journals for research articles[1]

There are many different international journals that accept research cases, each of which normally focuses on cases in a specific area of management discipline.

Research cases are often accepted in books and journals related to professional body organisations.

For example, this Handbook has already showcased the Academy of Management, which accepts case studies as part of its Dark Side of Business themed studies, (see Chapter 3). The Dark Side case series forms part of the Critical Management Studies Interest Group at the Academy of Management. This has led to both journal and book publications, including a global Dark Side annual competition (see https://cms.aom.org/cms/awards).

The starting point for many research case outputs is the presentation at a professional body conference. For example, the Academy of Marketing invites case studies as part of its call for papers to its annual conference. The organisation boasts more than 20 special interest groups, which draw scholars together around key marketing themes. It invites outputs from research initiatives which can take the form of a research case article for submission to its Journal of Marketing Management (see www.academyofmarketing.org).

Similarly, The European Operations Management Association has an annual conference which receives case based papers (see www.euroma-online.org/about-euroma/), and from which articles can be developed as research cases for the *Journal of Operations Management* (see https://onlinelibrary.wiley.com/journal/18731317) and the *International Journal of Operations and Production Management* (see https://www.emeraldgrouppublishing.com/journal/ijopm). This last journal recognises the research case study as that which 'describes actual interventions or experiences within organizations. It can be subjective and doesn't generally report on research. Also covers a description of a legal case or a hypothetical case study used as a teaching exercise'.

Journals dedicated to case studies often focus around specific management themes. For example, Emerald Emerging Markets Case Studies is a journal that receives case studies focusing on themes largely related to international economics.

The US-based Society for Case Research was formed in 1978 and produces three research case study journals: *Business Case Journal* (https://sfcr.org/bcj/), *Journal of Case Studies* (https://sfcr.org/jcs/) and the *Journal of Critical Incidents* (https://sfcr.org/jci/). Similarly, the North American Case Research Association produces the *Case Research Journal* (www.nacra.net/). The *Asian Case Research Journal* (www.worldscientific.com/worldscinet/acrj) is hosted by the Asian Academy of Management, and for more than 20 years, has provided a broad selection of cases which focus on companies operating in the Asia-Pacific. More recently, the Case Centre has launched its *Case Focus* journal which focuses on case studies in the Middle East and Africa (www.thecasecentre.org/educators/casefocus/).

Case study publications are not exclusively the preserve of the business community. For example, Taylor & Francis has produced Case Studies in Construction Management (www.taylorfrancis.com/books/9781351113632), Disaster Response and Emergency Management (www.taylorfrancis.com/books/9780429252006) and Infection Control (www.taylorfrancis.com/books/e/9780203733318).

Many case writing institutes also produce their own case journal or regular case bulletins. For example, Harvard Business School produces the *Harvard Business Review* (https://hbr.org/), and the Richard Ivey Business School produces the *Ivey Business Journal* (www.iveybusinessjournal.com). These and other case writing institutes are featured in greater detail in the next chapter.

Now that you have completed this chapter, you should know that:

1. Research cases submitted for journal publication are structured significantly differently to cases used for teaching. Often, no teaching note is required.
2  Many professional body organisations accept research cases for submission as a journal article.

## Note

1  While website links are accurate at point of publication, these can change over time. For regular updates on these case development resources see the additional Support Material that accompanies this book, which can be found at www.routledge.com/9780367426965.

# 18

# ORGANISATIONS SUPPORTING CASE DEVELOPMENT

Many different organisations supporting case development have been mentioned in the previous chapters of this Handbook. This chapter seeks to provide a repository of case development resources. Unavoidably, the organisations listed and the website links provided are likely to change from time to time, so for more regular updates on these case development resources see the additional Support Material that accompanies this book, which can be found at www.routledge.com/9780367426965.

## Asian Business Case Centre, Nanyang Business School, Singapore

The Asian Business Case Centre (ABCC) was formed in 2000 to develop an Asian case repository with initial support from the Richard Ivey School of Business, Canada. As well as holding a regional Asian Management Case Collection, it delivers case training workshops and produces casebooks. Given its close proximity to China, ABCC has translated many cases into Chinese to broaden its appeal across Asia. It has established distribution partnerships with Harvard Business Publishing, Ivey Publishing and The Case Centre. (www.asiacase.com)

## Asia Case Research Centre, University of Hong Kong

Formerly known as the Centre for Asian Business Cases, the Asia Case Research Centre (ACRA) was established in 1997 and has developed a broad range of case based resources (including multimedia cases) for wider circulation across Asia. ACRA run an annual Asia Pacific Business Case Competition which attracts participants from across the world. The Centre also delivers case teaching workshops and case writing guides (www.acrc.hku.hk).

## The Case Centre, UK

Created in 1973, The Case Centre is the independent home of the case method. A not-for-profit organisation and registered charity, it is dedicated to advancing the case method worldwide. It was formerly known as the Case Clearing House of Great Britain and Ireland, and then the ECCH. From its offices at Cranfield University, UK and Babson College, USA, the organisation holds and distributes the world's largest and most diverse collection of management cases, articles, book chapters and teaching materials. This includes the collections of Harvard Business School, ICFAI Business School, INSEAD and Ivey Business School, among many others. Items are available in a range of different media and languages. Discover more about the collection at www. thecasecentre.org/cases.

To support case teachers, writers and learners The Case Centre also:

- delivers case workshops and webinars www.thecasecentre.org/workshops
- runs case competitions www.thecasecentre.org/starquality
- offers scholarships at www.thecasecentre.org/scholarships
- hosts Learning with Cases: An Interactive Study Guide www.thecasecentre. org/guide.

## The Case Development Centre, Rotterdam School of Management, The Netherlands

The Case Development Centre was established in 2008 to support the development of case studies in management education by working alongside authors and organisations to produce high quality teaching outputs including teaching notes and case competitions. They provide a range of learning resources to support the case writing process and hold their own case collection (see www.rsm.nl/cdc/case-catalogue/). Not only are cases developed for class-based learning, but they also work with businesses to develop cases to showcase good practice or for internal business training and development purposes. (https://www.rsm.nl/cdc)

## Case Method Institute, Washington, USA

The Case Method Institute supports training and development programmes aimed at enhancing the capacity for individuals to hone their case teaching and writing skills, by offering a range of coaching and training services. (http://casemethodinstitute.com)

## China Europe International Business School, Shanghai, China

The Case Development Centre at the China Europe International Business School was established in 2001 to provide a range of case resources with a specific focus on business in China. They have since partnered with the Harvard Case Library, Ivey Publishing and The Case Centre to provide wider distribution opportunities for its China-focused cases. (https://www.ceibs.edu)

## Darden Business Publishing, University of Virginia, USA

The Darden case collection includes more than 3,000 cases, teaching notes and case articles. Darden established its publishing activities in 2003 and more recently has particularly invested in the development of multimedia and simulation cases. It is one of the largest publishers of case resources in the USA. It has also produced a number of articles on the case writing and teaching process. (http://store.darden.virginia.edu)

## European Foundation for Management Development, Brussels, Belgium

The European Foundation for Management Development (EFMD) describes itself as a membership driven, global network of almost 1,000 institutions from more than 90 institutions in six continents. The EFMD provides a world-renowned quality-accreditation scheme and plays host to an annual writing case competition. (www.efmdglobal.org)

## Harvard Business Publishing, Cambridge, USA

Arguably the home of the management case study. Harvard produced its first book of business and management case studies in 1921 and has been developing cases ever since. Harvard Case Studies are available to purchase for use in your own institute from Harvard Business Publishing, and its collection also includes books, teaching bundles, multimedia resources and business simulations, articles and magazine issues. Harvard also hosts competitions (see www.thecasecompetition.org) and runs a regular open programme of case teaching and writing workshops both at its base in Cambridge, Massachusetts and at centres across the world. (https://store.hbr.org)

## IBS Case Development Centre, Hyderabad, India

The IBS Case Development Centre (CDC) boasts Asia Pacific's largest case collection for business and management, including best-selling and award-winning cases, case books and case packs (including cases, teaching notes and structured assignments). IBS CDC was launched in 2003 and has developed a repository of more than 5,000 cases, including multimedia case and movie-based cases. (http://ibscdc.org)

## IE Publishing, IE Business School, Madrid, Spain

The IE Business School has been actively promoting the case method for more than 40 years and has developing a publishing outlet for development and circulation of case studies. More recently, it has invested significantly in the development of multimedia, simulations and online case studies. IE manages a case catalogue and hosts an annual case contest. (https://iepublishing.ie.edu/en)

## IMD, Lausanne, Switzerland and Singapore

With over 50 years of experience of developing cases, IMD Lausanne is one of the leading case producing institutions to emerge from Europe. Now with a second campus in Singapore, IMD has looked to develop, deliver and showcase case teaching and its case collection to a global executive audience. (www.imd.org)

## INSEAD Publishing (France, Singapore, United Arab Emirates, USA)

INSEAD has a long-standing reputation for producing high-quality, best-selling, award-winning cases of all types (including some found in this book). INSEAD features frequently in the global best-selling lists for its cases across many disciplines, and more recently it has pioneered the development of integrated case learning with Virtual Reality as part of its experimental, immersive, innovative learning initiative. (https://publishing.insead.edu/)

## Ivey Publishing, Richard Ivey Business School, Canada

Ivey Publishing holds a vast database of case studies and teaching notes produced by faculty from the Richard Ivey Business School since 1923, as well as from external case writers. Ivey publishing also holds a number of other case collections, for which it has distributing rights. These collections include Harvard and Darden, as well as other collections from China, Singapore, South Africa and India. Individual authors can submit cases to Ivey, and if accepted, then the author is paid royalties on any sales, and the copyright for the case remains with Ivey. Ivey produces specific submission guidelines for the layout and formatting of cases and teaching notes and also produces training materials and textbooks on the Ivey case method, as well as running workshops for case teachers and writers. (www.iveycases.com)

## North American Case Research Association, USA

The North American Case Research Association (NACRA) is a membership-based organisation which brings together hundreds of case writers, researchers and tutors to support the case development process. It is responsible for the *Case Research Journal* and a regular case newsletter, provides fellowships and competitions and hosts an annual conference. It is affiliated to a network of localised case research associations based across the USA, Canada, Mexico and the Caribbean. (www.nacra.net)

## Society for Case Research

The Society for Case Research (SCR) originated in the USA as a membership-based organisation, established in 1978, to support case research, writing and teaching. The SCR publishes three scholarly journals, the *Business Case Journal*, the *Journal of Case Studies* and the *Journal of Critical Incidents*. The SCR also hosts an annual conference and publishes its proceedings, as well as a members' newsletter. (https://sfcr.org)

## Network

### *The Future of Management Education Alliance*

Established in 2018, the Future of Management Education Alliance is an alliance of global business schools, with a strong reputation for case based learning, comprising Imperial College Business School, ESMT Berlin, the BI Norwegian Business School, the Lee Kong Chian School of Business at Singapore Management University, the IE Business School, EDHEC Business School, the University of Melbourne and Ivey Business School as a knowledge-sharing network looking to pioneer online learning. (www.fome.group)

# 19

# CONTRIBUTING RESOURCES AND REFERENCES

This chapter brings together all the contributing resources which have helped to make this publication possible. Some of these have been sourced from journals, articles, webpages as well as other case books. The use of case studies, handouts or extracts of cases have also been made possible by the kind support of the following:

## 19.1 Individual supporters

1. Todd Bridgman, Associate Professor of Management, Victoria Management School, New Zealand, for his case: 'Trimming the FAT: change at the Ministry of Foreign Affairs and Trade ', authored by T. Bridgman and R. Berry, (Victoria University of Wellington). Available at: www.thecasecentre.org/educators/products/view?id=149596.
2. Anne-Marie Carrick, Senior Research Associate, INSEAD, Fontainebleau, France, for her case: 'Crisis at the Mill: Weaving an Indian Turnaround − Alvarez & Marsal', authored by C. Zeisberger & A.M. Carrick, © INSEAD. Available at: https://publishing.insead.edu/case/alvarez-marsal.
3. Pierre Chandon, The L'Oréal Chaired Professor of Marketing, Innovation and Creativity, INSEAD-Sorbonne Université Behavioural Lab, France, for his case: 'Unilever in Brazil (1997–2007): Marketing Strategies for Low-income Consumers', authored by P. Chandon & P.P. Guimaraes. © INSEAD. Available at: www.thecasecentre.org/educators/products/view?id=62368.
4. Direnç Erşahin, TED University, Ankara, Turkey, for his case and teaching note: 'Ereuna Research - Ethical Dilemmas with Big Data Analytics', authored by D. Erşahin (Ted University); S. Andrews (University of Worcester); N. Wasti (Middle East Technical University), © Ted University. Available at: www.thecasecentre.org/educators/products/view?id=165593.
5. Sandra Vandermerwe and Marika Taishoff, for their case: '*Amazon.com: Marketing a New Electronic Go-between Service Provider*', authored by M. Taishoff and S. Vandermerwe © Imperial College London. Available at: www.thecasecentre.org/educators/products/view?id=22628.

6. Tsai Terence, CEIBS, China for his case: "*Hard Choices: Best Buy and Five Star in China (A)*", authored by T. Tsai, J. Zhu and L Xu, © China Europe International Business School (CEIBS). Case ref: 302–318-1 available at: www.thecasecentre.org/educators/products/view?id=157674.

7. The Case Centre, UK for Monarch Airlines case examples from its online interactive study guide. Available at: www.thecasecentre.org/guide.

8. Tao Yue, Rotterdam School of Management, The Netherlands for her handout: 'Ten Questions to Ask Yourself Before Writing a Teaching Case', authored by T. Yue © The Rotterdam School of Management Case Development Centre, (Erasmus University). Available at: www. rsm.nl/fileadmin/Images_NEW/CDC/CDC_Ten_Questions_to_Ask_Yourself_Before_ Writing_a_Teaching_Case.pdf.

## 19.2 References

Abell, D. (1997) *What Makes a Good Case*. Lausanne: IMD. Ref IMD-3–731.

Ballantyne, B., Bain, J.D. and Packer, J. (1999) 'Researching university teaching in Australia: Themes and issues in academics' reflections'. *Studies in Higher Education*, 24:2, pp. 237–257, doi:10.1080/03075079912331379918.

Barnes, L.B., Christensen, C.R. and Hansen, A.J. (1994) *Teaching and the Case Method*. 3rd edn. Boston, MA: Harvard Business Publishing.

Bayram, L. (2012) 'Use of Online Video Cases in Teacher Training'. *Procedia - Social and Behavioral Sciences*, 47, pp. 1007–1011. Amsterdam: Elsevier.

Betts, J. (2004) 'Theology, therapy or picket line? what's the 'good' of reflective practice in management education?'. *Reflective Practice*, 5(2), pp. 239–251.

Bolton, G. and Delderfield, R. (2018) *Reflective Practice: Writing and Professional Development*. 5th edn. London: Sage Publications.

Boud, D. and Soloman, N. (eds.) (2001) *Work-based Learning: A New Higher Education*. Buckingham: Open University Press.

Bramley, C. (2015) *Involve me: …and I Will Understand*. 2nd edn. London: Sanctum Publishing.

Bridgman, T. (2010). 'Beyond the manager's moral dilemma: Rethinking the 'ideal-type' business ethics case'. *Journal of Business Ethics*, 94(5), pp. 311–322.

The Case Centre. (2008) *Multimedia - powering the real world into the classroom*. Available at: https://www.thecasecentre.org/educators/casemethod/resources/features/multimedia (Accessed 2 May 2020).

The Case Centre. (2019) *Bestselling Cases in 2019*. Available at: www.thecasecentre.org/files/ mailings/bestsellers/2019bestsellingcases-infographic.jpg. (Accessed 4 April 2020).

Charlebois, S., & Foti, L. (2017). 'Using a Live Case Study and Co-opetition to Explore Sustainability and Ethics in a Classroom: Exporting Fresh Water to China'. *Global Business Review*, 18(6), pp. 1400–1411. https://doi.org/10.1177/0972150917713086.

Clark, S. (1996) 'A Very Big Gig'. *The Sunday Telegraph*, 17 November 1996.

Clawson, J.G. (1995) *Case Method*. Charlottesville, VA: Darden Business Publishing. Ref UVA-PHA-0032.

Clawson, J.G. and Weatherford, L. (1995) *Teaching Notes*. Charlottesville, VA: Darden Business Publishing. Available at: https://www.thecasecentre.org/educators/products/ view?id=200 (Accessed 10 April 2020)

Corey, E.R. (1998) *Case Method Teaching*. Boston, MA: Harvard Business Publishing. Ref: 9–581–058. Available at: www.thecasecentre.org/educators/products/view?id=48275 (Accessed 2 February 2020).

Costley, C., Elliott, G. and Gibbs, P. (2010) *Doing Work Based Research: Approaches to enquiry for insider-researchers*. London: Sage Publications.

Covey, S.R. (1999) *The 7 Habits of Highly Effective People*. London: Simon & Schuster UK.

Elam, E.L.R. and Spotts, H.E. (2004). 'Achieving marketing curriculum integration: A live case study approach'. *Journal of Marketing Education*, 26(1), pp. 50–65.

Ellet, W. (2018) *The Case Study Handbook: A Students Guide*. Revised edn. Boston, MA: Harvard Business Publishing.

Elliott, G. (1999) *Lifelong Learning: The Politics of the New Learning Environment*. London: Jessica Kingsley.

Erskine, J.A., Leenders, M.R. and Mauffette-Leenders, L.A. (2003) *Teaching with Cases*. 3rd edn. London, ON: Ivey Publishing.

Farhoomand, A (2004) 'Writing Teaching Cases – A Quick Reference Guide'. *Communications of the Association for Information Systems*, 13, pp. 103–107. www.acrc.hku.hk/Content/Document/case.writing.guide.pdf (Accessed 21 July 2020).

Fawcett S.E. and Fawcett, A.M. (2011) 'The "Living" Case: Structuring Storytelling to Increase Student Interest, Interaction, and Learning'. *Decision Sciences Journal of Innovative Education*. 9(2), May 2011, pp. 287–298.

Fenton-O'Creevy, M. (2019) *Teaching with Cases Online – Practical and Pedagogical Considerations* (ed. Simmons), E.) Available at: www.thecasecentre.org/educators/casemethod/resources/features/teachcasesonline-landscape2 (Accessed 4 April 2020).

Gabaldón, P. (2020) *Tips to Go Online During Covid-19 Crisis*. Available at: https://iepublishing.ie.edu/en/news/post/tips-to-go-online-during-covid-19-crisis (Accessed 24 July 2020).

Gentile, M.C. (1990) *Twenty-Five Questions to Ask as You Begin to Develop a New Case Study*. Boston, MA: Harvard Business Publishing. Ref 0–391–042. Available at: www.thecase-centre.org/educators/products/view?id=46867. (Accessed 02 February 2020)

Gibbons, M., Limoges, C., Nowotney, H., Schwartzman, S., Scott, P. and Trow, M. (1994) *The New Production of Knowledge: The Dynamics of Science and Research in Contemporary Societies*. London: Sage Publications.

Gibbs, P. and Garnett, J. (2007) 'Work based learning as a field of study', *Research in Post-Compulsory Education*, 12(3), pp. 409–421.

Gragg, C. I. (1940) 'Because Wisdom Can't be Told', *Harvard Alumni Bulletin* (19 October 1940).

Green, A. and Erdem, M. (2016) 'Bridging the Gap Between Academic and Industry in Hospitality: Using Real Life Case Studies'. *Developments in Business Simulation and Experiential Learning*, Volume 43, pp. 43–46.

Greer, W.R. (1985) 'Malcolm Perrine McNair, 90, Retailing Expert at Harvard'. *The New York Times*, 10 September 1985.

Hammond, J.S. (2002) *Learning by the Case Method*. Boston, MA: Harvard Business School.

Harris, L.R. and Brown, G.T.L. (2013) 'Opportunities and obstacles to consider when using peer- and self-assessment to improve student learning: Case studies into teachers' implementation'. *Teaching and Teacher Education*. 36, pp. 101–111. doi:10.1016/j.tate.2013.07.008.

Harvard Business School. (2020) Master Business Essentials with Harvard Business School's Online CORe Program. Available at: https://online.hbs.edu/courses/core/ (Accessed 30 July 2020).

Heath, J. (2015) *Teaching and Writing Cases – A Practical Guide*. 4th edn. Bedford: The Case Centre.

Heckman, R. and Annabi, H. (2005). 'A content analytic comparison of learning processes in online and face-to-face case study discussions'. *Journal of Computer-Mediated Communication*, 10(2).

Hersey, P. and Blanchard, K. H. (1969). 'Life cycle theory of leadership'. *Training and Development Journal*, 23(5), pp. 26–34.

INSEAD. (2020a) Experiential, Immersive, Innovative Learning via Virtual Reality at INSEAD. Available at: www.insead.edu/executive-education/virtual-reality (Accessed 20 July 2020).

INSEAD. (2020b) INSEAD GO-Live. Available at: www.insead.edu/executive-education/go-live (Accessed 27 July 2020).

Ivey Publishing. (2020). *10 Tips for Taking Case Classes Online*. Available at: www.iveycases.com/News/10-tips-for-taking-case-classes-online (Accessed 30 July 2020).

Jack, A. (2018) 'Why Harvard's case studies are under fire'. *Financial Times*. Available at: www.ft.com/content/0b1aeb22-d765-11e8-a854-33d6f82e62f8 (Accessed 10 April 2020).

Jones, M.D. and Baltzersen, M. (2017) 'Using twitter for economics business case discussions in large lectures'. *International Review of Economics Education*, 26, pp. 14–18. Available at: www.sciencedirect.com/science/article/pii/S1477388017300488 (Accessed 17 July 2020).

Jones, O and Kerr, M.A. (2012) 'Refreshment by the case: Use of multimedia in case study assessment'. *The International Journal of Management Education*, 10(3), pp. 186–200. doi:10.1016/j.ijme.2012.07.002.

Kennedy, L., Cole, C. and Carter, S. (1999) 'The false focus in online searching: The particular case of undergraduates seeking information for course assignments in the humanities and social sciences', *Reference & User Services Quarterly*, pp. 267–273.

Kirby, P. (2015). *Levels of Success: The Potential of UK Apprenticeships*. London: Sutton Trust.

Kupp, M. and Mueller, U. (2020) 'Moving Case Teaching Online Quickly – Shared Experiences'. Available at: https://youtu.be/7JlniWDf7uo. Accessed 21 July 2020.

Kyei-Blankson, L., Godwyll, F. and Nur-Awaleh, M.A. (2014) 'Innovative blended delivery and learning: exploring student choice, experience, and level of satisfaction in a hyflex course'. *International Journal of Innovation and Learning*, 16(3). doi:10.1504/IJIL.2014.064728.

Kyro, P. (2015) 'The conceptual contribution of education to research on entrepreneurship education', *Entrepreneurship and Regional Development*, 27(9–10), pp. 599–618.

Lee, A. (2020) 'Moving Case Teaching Online Quickly – Best Practice'. Available at: https://youtu.be/VgJDU4E38T4 (Accessed 30 July 2020).

Lenger, A. (2008). 'Regional innovation systems and the role of state: institutional design and state universities in Turkey', *European Planning Studies*, 16(8), pp. 1101–1120.

Lefevre, D. (2019) *Teaching with Cases Online - Practical and Pedagogical Considerations* (ed. Simmons, E.) Available at: www.thecasecentre.org/educators/casemethod/resources/features/teachcasesonline-landscape2 (Accessed 4 April 2020).

Levy, D. (2020) 'Digital Learning: The Synchronous vs. Asynchronous Balancing Act'. Available at: https://hbsp.harvard.edu/inspiring-minds/the-synchronous-vs-asynchronous-balancing-act (Accessed 18 August 2020).

Liu, J., Socrate, S. and Pacheco, J. (2020) 'Guide to Transitioning to Remote Teaching (Part I)'. Available at: https://meche.mit.edu/meche-virtual-resources/educational-resources-teaching-assistants#slides (Accessed 30 July 2020).

McKenna, S. (1999) 'Organisational learning: "live" case studies and the consulting process'. *Team Performance Management*, 5(4), pp. 125–135. doi:10.1108/13527599910283439.

McNair, M.P. (1971) 'McNair on Cases'. *Harvard Business School Bulletin*, July/August 1971.

Mehrabian, A. (1981). *Silent Messages: Implicit Communication of Emotions and Attitudes*. Belmont, CA: Wadsworth.

Mollett, A., Moran, D. and Dunleavy, P. (2011) 'Using Twitter in university research, teaching and impact activities'. Impact of social sciences: maximizing the impact of academic research, LSE Public Policy Group, London School of Economics and Political Science.

Mueller, P. A., and Oppenheimer, D.M. (2014). 'The pen is mightier than the keyboard: Advantages of longhand over laptop note taking'. *Psychological Science*, 25(6), pp. 1159–1168. doi:10.1177/0956797614524581.

Muilenburg, L.Y. and Berge, Z.L. (2005) 'Student Barriers to Online Learning: A Factor Analytic Study'. *Journal of Distance Education*, 26(1), pp. 29–48. doi:10.1080/01587910500081269.

Mullane, P. (2019) 'Teaching with cases online - practical and.pedagogical considerations', (ed. Simmons, E.). Available at: www.thecasecentre.org/educators/casemethod/resources/features/teachcasesonline-landscape2 (Accessed 4 April 2020).

Murray, K. (1991) 'Notes and Case Studies: "A Live Case Study"', *British Journal of Education & Work*, 4(3), pp. 81–85. doi:10.1080/0269000910040306.

Mwasalwiba, E.S. (2010) 'Entrepreneurship education: a review of its objectives, teaching methods, and impact indicators', *Education + Training*, 52(1), pp. 20–47. doi:10.1108/00400911011017663.

Narayanan, V.G. and Schiano, B. (2020) *Exploring the Challenges and Opportunities in Online Case Teaching: Insights from Two Case Teaching Experts*. Available at: http://academic.hbsp.harvard.edu/exploring-the-challenges-and-opportunities-in-online-case-teaching (Accessed 13 June 2020).

Ohlsson-Corboz, A.V. (eds Simmons, E.) (2017) *Using Cases with Undergraduates*. Available at: www.thecasecentre.org/educators/casemethod/resources/features/using-caseswithundergraduates (Accessed 24 July 2020).

Pérez-Bennett, A., Davidsen, P. and López, L.E. (2014) 'Supercharging case-based learning via simulators: Achieving double-loop learning with case-sims', *Management Decision*, 52 (9), pp. 1801–1832. doi:10.1108/MD-09-2013-0499.

Raelin, J.A. (1997) 'A Model of Work-Based Learning'. *Organisation Science*, 8(6) pp. 563–709. doi:10.1287/orsc.8.6.563.

Rangan, V.K. (1996) 'Choreographing a Case Class'. Ref 9–595–07. Available at: www.thecasecentre.org/educators/products/view?id=44687 (Accessed 4 April 2020).

Rapp, A. and Ogilvie, J. (2019) 'Live Case Studies Demystified'. Available at: https://hbsp.harvard.edu/inspiring-minds/live-case-studies-demystified (Accessed 19 April 2020).

Raufflet, E. and Mills, A.J. (2017) *The Dark Side – Critical Cases on the Downside of Business*. Abingdon: Routledge.

Shapiro, B.P. (1984) *Hints for Case Teaching*. Boston, MA: Harvard Business Publishing. Ref: 9–585–012.

Schiano, B. and Andersen, E. (2017) 'Teaching with Cases Online'. Available at: https://s3.amazonaws.com/he-product-images/docs/Article_Teaching_With_Cases_Online.pdf (Accessed 4 April 2020).

Schiano, B. and Ellet, W. (2019) 'Case Teaching: The Perfect Opening Question'. Available at: https://hbsp.harvard.edu/inspiring-minds/the-perfect-opening-question? (Accessed 4 April 2020).

Schmenner, R.W. (2002) 'Thoughts on Case Teaching'. IMD Ref: IMD-3–1052. Available at: www.thecasecentre.org/educators/products/view?id=11718 (Accessed 4 April 2020).

Schonell, S and Macklin, R (2018): 'Work integrated learning initiatives: live case studies as a mainstream WIL assessment'. *Studies in Higher Education*. Available at: doi:10.1080/03075079.2018.1425986 (Accessed 2 February 2020).

Sklar, J. (2020) '"Zoom fatigue" is taxing the brain. Here's why that happens'. *National Geographic*. Available at: www.nationalgeographic.com/science/2020/04/coronavirus-zoom-fatigue-is-taxing-the-brain-here-is-why-that-happens (Accessed 30 July 2020).

Sridharan, A. (2019) 'Teaching with cases online - practical and pedagogical considerations', (ed. Simmons, E.). Available at: www.thecasecentre.org/educators/casemethod/resources/features/teachcasesonline-landscape2 (Accessed 4 April 2020).

Van der Ham, V. (2016) *Analysing a Case Study*. New York, NY: Palgrave MacMillan.

Vedpuriswar, A.V. (2003a) *The Case Method of Learning*. Hyderabad: ICMR Centre for Management Research. Ref 303–169–6.

Vedpuriswar, A.V. (2003b) *Developing Cases*. India: ICMR Centre for Management Research. Ref 303–168–6.

Velenchik, A.D. (1995) 'The case method as a strategy for teaching policy analysis to undergraduates', *Journal of Economic Education*, 26(1), pp. 29–38.

Willmot, P., Bramhall, M., Radley, K. (2012) 'Using digital video reporting to inspire and engage students'. Available at: www.uq.edu.au/teach/video-teach-learn/ped-benefits. html (Accessed 24 July 2020).

Yemen, G. (2012) *What Kind of Business Case Studies are we Writing?*Charlottesville, VA: Darden University Press. Ref UVA-PHA-0064.

Yue, T. (2016a) 'How to Write a Good Teaching Case', Rotterdam School of Management. Available at: www.rsm.nl/fileadmin/Images_NEW/CDC/CDC_How_to_Write_a_Good_Teaching_Case_.pdf (Accessed 20 April 2020).

Yue, T. (2016b) 'How to Write a Good Teaching Note'. Rotterdam School of Management. Available at: www.rsm.nl/fileadmin/Images_NEW/CDC/CDC_How_to_Write_a_Good_Teaching_Note.pdf (Accessed 20 April 2020).

# 20

# CASE MATERIALS

The final chapter contains case materials that can be used as examples and illustrations. The three full cases include one field research case (Trimming the FAT: change at the Ministry of Foreign Affairs and Trade), one desk research case (Monarch Airlines) and one case based on the author's personal experiences (Ereuna Research – Ethical Dilemmas with Big Data Analytics). In addition, there is an accompanying teaching note for the Ereuna Research case and links to an annotated version of the Monarch Airlines case.

## 20.1 A Field Research Case: Trimming the FAT – change at the Ministry of Foreign Affairs and Trade

### A LEADER TO BREAK THE MOULD

On 21 March 2012 John Allen, Chief Executive of the New Zealand Ministry of Foreign Affairs and Trade (MFAT) received an unusual letter.[1] It came from Foreign Affairs Minister Murray McCully, and it set out, over four pages, the Minister's significant concerns about Allen's proposals to radically reform the Ministry, which had first been outlined in an internal consultation document and subsequently explained at a press conference. The proposal would see 305 of the 1,340 staff lose their jobs and a further 600 need to reapply for their positions. Major changes to the employment conditions of diplomats – including entitlement reductions and loss of security of tenure – and closures of posts were also proposed.[2] The change proposal had sparked not only political controversy, but a furious and very public revolt from the diplomatic community itself, including an unprecedented series of leaks from within the Ministry.

McCully took the unusual step of releasing his letter to Allen to the media. The public nature of the criticism and the very detailed exposition of the Minister's concerns about both Allen's proposals and his handling of the change process itself were uncommon. The media speculated that McCully had lost confidence in Allen and wanted him sacked. McCully denied this, but he left no doubt that he held Allen to blame for the turmoil. It was not the first time that McCully had so publicly clashed with those reporting to him, having resigned as Tourism Minister in 1999 after a major fall-out with the Tourism Board.[3]

When Allen, the former New Zealand Post Chief Executive was made head of MFAT in

2009, it was celebrated as an "inspired move" in the local *Dominion Post*'s editorial:

> "Foreign Affairs in this country has mostly been the preserve of diplomats and cast-out politicians. The Ministry has never been led by a businessman, or anyone who has not earned his spurs by patiently crafting elegant papers on arcane aspects of foreign policy...[John Allen] has instead been a successful commercial operator, who straddles easily the white line between the public service and private sector sides of his SOE operations."[4]

Tipping the announcement several weeks earlier the *New Zealand Herald*'s foreign affairs commentator Fran O'Sullivan said that Allen would:

> "not only break the mould as the first business person appointed to lead the Ministry...he will also be a key driver in a huge transformational programme designed to leverage 'New Zealand Inc', so New Zealand's vital economic and business interests are better projected offshore."[5]

There is little to be found on the public record about what the MFAT community thought of the appointment, but it was evident that McCully, adept at off-the-record media briefings, had successfully billed Allen's arrival. As the Opposition's spokesman for the portfolio for nine years before becoming the minister, McCully had, for some time, set his sights on a Foreign Affairs shake-up. He evidently believed the appointment of an "outsider" with no MFAT "baggage" would be a key component of the transformation. O'Sullivan's "scoop" knowingly asserted that the State Services Commission (SSC), the central government agency which employs public service chief executives, had been "encouraged to look at the top job in an 'expansive way.'"[6]

Allen had an impressive CV, good entrepreneurial skills and plenty of charisma. When announcing his appointment as head of New Zealand Post, then NZ Post Board chairman and former Prime Minister Jim Bolger said that Allen had successfully grown the profitability of NZ Post's core business and "had a tremendous ability to inspire those around him."[7] O'Sullivan labelled him an "accomplished after-dinner speaker and exceptional dinner party host who works the Wellington scene well." A lawyer by profession, he was a partner at a local law firm before being recruited to New Zealand Post on secondment in 1994. He enjoyed a rapid rise up the ranks before beating international competitors to become its chief executive in 2003. On paper and by reputation, Allen seemed to possess many of the credentials needed for the MFAT job. McCully wanted to transform the Ministry, and Allen displayed all the characteristics of a transformational leader. What he did not have, and which marked him apart from all his predecessors, was experience, not just in foreign affairs, but in the core public service.

## Change afoot at MFAT

Allen arrived at MFAT less than a year after the National Party won enough seats in the 2008 election to become the new Government, and as the effects of the global financial crisis were starting to bite. The Government embarked on a determined belt-tightening campaign, drawing flak from public service unions and the Opposition, which argued that the financial crisis was being used to divert attention from an ideological agenda to reduce the size of the public sector. A cap on staffing numbers was imposed in December 2008, requiring all agencies to reduce staff, as well as the size of their operating budgets. [8] Sector-wide reform, with a focus on value-for-money and better public services, was a clear Government imperative, although the scale of change sought by the Government within individual agencies differed. In 2010 the SSC published an independent review of MFAT,[9] around the same time as the Ministry's own Statement of Intent 2010–2013 was published.[10] Both documents identified the need for considerable reform of the Ministry and pointed to the *MFAT 20/20* change programme, which was already under way. The SSC report on MFAT was one of the first four Performance Improvement

Framework (PIF) reviews – an initiative spearheaded by central agencies to drive performance improvements across government.[11] The review rated MFAT's management as needing development in vision, strategy and purpose, leadership and governance, culture and values and engagement with ministers. Its financial and resource management rated poorly, and the review identified the need for a more "proactive and strategic" Ministry that was able to make "hard resource allocation decisions".

The PIF review listed a range of factors challenging the Ministry, including cost pressures and the emergence of new international strategic priorities. It observed that MFAT had experienced little change of late, which meant that its change management capacity was under-developed. Therefore, the need for rapid change to reduce uncertainty, demonstrate direction and generate results would have to be balanced against the organisation's capacity to change, the PIF review warned. It noted that MFAT had a strong culture of professionalism, which encouraged high standards and valued on-the-job development through its practice of rotating generalist diplomats between postings overseas (Exhibit A) and in Wellington. However, while this process was competitive, it had created a culture that was "relatively closed, individualistic, hierarchical and risk averse." The review recommended that MFAT's management be strengthened, with more attention to be given to addressing under-performance of staff. Career progression and talent management appeared to be under-developed, and senior staff were not leaving the organisation, thereby impeding succession processes.

## A diplomatic crisis

While Allen and his senior leadership team had been busy, as had the PIF review team and no doubt the Minister, little of this activity was subject to the public gaze until April 2011, when McCully first outlined the scale of reform envisaged in a speech and admitted it was already ruffling diplomatic feathers.[12] McCully emphasised the Government's fiscal pressures and the new strategic trading priorities for the Ministry, which required "dramatically changing" the way that MFAT did business, including "changing the size and configuration of our posts".[13] There would need to be "significant economies in back office services in Wellington, and the elimination of many seconded administrative positions in overseas posts." Changes would have "profound implications for Ministry staff" and would include opening up more heads of mission roles to non-ministry staff. McCully described the changes as "opening some doors and windows" at MFAT. He said:

> "The Ministry has a track record of losing too many talented younger people because they have been forced to wait far too long for their opportunities. We need to acknowledge that experience in the private sector, or another relevant government agency, can bring significant

benefits for our diplomats. We should not just facilitate but reward this type of career development."[14]

By late 2011 the MFAT *Briefing for the Incoming Minister* (BIM) was describing the 20/20 change programme as "the most profound structural, cultural and technological reform in the Ministry's history."[15] Significant operating savings were identified, and job losses were inevitable. The BIM was not immediately released, and when it was, the $40 million total for savings – subsequently leaked – was blacked out.[16] In February 2012 John Allen held a press conference to explain the internal release of a consultation document outlining the proposed job losses and other substantial employment changes. It was then that the matter became the subject of public debate. Allen explained the proposal to cut 305 jobs, with a further 600 staff to reapply for jobs in new specialist roles. There would be significant reductions in offshore allowances paid to diplomats with families[17] and no guarantee of jobs, once they returned to New Zealand. Outsourcing of some services was planned, and further diplomatic posts would be closed and replaced by regional hubs.[18]

Within a week, the Foreign Service Association (FSA), one of two unions representing diplomatic staff, released the details of an internal survey, which found that nearly three-quarters of staff working overseas were either considering ending their posting early or resigning as a consequence of the proposed changes. Association president and MFAT staff member Warren Fraser said that two-thirds of Wellington-based staff said that they would be less likely to consider an overseas posting abroad and a further quarter said they were considering resignation.[19]

> "The Ministry is proposing to offer peanuts to work long hours in often unglamorous locations where staff partners often can't or aren't allowed to work. If it proceeds … staff will desert the Ministry in droves."

On the following day Allen was grilled by opposition parties at a parliamentary committee reviewing MFAT's financial performance. The attack was led by Labour's Phil Goff, a former Foreign Affairs Minister, whose ongoing relationships with Ministry insiders had already resulted in him being leaked documents.

Allen described the FSA survey as an "interesting early snapshot…undertaken almost immediately after the release of the material."

> "My view is that we will get, as I said to you, a great deal of constructive and useful feedback from people as we move forward. The intention of us all is to build a ministry which can have pride in its past, but is not so linked to the past that it can't reinvent itself to be similarly successful in the future."[20]

Allen also referenced the PIF report and the "significant weaknesses" that it identified. He noted that the proposed changes reflected "not only the insight of that report but the insight of decades of other reports which have been prepared for the ministry and simply not implemented." He explained that the Ministry could not afford to continue to pay overseas allowances which compensated for the loss of a partner's income.

In the ensuing weeks, the Labour opposition leader David Shearer revealed that a contracted change management advisor had, as part of a workshop on "getting yourself through change", recommended MFAT staff take a hot bath, pray or meditate to reduce stress, or to get a pet, as their love was unconditional.[21] There were further leaks of information to Goff, including confidential cables from top diplomats to Allen criticising the change plans.[22] In March 2012 the partners of overseas diplomats released an open letter[23] (Exhibit B), urging Allen to "reconsider this proposed dismantling of the foreign service" and expressing their dismay at the lack of consultation with them. The letter described a Ministry at "tipping point" and warned that if the changes were implemented, "partners will no longer be able to support our spouses continuing their careers with MFAT."

## The Government steps in

By 21 March the *New Zealand Herald* was reporting the imminent release of McCully's letter, surmising Allen had "cocked up" with the "cookie cutter" approach taken to the restructuring.[24] The Minister, the paper reported, "reckons that as the purchaser of the ministry's services he is entitled to get deeply engaged with the scope of the restructuring. But he can't run the operational side." McCully's letter, subsequently released, expressed exactly this line of reasoning, while also explaining his need to have regard for the "management of political risk, given the highly politicised commentary that this process has attracted."[25]

McCully also attempted to distance himself from the flak that the proposal had generated:

> "At the time the document was released to staff I stated publicly that the change proposals were a genuine attempt to modernise the Ministry...as we both know, change is overdue... Prior to the release of the consultation documents to staff I was forthright in my views about some aspects of the reform proposals. It would be fair to say that the consultation process has seen strong criticism directed at many of those same features of the change process. Now that the obligatory consultation process is coming to an end it is important that key decisions are made quickly, to adopt changes where they will provide long term benefits and suspend change debate where they will not."

The *Trans Tasman* political newsletter, a well-read weekly summary of goings-on at the Beehive,[26] immediately speculated that a humiliated Allen might be considering resigning[27] but there was no sign of that. Days after McCully's letter, Goff released a leaked letter in Parliament, in which all but four overseas diplomats petitioned Allen to reverse his plans.[28] Former senior diplomat and foreign affairs commentator Terence O'Brien published an uncharacteristically savage commentary in the *Dominion Post*, claiming that the culture of MFAT was being threatened by the personal beliefs of the Minister, which ran counter to what was regarded as international "best practice". O'Brien believed that there had been "a seeming collapse of mutual trust and respect which may now only be repaired by change among the main actors involved."[29]

In early May three Cabinet papers detailing the proposed revised changes were leaked to the opposition's Goff, sparking Government fury and the launch of an SSC inquiry into the leaks, promptly labelled a witch-hunt by opponents. The matter had now escalated to Prime Ministerial level, with John Key and his officials reported to be taking a "hands-on role"[30] in the restructuring, which included giving Allen a "top-level grilling." Key told reporters the Cabinet had "not fully sighted" the initial change proposals and wanted to ensure the final changes were "appropriate." He was also extremely critical about the leaks, noting that only about 20 people had access to the material and that he was "deeply disappointed because at the end of the day these are people charged with diplomacy and ....upholding the highest standards by virtue of the job and they completely failed the test."[31]

## Allen changes course

In May 2012 the final change proposals were announced. A scaled back restructure was reported,[32] with the job cuts reduced from 305 to 79 and many of the proposed entitlement cuts reversed. The FSA described the process as shambolic, with Fraser noting "the saving grace of late is that John and his team have remembered they can talk to staff."[33] Allen believed "the process has gone very well", with the scaling-back of the proposals a demonstration that the consultation process had been genuine. Prime Minister Key was not so positive. Asked if the restructuring had been botched, he said that many changes that his Government had made had gone smoothly "and whatever way you define this, this hasn't and we need to learn some lessons from this."

Had the appointment of Allen been a mistake, given his lack of relevant experience? Did he and his senior leadership team take sufficient heed of the PIF review's warnings about the need for caution around the speed and size of change? Was the Minister to blame for interfering in the change programme? Should MFAT staff have been more open to seeing the benefits of the change? Or was the change programme itself the problem?

Exhibit A: Countries where New Zealand has Embassies and High Commissions (as at March 2012)

| Australia | Hong Kong | Papua New Guinea | Thailand |
|---|---|---|---|
| Austria | India | Philippines | Timor-Leste |
| Belgium | Indonesia | Poland | Tonga |
| Brazil | Iran | Russia | Turkey |
| Canada | Italy | Samoa | United Arab Emirates |
| Chile | Japan | Saudi Arabia | United Kingdom |
| China | Kiribati | Singapore | United Nations (Geneva) |
| Cook Islands | Korea | Solomon Islands | United Nations (New York) |
| Egypt | Malaysia | South Africa | United Nations (Vienna) |
| European Union | Mexico | Spain | United States of America |
| Fiji | Netherlands | Sweden | Vanuatu |
| France | New Caledonia | Switzerland | Viet Nam |
| Germany | Niue | Taiwan | World Trade Organisation |

Exhibit B: Excerpt from MFAT partners' letter of 12 March 2012 to John Allen[34]

Dear John,

MFAT spouses and partners have a unique perspective on the likely impacts of the Ministry's proposed restructuring on the careers of our partners and the effectiveness of New Zealand's diplomacy.

MFAT partners have been explicitly excluded from the consultation process but we are determined to be heard on issues that will directly influence our willingness to continue to make the sacrifices and contributions that being the partner of an MFAT officer demands. More than 180 partners have come together using social media to share our grave concerns about the proposed restructuring.

Given the lack of any formal avenue to convey our views, we have chosen to present them in this open letter. Consistent with the past practice of constructive dialogue and consultation with partners, we ask that MFAT:

- Reconsider the path on which it is setting the organisation with this proposed dismantling of the professional foreign service;
- Recognise MFAT partners as key stakeholders in the future of MFAT;
- Initiate a consultation process with MFAT partners on the impacts and implications of the proposed restructuring;
- Allow the Family Liaison Co-ordinator to communicate and liaise with MFAT partners freely throughout the consultation on the restructuring.

**What value can partners add to this consultation?**

As MFAT partners we have a thorough understanding of the demands of a diplomatic career, and a legitimate voice in commenting on the likelihood that the restructuring will succeed in its aim of retaining good staff.

All MFAT partners and families have felt and absorbed the consequences of accompanying MFAT staff overseas. We have:

- travelled and served in inhospitable and insecure environments;
- accepted disruption to careers and schooling;
- absorbed loss of income and pension; and
- suffered the impacts of long absences from family and friends.

In doing so we have committed ourselves to supporting the career of our MFAT partner and sharing in their responsibility to represent New Zealand in the manner that Government Ministers, government agencies, businesses and citizens in trouble expect. We have done this with pride, buoyed by the knowledge that we were contributing to the Ministry's work to help New Zealand get ahead and to secure New Zealand's future in a rapidly changing worked. We have done this confident that the Ministry acknowledged and valued our contributions. But a tipping point has now been reached.

Source: 'Trimming the FAT: change at the Ministry of Foreign Affairs and Trade – Bridgeman & Berry'. Reproduced with permission.

## 20.2 A Desk-Based Case: Monarch Airlines

### MONARCH AIRLINES[35]

"We're delighted to announce the biggest investment in our history and, building on our successful turnaround, we are now able to approach the future with great confidence. We're pleased to say that we are going to make over £40m profit this year, we made over £70m last year," boasted a very confident Monarch chief executive, Andrew Swaffield, on the announcement of a £165m investment from Greybull Capital to secure the business in October 2016.

Justifying the investment, he went on to confirm: "We needed to make sure that we had secured sufficient funding to ensure a confident future for Monarch and that's what we have done. We have secured the biggest investment in our history, which is very much about looking forward now; and we are renewing our fleet in 2018 into brand new Boeing 737 MAX-8's which are 22% more fuel efficient than our current fleet and require 80% less maintenance expenditure. So, we're on the brink of transformation in terms of economics and the customer experience of our airline."

By early 2017 Monarch was experiencing a growth in ticket sales and boasted an operating profit. However, in less than 11 months since the Greybull bailout, Swaffield was once again under the media spotlight, describing himself as "absolutely devastated" by the announcement of the collapse of Monarch

Airlines on 2 October 2017, after more than 50 years in operation as the UK's longest-serving airline. The news left more than 110,000 customers stranded or with tickets that were no longer valid and led to a global repatriation of travellers. How could such an optimistic chief executive get it so wrong? Was this down to bad management decision-making or poor strategic planning, or was it due to factors outside of the control of the organisation? Could the collapse have been prevented or was it simply an unavoidable disaster waiting to happen?

## The formation of the Monarch family dynasty

Monarch was founded by the Swiss-based Mantegazza family in 1968, as a low-cost airline that helped to bolster the rapid expansion of package holidays. Dozens of tour operators used its services, as well as its 'in-house' Cosmos holiday firm. Initially Monarch's business model was created to service the boom in package holidays. Its first charter flight took off from Luton airport in the UK, and there were soon flights leaving from Gatwick, Manchester and Glasgow. For the following 30 years, Monarch appeared to thrive, owing largely to good management, a high-quality product and expanding travel horizons. By the mid-1990s Monarch had launched a scheduled operation, which served a range of Mediterranean destinations.

However, that business model was challenged by the internet and the introduction of online purchasing, which meant that holidaymakers could now book their own holidays. This changing online landscape coincided with the rise of low-cost airlines such as easyJet, founded in 1995, which offered passengers cheap alternatives to charter flights. Passenger numbers on charter flights operated by British airlines fell by two-thirds between 2001 and 2016, while the overall number of passengers increased. Although Monarch had acquired scheduled operating licences since 1985, it ceased offering charter and long-haul flights in only 2015 (see Exhibit 1).

In response, Monarch sought to adapt to the online requirements of a modern airline with significant investment in online and social media as part of its cross-functional social customer care strategy. As a consequence, by 2015 Monarch was able to boast an average of 8.8 out of 10 for its customer satisfaction rating on Twitter.

However, rather than competing head-on with new arrivals, such as easyJet and Ryanair, with their no-frills model, Monarch elected for an upmarket offering, with everything from free newspapers to four-course meals included in fares, which, at the time, were about twice as high as easyJet's.

As the no-frills, low-cost airline revolution evolved, Monarch was left struggling to cope with such a changing and highly competitive market. In 2009 the Mantegazza family had invested £45m in the business, followed by a further £75m in 2011, to maintain Monarch as a going concern. Family patriarch Sergio Mantegazza was understood to have become impatient with the airline's financial troubles after Monarch asked for a third bail-out in July 2014. The family agreed a further investment of £50m to bolster business before agreeing to sell most of the airline in October 2014, to Greybull Capital, a private equity firm.

On the sale of Monarch, Fabio Mantegazza, speaking on behalf of the family, saidd that "We are very proud to have created one of the most loved aviation brands in the UK over the past 46 years. We think that now is an appropriate time to allow new shareholders to take Monarch into the future, with secure financial backing and clear strategic goals and we wish the Group every success." Fabio confirmed that his octogenarian father had thanked him on receiving news of the successful sale and said that "He was relieved." The Mantegazza family considered it a "privilege" to have achieved an exit that kept the business alive. Fabio concluded that a liquidation would have been "a very regrettable outcome."

## Greybull and Swaffield join Monarch in 2014

Andrew Swaffield was lured to join Monarch in 2014 as the chief executive, having previously worked as the former boss of Avios, the reward programme of rival British Airways. After reviewing Monarch's financial position, he discovered that as much as £60m would be needed to shore up the airline's finances. As this extra injection of capital was rejected by the Mantegazza family, Swaffield was forced to hunt for investors elsewhere in what become known as Project Sandringham. Swaffield noted that "it wasn't what I had signed up for but I knew we had to make it work and I had a strong instinct it could be done." The business plan was torn up, and managing director Iain Rawlinson left his office, leaving Swaffield to find a way out for the business. The urgency of the situation soon became clear: "We were given the option to find another investor or shut down and we had just 12 weeks to do so." Monarch had been close to collapse when turnaround group Greybull Capital took control from the Mantegazza family by acquiring a 90% stake in Monarch in October 2014.

The 90% stake purchased by Greybull represented the dawn of a new season for Monarch, about which Swaffield said: "I am delighted to welcome the Greybull team as the new owners of the Monarch Group. We have a shared vision for the strategic direction and prospects for the business, and I am looking forward to working with them to implement the exciting plans for building our future."

Following Swaffield's arrival and the Greybull investment, Monarch embarked on £200m of cost cuts to bolster its finances, resulting in a swing to a £19.2m pre-tax profit at the end of October 2015, from a £57.3m loss 12 months earlier. This cost-cutting included the scrapping of its operations from East Midlands Airport, reducing its fleet from 42 aircraft to 33, cutting 700 jobs and slashing pay by between 30-35%. It also shifted the carrier's focus to scheduled flights and cut long-haul routes.

Under Swaffield's leadership, the airline ceased long haul routes to focus on the European low-price market. He assured the public that they remained committed to customer service, saying: "We're not just here to fly you from A to B – our aim is to make your journey as smooth as possible, from the second your flight is booked to the moment you arrive home." In subsequent marketing drives, the company rewarded customer politeness with free upgrades among a range of customer service improvements, including the provision of extra legroom and priority check-in rewards (normally worth more than £50) for passengers who were friendly when they booked flights by phone.

According to Nils Christy, Monarch's chief operating officer, the business basis for the kindness-reward model was informed by a study conducted by Goldsmith University into the links between being nice and happiness, health and success. Christy claimed: "Our customer services staff are already nice – now they can reward those who are positively nice to them, too." Monarch said that the initiative was part of a year-long campaign "to promote traditional values of chivalry, courtesy and respect." Christy added: "Everyone benefits from niceness. Planes depart more punctually, staff and customers are happier and it improves the travelling experience for everyone."

## The Arab Spring

The following year was an unpredictably difficult one for Monarch, which suffered from turmoil in the Middle East and Europe. Monarch had to stop operating services to Tunisia shortly after a terrorist attack in the resort of Sousse on 26 June 2015, which left 38 tourists (most of them British nationals) dead. Furthermore, after a bomb brought down a Russian Metrojet airliner in the Egyptian resort of Sharm el Sheikh on 31 October 2015, Monarch was one of the carriers forced to cancel its charter flights to what was once a staple destination of winter sun. One of its most important markets was the Red Sea, but all travel to this year-round sun destination was suspended. Monarch also experienced a 50% drop in bookings to Greece because of the financial crisis there.

Monarch had intended to resume its flights to Egypt on 14 February 2016, but was forced to suspend services by at least a further few months until the British Foreign and Commonwealth Office changed its no-fly warning. Meanwhile, tensions in the region and an ongoing refugee crisis had affected Britons' appetite for holidays in Cyprus and Turkey, both of which were major destinations for Monarch. During the first half of 2016 as the security situation in Turkey deteriorated, Monarch and its rivals shifted capacity west to Spain and Portugal, depressing fares in a key market.

## Early warning signs in 2016

While initially stating in October 2014 that they saw Monarch as a "long-term investment", by March 2016 Greybull Capital sent a wave of uncertainty through Monarch as they appointed Deutsche Bank to explore the company's growth options in Europe, which could pave the way to include selling or merging with a distressed airline. At this point, budget airline rivals such as easyJet and Norwegian Air Shuttle were being looked at as potential buyers, and the company also considered Air Berlin as a possible target for a merger. Having taken Monarch from a place of debt to profit in a 17-month period, it was likely that Greybull would be set to make a significant return on any sale. This coincided with Greybull nearing completion on the final stages of agreeing to purchase Tata Steel UK's Scunthorpe works.

However, by June 2016 financial accounts showed Monarch was still highly dependent on shareholder funding, and so the airline went out to speak to external investors. In accounts filed with Companies House, the parent firm, Monarch Holdings, said that it was looking to secure finances totalling £35m either from owner Greybull Capital or an outside lender. This prompted the airline to issue a 'going concern' warning in its annual report because the financing was yet to be agreed. Swaffield played down the significance of this, stating that this was not unusual: "The business has been heavily returned to profit but unsurprisingly profit and cash are not the same thing." He added that the accounts were "just simply making the point that we're still dependent, unsurprisingly, on support from our shareholder" and that in its 2014 accounts the carrier had issued a similar warning.

Swaffield believed that Brexit meant it was unlikely they would find funding from any firm other than Greybull, but nonetheless remained positive in his outlook: "We are on track to deliver what I think will be our second most profitable year in our history."

His subsequent confident announcement of a future "on the brink of trans-formation" for Monarch followed an injection of a £165m investment from its majority shareholder, Greybull Capital, to secure the business in October 2016 and to enable it to invest in new planes. When challenged about likely profits falling by £30m compared with the previous year, Swaffield was quick to draw attention to the challenges posed with conflicts in Tunisia and Turkey, which had massively affected tourism in the region. Swaffield was now convinced that this new injection of funds was not a short-term fix but that Monarch was now ready to overcome the recent hurdles of terrorism and economic uncertainty: "The deal is built around a six-year business plan. By 2021, we will have the youngest fleet of any airline in Europe. The new aircraft are 22 per cent more fuel efficient and we spend £120m a year on fuel, so that's a significant saving."

He added that Monarch had a clear vision for its brand, which would combine low prices, punctuality and personal service. It wanted to position itself closer to airlines such as Norwegian Air Shuttle, rather than Ryanair, which would be achieved through a planned increase in its marketing spending: "Running an airline in Europe – home to some of the world's biggest low-cost carriers – is not for the faint of heart. But we're up for the fight – and you can bet on our future."

## Renewed hope in 2017

However, within three months, on 16 December 2016, Monarch issued yet another profits warning, confirming that its profits will be down by 35% in the trading year, describing the current trading environment as the "toughest ever." In 2016 the airline had flown 14% more customers, which would normally mean growth and progress in a business; however, there was a corresponding decrease in revenue of some £100m. In addition to dwindling revenues, Monarch also had increasing costs as a result of the weakened pound sterling. Monarch's fuel handling charges and lease payments were still being paid in US dollars. Since the Brexit referendum, the 10% decline of sterling against the dollar and more than 12% against the euro left Monarch paying about £50m a year more for its fuel and aircraft.

However, Swaffield remained upbeat stating: "The record investment in the business announced in October, enhanced marketing initiatives, including our first TV advertising campaign in three years, and continuing cost control means Monarch enters 2017 in a strong position." The company went on to confirm that new bookings for summer 2017 were up by some 40%.

Swaffield continued: "I'm very confident in our financial position now, which is the strongest it has ever been. When combined with the benefit of the restructure and the arrival of the new fleet, the business is in great shape."

Nonetheless, the European airline market remained highly saturated, with rivals Ryanair and easyJet fighting a vicious price war in the Mediterranean. These larger competitors in the low-cost travel sector had continued to experience passenger growth.

By August 2017 details of Monarch's annual accounts continued to paint a different picture. Nonetheless, Swaffield rejected suggestions that the group was in trouble after its accounts for the year to October 2016 showed a statutory loss of £291m, stating that the bulk of the losses related to "onerous" leases for aircraft, which left the Monarch group reporting a pre-tax profit of £12.9m before provision for "exceptional items." Swaffield attributed the headline deficit to "a very significant one-off loss" from writing off the costs of Monarch's current fleet. The airline would take delivery of the first of a new fleet of Boeing 737 MAX-8 aircraft in March 2018, having ordered 45 of the aircraft, and would phase out its existing fleet over three years. The losses were "the last legacy of the old Monarch." In summary, "Monarch's business will be so much more profitable with the new aircraft. There is a £100m benefit for us on the bottom line." Swaffield concluded: "I'm pretty happy with where we are."

## The end of Monarch and the future for Swaffield

At 3am on 2 October 2017, Monarch – the UK's fifth-largest airline – closed for business as it went into administration, with the British Government instigating what it called the "country's biggest ever peacetime repatriation" effort to fly about 110,000 passengers stranded abroad back home. At the time Monarch employed approximately 1,900 people.

The British Secretary of State for Transport, Chris Grayling, confirmed that "Monarch directors had informed the government that they couldn't carry on trading, which led the government to put into action its contingency plans." Grayling noted that although Monarch had achieved recent growth in passenger numbers, pressure to reduce flight prices, owing in part to the intense competition in the market, had contributed to the collapse of the airline.

This news coincided with similar announcements from Alitalia and Air Berlin. Alitalia was the first to go into administration; and Air Berlin, which had been Europe's tenth-largest airline, ceased flights on 26 October.

Monarch's chief executive Swaffield had received a salary of £583,000. Records at Companies House appeared to indicate that he had set up a new company just a few days before the Monarch collapse. Speaking on the final days of the company, he said: "Monarch was on a restructuring journey. We were pursuing multiple options, including the sale of the entire company, including the sale of assets and including other strategic options. Unfortunately, we reached the end of the runway."

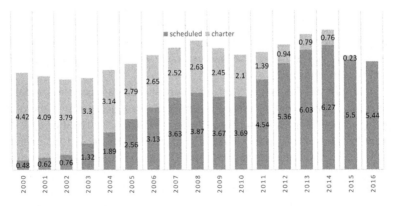

Exhibit 1: Monarch passenger figures (Source: CAA)

EEA Scheduled Services 2016

| Passenger Service | Aircraft Km , (000) | Stage Flights | A/C Hours | Number of Passengers Uplifted | Seat-Km Available , (000) | Seat-Km Used , (000) | As % of Avail | Cargo Uplifted Tonnes | Tonne-Km Available , (000) | Total , (000) | Tonnes-Km used | | | As % of Avail |
|---|---|---|---|---|---|---|---|---|---|---|---|---|---|---|
| | | | | | | | | | | | Mail , (000) | Freight , (000) | Passenger , (000) | |
| BA CITYFLYER LTD | 14,599 | 18,944 | 29,848 | 1,135,692 | 1,285,390 | 934,840 | 72.7 | 1 | 128,600 | 83,178 | - | - | 83,178 | 64.7 |
| BMI REGIONAL | 11,958 | 17,345 | 24,680 | 355,280 | 543,229 | 270,650 | 49.8 | 4 | 62,063 | 23,010 | - | 3 | 23,010 | 37.1 |
| BRITISH AIRWAYS PLC | 138,822 | 128,908 | 268,027 | 15,774,942 | 21,871,265 | 17,666,474 | 80.8 | 33,831 | 2,374,138 | 1,682,923 | 6,696 | 41,556 | 1,682,923 | 70.9 |
| EASTERN AIRWAYS | 658 | 1,414 | 1,661 | 32,607 | 32,529 | 15,664 | 48.2 | - | 3,253 | 1,932 | - | - | 1,332 | 40.9 |
| EASYJET AIRLINE COMPANY LTD | 424,697 | 369,594 | 749,381 | 54,057,045 | 70,873,750 | 63,393,165 | 89.4 | - | 6,024,244 | 5,388,514 | - | - | 5,388,514 | 89.4 |
| FLYBE LTD | 35,928 | 54,013 | 83,449 | 3,165,586 | 3,278,370 | 2,202,705 | 67.2 | 23 | 357,183 | 187,247 | - | 11 | 187,247 | 52.4 |
| JET2.COM LTD | 79,913 | 39,692 | 125,979 | 6,389,690 | 14,647,411 | 13,320,215 | 90.9 | - | 1,384,202 | 1,132,242 | - | - | 1,132,242 | 81.8 |
| LOGANAIR LTD | 286 | 652 | 788 | 20,201 | 13,574 | 9,759 | 71.9 | - | 1,452 | 827 | - | - | 827 | 57.0 |
| MONARCH AIRLINES | 54,275 | 28,185 | 85,406 | 4,312,085 | 10,971,219 | 8,321,335 | 75.8 | 552 | 1,154,322 | 707,710 | - | 1,391 | 706,319 | 61.3 |
| THOMAS COOK AIRLINES LTD | 54,022 | 21,675 | 79,776 | 4,362,575 | 12,235,993 | 10,975,901 | 89.7 | 316 | 1,210,086 | 933,750 | - | 903 | 932,847 | 77.2 |
| THOMSON AIRLINES LTD | 789 | 416 | 1,196 | 92,113 | 184,121 | 174,294 | 94.7 | - | 22,364 | 14,816 | - | - | 14,816 | 66.2 |
| VIRGIN ATLANTIC AIRWAYS LTD | - | - | - | 1 | - | - | - | - | - | - | - | - | - | - |
| Total Passenger Services | 815,848 | 680,838 | 450,190 | 89,697,817 | 135,937,850 | 117,285,001 | 86.3 | 34,727 | 12,721,906 | 10,155,550 | 6,696 | 43,865 | 10,104,989 | 79.8 |
| Cargo Only Services | | | | | | | | | | | | | | |
| BRITISH AIRWAYS PLC | 1,275 | 1,428 | 3,066 | - | - | - | - | 22,891 | 49,511 | 18,765 | - | 18,765 | - | 37.9 |
| Total Cargo Only Services | 1,275 | 1,428 | 3,066 | - | - | - | - | 22,891 | 49,511 | 18,765 | - | 18,765 | - | 37.9 |
| Grand Total | 817,123 | 682,266 | 453,256 | 89,697,817 | 135,937,850 | 117,285,001 | 86.3 | 57,618 | 12,771,417 | 10,174,315 | 6,696 | 62,630 | 10,104,989 | 79.7 |

Exhibit 2: All EEA scheduled flights for 2016 (Source: CAA)

| Key performance indicators | 2016 | 2015 | Change |
|---|---|---|---|
| Revenue (£m) | 558.7 | 655.5 | (14.8)% |
| Total Airline capacity ('000) | 7,082 | 7,196 | (1.6)% |
| Total Airline booked passengers ('000) | 5,568 | 5,975 | (6.8)% |
| Airline load factor | 78.60% | 83.00% | (5.3)% |
| Average number of aircraft | 33.8 | 35.3 | (4.2)% |
| EBITDA - underlying (£m) | 46.6 | 64.8 | (28.1)% |
| EBITDAR - underlying (£m) | 125.7 | 134.7 | (6.8)% |
| On Time Performance | 78% | 82% | (4)% |

Exhibit 3: Revenue and other KPIs for Monarch 2015 and 2016 (Source: Companies House Annual Report)

Source: 'Monarch Airlines – Andrews & The Case Centre'. Produced as part of the Online Interactive Study Guide. Available at: www.thecasecentre.org/guide. Reproduced with permission

An annotated version of the case is available in the Support Material, which can be found at www.routledge.com/9780367426965. This contains additional comments identifying how the chronology structure was developed. These notes also contain further ideas which shaped the other three case structures as well as identifying points for analysis. It was produced as part of the Online Interactive Study Guide. Available at: www.thecasecentre.org/guide. Reproduced with permission.

## 20.3 An Armchair Case based on Personal Experience: Ereuna Research – Ethical Dilemmas with Big Data Analytics[36]

Ahmet Meraklı was used to finding himself in situations where difficult and often risky decisions had to be made. After all, speculation and risk were at the heart of the sector within which he operated, which saw some speculators reaping the rewards of risky choices, leaving behind more risk-averse competitors in a fast-changing sector. Working with big data would always be fraught with risk. And it seemed to Meraklı that there was no such thing as clear black and white – there were plenty of grey areas and blurred lines too! However, the blurred line that he was now examining left him with a dilemma. Should he continue to pursue the development of big data analytics for the purpose of greater gain and risk the criticism of those who challenge his actions on ethical grounds? Or was it time to take stock of the situation and put in place a more risk-averse response to safeguard his company's future reputation? With the latest updates on Turkish Personal Data Protection Law ready to be reviewed on his desk, he knew that a difficult decision had to be made.

\*\*\*\*\*\*\*\*\*\*

In October 2015 Meraklı, an economist and founder of Ereuna Research, brokered a strategic partnership with a promising start-up, Future Data. In recent years Ereuna had become increasingly popular, and by 2015 it was regarded as one of the most widely trusted research companies in Turkey.

After ten years of hard work, Meraklı had taken the company from nothing to become an accomplished sector leader. But Ereuna needed to adapt to changing market demands, and Meraklı was keen to diversify Ereuna's activities into cutting-edge research areas. As a priority, Ereuna was looking for a way to integrate large volumes of data generated through social networks into analytical opportunities. Thanks to its popularity, Meraklı's company was highly capable of accomplishing the early stages of data-processing – including data collection, preparation, and input – and yet it lacked the cutting-edge knowhow necessary for the later stages – data-processing, output and interpretation. In order to fill this gap, Meraklı decided to form a strategic partnership with a company with expertise in this field, and Future Data appeared to be the most suitable one.

Future Data was a small start-up founded by Dr Elif Budak. A data scientist, with a PhD in computer science, Budak was a full-time faculty member of a computer science department in one of Turkey's leading universities. She took advantage of market insights and her knowledge of data analytics and founded Future Data in her personal time. The start-up enabled her to conduct massive data-intensive research, which also informed her academic studies. Future Data focused on all forms of public big data and developed opportunities to process this big data in order to predict people's social trends and behaviours. A partnership with Ereuna would be really valuable for Future Data, as Ereuna had the volume and labour required for getting big data ready for Future Data's analysis. Having their own servers as an established company, Ereuna was capable of providing storage opportunity, which was quite essential for big data studies.

So, in late October 2015 contracts were signed, and the partnership was launched. The first four months of the partnership were spent building a framework for joint projects. In February 2016 Ereuna and Future Data launched their first project, which was designed to be built by Future Data. The project was the first concrete attempt by Future Data to implement massive social network data analysis that could be processed to predict young individuals' buying preferences. Ereuna willingly agreed to prepare the data, which would include cleaning the data, constructing data sets, and pre-processing them, and then to convert the data into a machine-readable form. Accordingly, it was agreed that Future Data and Ereuna would work on two large data sets: (i) the public data available on a new social media platform, which had recently become quite popular among university students; and (ii) a large data set addressing the consumption behaviours of students of Budak's university. The latter data set was provided to Budak by her university as part of another research project, which involved designing the future of their campus. In addition to its original intended use, Budak then had this data set anonymised by Future Data. This way, she thought that she could make the data available for a second purpose without sharing any private information of the students. The data collected from the popular social media platform included a fair amount of individual member information. While this information could be used for identification purposes by the project researchers, as the data was already public, Budak saw no compelling reason to anonymise it for use on this project. By combining these two data sets, Budak's intention was to capture metrics that could make a significant initial impact in the field.

Things worked even better than both companies expected. By November 2016 they started to evaluate the initial outcome of their project and the signs were highly promising. The social network data made it possible for them to trace the mood and emotions of the young community, which even by itself represented significant value. In addition, through data mining techniques, the anonymised data of the university students was analysed to find a correlation between the mood of the students and their consumption behaviour. The initial outcome was positive: students' buying preferences varied significantly during certain periods such as finals week and the Spring fest. The next step, which would be accomplished by Ereuna, was to design a research tool that could test the findings in the market. Confident of the likely impact of this research, Meraklı had already started talks with potential buyers of such information. Even at this early stage there was a surprisingly high level of interest. Meanwhile, Budak was excited for another reason. She had drafts for two academic articles addressing their findings, which had also been accepted for presentation at two significant international conferences. By the end of 2016 both parties were optimistic about the opportunities that 2017 would bring.

Budak wasted no time preparing and submitting her two articles, which were sent to two top-level academic journals. Given their findings, she was almost certain of being accepted for publication. In April 2017 Budak also delivered her first conference presentation, highlighting Ereuna as her key sponsor. The paper received a high level of interest. As a result, a number of researchers requested replication data sets from Budak. However, the researchers also noted that the use of these data sets generated some questions about the methodology, mainly concerning the ethical viability of the study. From Budak's perspective, the project was a product of her start-up which, unlike her university work, was free from the requirements of an ethical review board. Having reflected on the manner by which the data had been processed, she was sure that it was perfectly anonymised and that the participants of the study were not re-identifiable by any means. Nonetheless, some researchers still criticised Budak for using research-oriented data for a private sector project. Some of these critics believed that even full accomplishment of anonymisation would be insufficient to satisfy ethics committees that would normally monitor this type of usage.

As the impact of the discussion developed, Budak decided to address these critics and their concerns head-on by delivering a full explanation about the project and the articles that she had already submitted in another conference talk. During her presentation, she explained what the project was all about and also mentioned the paper that she was working on, which was based on public data retrieved from a social media platform.

In response to questions about the ethical implications, Budak claimed that the recent Turkish Personal Data Protection Law gave her the right to use the publicised data. To further endorse this, she referred to Article 5, 2d of the Law stating:

> "Personal data may be processed without obtaining the explicit consent of the data subject if the relevant information is revealed to the public by the data subject herself/himself (Article 5, 2d)."

However, her justification for the use of public data was far from convincing. In fact, she continued to receive even heavier criticism.

The critics' main argument was based on the premise that whilst the data subjects publicised their data for socialising and making new friends, it was subsequently used for a totally different purpose – forecasting the buying preferences – by Future Data. This second utilisation had not been knowingly permitted by the data subjects and therefore should require further consent. As a consequence, Budak, who had expected to leave the conference with resounding appreciation for her research, subsequently found herself to be the centre of a media-inflamed controversy, leading to calls from her Dean.

By the summer of 2017 Meraklı found himself becoming both increasingly excited and yet at the same time panicking about the impact of his ongoing research, which had supported the earlier findings of their joint project with Future Data. He was amazed at what the project on big data had enabled them to predict and achieve. However, increasing hostility to Budak's research was creating a dilemma for the partnership. Following all the criticism that Budak's conference talk had received, she was undecided whether or not to withdraw her articles. Concerned about the likely impact of Budak's actions on Ereuna's reputation, Meraklı found himself looking for alternative ways to secure his company's future. Should he ignore the critics and continue to work to promote the valuable findings of their joint project with Future Data? Or was it time to disassociate his company from its strategic partner? Meraklı was unsure what to do next.

Source: 'Ereuna Research - Ethical Dilemmas with Big Data Analytics – Erşahin, Andrews & Wasti'. Reproduced with permission.

## 20.4 Sample Teaching Note: Ereuna Research – Ethical Dilemmas with Big Data Analytics[37]

### I) SYNOPSIS

This case addresses a multi-dimensional, big data ethics dilemma. Ahmet Meraklı, owner of Ereuna Research, finds himself in a tricky situation, which can lead to both a major professional accomplishment and an ethical challenge. A joint project run by Ereuna Research and Future Data, a start-up founded by an academic specialising in data science, Dr Elif Budak, had just begun to generate valuable results through what some might see as a potentially controversial process.

### ii) Teaching objectives and target audience

#### Teaching objectives

The case aims to assist students in:

a  Developing an ethical perspective for various dimensions of data-based research (collecting, anonymising, mining, analysing, storing data).
b  Defining and discussing the concepts of privacy, anonymity, publicity, and research ethics in the context of data science.
c  Developing awareness about the privacy and publicity issues related to the personal information people share on the internet.

#### Target audience

The case would be most suitable for a Data Ethics course that is designed for a Data Science programme. It can also be useful for graduate students enrolled in a Research Ethics or Data Analytics module.

### iii) Case analysis and teaching plan

The case can be discussed in an inductive/abductive approach. Driving the students towards problem identification, analysis and critical thinking, as well as problem-solving would promote the achievement of potential learning objectives. Following a multi-dimensional discussion of ethics, data ethics and research ethics, students are expected to analyse Meraklı's dilemma and make a decision. Budak's action regarding her upcoming articles is also left at an impasse. Participants are invited to think about action plans for both parties while developing a grounded understanding of the situation.

One way of initialising the discussion is to address a broad description of ethics. The starting point of this path might be the meaning of the Greek word *ethos*. A general question such as "Is there a code illuminating how to live and how to behave?" can be deduced to the following: "Is there a 'proper' way to run a data-based project?"

The second step might be to engage participants to the topic of data ethics. To do this, it would be useful to address the data that they produce online and to identify related problems that they might have experienced. Students may be asked whether they really know the privacy policies of the online platforms they are using, to demonstrate how they are already part of this issue.

Following this conceptual section, the case can be introduced briefly. The first critical point to dwell on would be the transfer of anonymised data for a secondary purpose. The discussion might be advanced with the following questions:

- Do you find it appropriate to transfer data this way? If your answer is yes, please explain why. If you do not agree with it, please state what is wrong with it. Who is responsible for any inappropriateness in this case? Is it Budak or the boards of the university?
- What is anonymised data? Is it sufficient to anonymise a data set for any kind of secondary use of it?
- Once the data is anonymised, to whom does it belong? Can the participants of the university survey have a further claim on it? Or does the data belong to the researcher?

Once the discussion of the anonymisation of data is completed, the discussion could progress to exploring the difference between these opposing viewpoints. This can be addressed with the following question:

- Is there any difference between the ethical responsibilities of academia and the business world when it comes to a data-based research?

The class discussion could progress to consider what Meraklı and Budak (separately or jointly) should do next.

It could be appropriate to incorporate details of the legal aspects of data management, and the students could be invited to explore their interpretation of legal concepts in the context of this case situation. Exhibit A provides insights which could be used to inform this discussion.

## iv) Additional readings and references

Floridi, Luciano & Taddeo, Mariarosaria. (2016) "What is Data Ethics?", Philosophical Transactions of the Royal Society A374: 20160112. DOI: http://dx.doi.org/10.1098/rsta.2016.0360

Leetaru, Karev. (2016) "Are research Ethics Obsolete in the Era of Big Data?", Forbes, https://www.forbes.com/sites/kalevleetaru/2016/06/17/are-research-ethics-obsolete-in-the-era-of-big-data/#284246e37aa3

Weaver, Matthew. (2018) "Cambridge University Rejected Facebook Study over 'Deceptive' Privacy Standards," The Guardian, https://amp.theguardian.com/technology/2018/apr/24/cambridge-university-rejected-facebook-study-over-deceptive-privacy-standards

## v) Feedback

The case was first delivered during the April 2018 meeting of Case Study Alliance Turkey Project in Ürgüp. The audience said that it sets the scene for various discussions, and it would be good to structure them, and for this aim, the tutor might wish to create a flowchart based on student feedback to enable its utilisation, capturing key comments and concepts raised in the discussion.The second run of the case took place in May 2018 at a Data Science course at TED University. The students of the Applied Data Science Master Program found the case quite interesting and declared that it would be helpful for them to consider ethical issues while they collect data for their theses. Students were able to associate with the issues raised in the case and the actual problems that they faced with data that they had provided on online platforms. In-class discussion demonstrated that any data-based research is replete with ethical considerations, and the legal and deontological boundaries – both academic and professional – should be carefully considered by researchers.

### Exhibit A: Turkish Personal Data Protection Law no. 6698

#### Purpose

ARTICLE 1 – (1) The purpose of this Law is to protect the fundamental rights and freedoms of persons, privacy of personal life in particular, while personal data are processed, and to set forth obligations of natural and legal persons who process personal data and procedures and principles to comply with for the same.

#### Scope

ARTICLE 2 – (1) The provisions of this Law shall apply to natural persons whose personal data are processed and natural or legal persons who process such data wholly or partly by automatic means or otherwise than by automatic means which form part of a filing system.

## Definitions

**ARTICLE 3** – (1) In practice of this Law, the terms used herein shall have the following meanings:

a) **Explicit Consent**: Freely given specific and informed consent;
b) **Anonymisation**: Rendering personal data by no means identified or identifiable with a natural person even by linking with other data;
c) **President**: President of the Board of Protection of Personal Data;
ç) **Data subject**: Natural person whose personal data are processed;
d) **Personal Data**: Any information relating to an identified or identifiable natural person;
e) **Processing of personal data**: Any operation which is performed upon personal data such as collection, recording, storage, preservation, alteration, adaptation, disclosure, transfer, retrieval, making available for collection, categorization or blocking its use by wholly or partly automatic means or otherwise than by automatic means which form part of a filing system;
f) **Board**: The Board of Protection of Personal Data;
g) **Authority**: The Authority of Protection of Personal Data;
ğ) **Data processor**: Natural or legal person who processes personal data based on the authority granted by and on behalf of the data controller;
h) **Filing system**: Any recording system through which personal data are processed by structuring according to specific criteria;
ı) **Data controller**: Natural or legal person who determines the purposes and means of the processing of personal data, and who is responsible for establishment and management of the filing system.

## SECTION II

### PROCESSING OF PERSONAL DATA

General Principles

**ARTICLE 4** – (1) Personal data shall only be processed in accordance with the procedures and principles set forth by this Law or other laws.

(2) The below principles shall be complied with when processing personal data:

a) Being in conformity with the law and good faith;
b) Being accurate and if necessary, up to date;
c) Being processed for specified, explicit, and legitimate purposes;
ç) Being relevant, limited and proportionate to the purposes for which data are processed;

d) Being stored only for the time designated by relevant legislation or necessitated by the purpose for which data are collected.

## Conditions for Processing of Personal Data

**ARTICLE 5** – (1) Personal data shall not be processed without obtaining the explicit consent of the data subject.

(2) Personal data may be processed without obtaining the explicit consent of the data subject if one of the below conditions exists:

a) It is expressly permitted by any law;
b) It is necessary in order to protect the life or physical integrity of the data subject or another person where the data subject is physically or legally incapable of giving consent;
c) It is necessary to process the personal data of parties of a contract, provided that the processing is directly related to the execution or performance of the contract;
ç) It is necessary for compliance with a legal obligation which the controller is subject to;
d) The relevant information is revealed to the public by the data subject herself/himself;
e) It is necessary for the institution, usage, or protection of a right;
f) It is necessary for the legitimate interests of the data controller, provided that the fundamental rights and freedoms of the data subject are not harmed.

## Conditions for Processing of Special Categories of Personal Data

**ARTICLE 6** – (1) Data relating to race, ethnic origin, political opinions, philosophical beliefs, religion, sect or other beliefs, appearance and dressing, membership of association, foundation or trade-union, health, sexual life, criminal conviction and security measures, and biometrics and genetics are special categories of personal data.

(2) It is prohibited to process special categories of personal data without obtaining the explicit consent of the data subject.

(3) Personal data indicated in paragraph 1, other than personal data relating to health and sexual life, may be processed without obtaining the explicit consent of the data subject if processing is permitted by any law. Personal data relating to health and sexual life may only be processed without obtaining the explicit consent of the data subject for purposes of protection of public health, operation of preventive medicine, medical diagnosis, treatment, and care services, planning and management of health services and financing by persons under the obligation of secrecy or authorized institutions and organizations.

(4) It is additionally required to take the adequate measures designated by the Board when special categories of personal data are processed.

## Deletion, Destruction, and Anonymization of Personal Data

**ARTICLE 7** – (1) Personal data that is processed in accordance with this Law or relevant other laws shall be deleted, destroyed or anonymised either *ex officio* or upon request by the data subject in case the reasons necessitating their processing cease to exist.

(2) Provisions of other laws relating to deletion, destruction, and anonymization of personal data are reserved.

(3) Procedures and principles relating to deletion, destruction and anonymization of personal data shall be set forth by a regulation.

## Transfer of Personal Data

**ARTICLE 8** – (1) Personal data shall not be transferred without obtaining the explicit consent of the data subject.

(2) Personal data may be transferred without obtaining the explicit consent of the data subject if one of the conditions set forth under the following exists:

a) The second paragraph of article 5;
b) On the condition that adequate measures are taken, the third paragraph of article 6.

(3) Provisions of other laws relating to the transfer of personal data are reserved.

## Transfer of Personal Data Abroad

**ARTICLE 9** – (1) Personal data shall not be transferred abroad without obtaining the explicit consent of the data subject.

(2) Personal data may be transferred abroad without obtaining the explicit consent of the data subject if one of the conditions set forth in the second paragraph of article 5 or third paragraph of article 6 is present and:

a) If the foreign country to whom personal data will be transferred has an adequate level of protection;
b) In case there is not an adequate level of protection, if the data controllers in Turkey and abroad commit, in writing, to provide an adequate level of protection and the permission of the Board exists.

(3) The countries where an adequate level of protection exist shall be declared by the Board.

(4) The Board shall decide whether there is adequate level of protection in a foreign country and whether approval will be granted in terms of indent (b) of the second paragraph by evaluating if:

a) The international agreements to which Turkey is a party;
b) Reciprocality regarding transfer of personal data between the country requesting personal data and Turkey;
c) With regard to each present transfer of personal data, nature of personal data and purpose of processing and retention;
ç) Relevant legislation and practice of the country to whom personal data will be transferred;
d) Measures committed by the data controller in the country to whom personal data will be transferred;

and if it requires, by obtaining the opinion of relevant public institutions and organizations.

(5) Save for the provisions of international agreements, in cases where interests of Turkey or the data subject will be seriously harmed, personal data shall only be transferred abroad upon the approval of the Board by obtaining the opinion of relevant public institutions and organizations.

(6) Provisions of other laws relating to the transfer of personal data abroad are reserved.

## SECTION III

### *RIGHTS AND OBLIGATIONS*

### Data Controller's Obligation to Inform

**ARTICLE 10** – (1) Data controller or the person it authorized is obligated to inform the data subjects while collecting the personal data with regard to:

a) The identity of the data controller and if any, its representative;
b) The purposes for which personal data will be processed;
c) The persons to whom processed personal data might be transferred and the purposes for the same;
ç) The method and legal cause of collection of personal data.
d) The rights set forth under article 11.

Rights of Data Subject
**ARTICLE 11** – (1) Everyone, in connection with herself/himself, has the right to:

a) Learn whether or not her/his personal data have been processed;
b) Request information as to processing if her/his data have been processed;
c) Learn the purpose of processing of the personal data and whether data are used in accordance with their purpose;
ç) Know the third parties in the country or abroad to whom personal data have been transferred;

d) Request rectification in case personal data are processed incompletely or inaccurately;

e) Request deletion or destruction of personal data within the framework of the conditions set forth under article 7;

f) Request notification of the operations made as per indents (d) and (e) to third parties to whom personal data have been transferred;

g) Object to occurrence of any result that is to her/his detriment by means of analysis of personal data exclusively through automated systems;

ğ) Request compensation for the damages in case the person incurs damages due to unlawful processing of personal data by applying to the data controller.

## Obligations Regarding Data Security

**ARTICLE 12** – (1) Data controller shall take all necessary technical and organizational measures for providing an appropriate level of security in order to:

a) Prevent unlawful processing of personal data;
b) Prevent unlawful access to personal data;
c) Safeguard personal data.

(2) In case personal data are processed on behalf of the data controller by another natural or legal person, the data controller shall be jointly liable with such persons with regard to taking the measures set forth in the first paragraph.

(3) The data controller is obligated to carry out or have carried out necessary inspections within his institution and organization in order to ensure implementation of the provisions of this Law.

(4) Data controller and persons who process data shall not disclose and misuse personal data they learned contrary to the provisions of this Law. This obligation shall continue after leaving office.

(5) In case processed personal data are acquired by others through unlawful means, the data controller shall notify the data subject and the Board of such situation as soon as possible. The Board, if necessary, may declare such situation on its website or by other means which it deems appropriate.

## SECTION IV

## *APPLICATION, COMPLAINT, DATA CONTROLLERS' REGISTRY*

## Application to Data Controller

**ARTICLE 13** – (1) The data subject shall convey her/his requests relating to the enforcement of this Law to the data controller in writing or by other means designated by the Board.

(2) The data controller shall conclude the requests included in the application free of charge and as soon as possible considering the nature of the request and within 30 days at the latest. However, in case the operation necessitates a separate cost, the fee in the tariff designated by the Board may be collected.

(3) The data controller shall accept the request or reject it by explaining the reason and notify the data subject of its reply in writing or electronically. In case the request included in the application is accepted, it shall be fulfilled by the data controller accordingly. In case the request is resulted from the fault of the data controller, the collected fee shall be returned to the data subject.

## Complaint to the Board

**ARTICLE 14** – (1) In case the application is rejected, replied insufficiently, or not replied in due time; the data subject may file a complaint with the Board within 30 days following the date he/she learns the reply of the data controller and in any event, within 60 days following the date of application.

(2) Complaint remedy cannot be applied to without exhausting the application remedy set forth under article 13.

(3) Compensation rights of the ones whose personal rights are violated are reserved.

## Procedures and Principles of Inspection Ex Officio or upon Complaint

**ARTICLE 15** – (1) The Board shall conduct necessary inspection within the scope of its remit either *ex officio* in case it learns the allegation of a violation or upon complaint.

(2) Notices and complaints which do not meet the conditions set forth under the 6th article of The Law on the Exercise of the Right to Petition numbered 3071 and dated 1/11/1984 shall not be inspected.

(3) Except for the information and documents that constitute state secrets; data controller shall submit the information and documents requested by the Board related to its subject of inspection in 15 days and if necessary, provide for examining on-site.

(4) Upon complaint, the Board inspects the request and replies to those concerned. If not replied within sixty days following the date of the complaint, the request shall be deemed to be rejected.

(5) As a result of the inspection conducted either *ex officio* or upon complaint, in case it is understood that a violation exists, the Board decides that the illegalities it identified shall be eliminated by the data controller and serves it to those concerned. This decision shall be fulfilled accordingly without delay and within 30 days at the latest as from the notice.

(6) As a result of the inspection conducted either *ex officio* or upon complaint, in case it is determined that the violation is prevalent, the Board shall adopt a

resolution and publish it. The Board, if necessary before adopting the resolution, may obtain the opinion of relevant public institutions and organizations.

(7) In case serious or irreparable losses occur and illegality clearly exists, the Board may decide processing of data or transfer of data abroad to be ceased.

## Data Controllers' Registry

**ARTICLE 16** – (1) Under the supervision of the Board, Data Controllers Registry shall be kept by the Presidency in a publicly available manner.

(2) Natural or legal persons who process personal data shall register with the Data Controllers Registry prior to commencing processing. However, considering objective criteria that shall be designated by the Board such as the characteristics and the number of data to be processed, whether or not data processing is based on any law, or whether data will be transferred to third parties, the Board may set forth exemptions to the obligation to register with the Data Controllers Registry.

(3) Registry application to the Data Controllers Registry shall be made with a notification including the following matters:

a) Identity and address information of the data controller and of the representative thereof, if any.
b) The purposes for which personal data will be processed.
c) The group or groups of persons subject to the data and explanations regarding data categories belonging to these persons.
ç) Recipient or groups of recipients to whom personal data may be transferred.
d) Personal data which is envisaged to be transferred abroad.
e) Measures taken for the security of personal data.
f) The maximum period of time necessitated by the purposes for which personal data are processed.

(4) Changes to the information provided as per the third paragraph shall be immediately reported to the Board.

(5) Other procedures and principles relating to the Data Controllers Registry shall be regulated by a regulation.

Source: 'Ereuna Research – Ethical Dilemmas with Big Data Analytics. Teaching Note – Erşahin, Andrews & Wasti'. Reproduced with permission.

## Notes

1 Young, A. "McCully expresses confidence in John Allen." *New Zealand Herald*, 23 March 2012.
2 Cheng, D. "Ministry to lose fifth of staff in radical cuts." *New Zealand Herald*, 24 February 2012.
3 www.nzherald.co.nz/nz/news/article.cfm?c_id=1&objectid=5832.
4 Editorial. *Dominion Post*. 19 May,2009.

5 O'Sullivan, F. "Allen appointment a new direction." *New Zealand Herald*, 9 May 2009.

6 O'Sullivan, F. "Allen appointment a new direction." *New Zealand Herald*, 9 May 2009.

7 Bolger, J. Media statement. *NZ Post*. 8 May 2003.

8 Coleman, J. Media statement. "Core public service numbers continue to shrink." 30 August 2012.

9 Performance Improvement Framework: Formal Review of the Ministry of Foreign Affairs and Trade – September 2010. www.ssc.govt.nz The reviewers were the international consultant, former head of Treasury and of the ANZ Bank, Dr Murray Horn; PriceWaterhouseCoopers organisational change expert Debbie Francis, and recently retired former ambassador John Wood.

10 MFAT Statement of Intent 2010–2013. www.mfat.govt.nz

11 www.ssc.govt.nz/sites/all/files/CAB-PAPER-The-Performance-Improvement-Framework_2.PDF

12 Watkins, T. "Feathers ruffled in diplomatic shake-up". Dominion Post. 6 April 2011.

13 "While 80 percent of New Zealand's exports go to Asia and Australia, and only 20 percent to Europe and the United States, ...more than half our overseas diplomats are in the UK, Europe and the US." "Ruckus self-inflicted", *The Press*, 9 April 2012, p. A14.

14 McCully, M. "Speech to the NZ Institute of International Affairs." 5 April 2011.

15 Briefing to the Incoming Minister of Foreign Affairs. September 2011 www.mfat.govt.nz.

16 Trevett, C. "$15m more fat likely to be stripped from MFAT," New Zealand Herald. 2 March 2012.

17 Leaked figures cited "as much as $440,000 a year for rental accommodation", schooling costs of up to "$213,000 a family" and allowances "totalling well over $100,000." Watkins, T. "Diplomats' hefty perks revealed," www.stuff.co.nz/national/politics/6629834/Diplomats-heft-perks-revealed.

18 www.stuff.co.nz/national/politics/6466526/Foreign-Affairs-Ministry-confirms-305-jobs-to-go.

19 www.scoop.co.nz/stories/PO1202/S00316/mfat-faces-diplomat-crisis-says-survey.htm.

20 Uncorrected transcript of Foreign Affairs, Defence and Trade Committee's Financial Review of the Ministry of Foreign Affairs and Trade. 1 March 2012. (Released by committee clerk on request).

21 Small, V. Stressed MFAT staff told to 'get a pet', Dominion Post, 7 March, 2012.

22 Young, A. "MFAT staff cable leaks continue." *New Zealand Herald*. March 9, 2012.

23 http://pacific.scoop.co.nz/2012/03/mfat-partners-letter-to-ceo-on-proposed-restructuring.

24 O'Sullivan, F. "No diplomatic immunity from McCully." *New Zealand Herald*. 21 March 2012.

25 Young, A. "McCully expresses confidence in John Allen." New Zealand Herald, 23 March 2012. (Letter posted online in story.)

26 New Zealand Government ministers' offices are primarily located in a building designed in the shape of a Beehive. The Beehive has become the colloquial term for the seat of political power.

27 Young, A. "McCully expresses confidence in John Allen." New Zealand Herald. 23 March 2012.

28 Young, A. "All but four diplomats condemn cuts to MFAT." *New Zealand Herald*. 29 March 2012.

29 O'Brien, T. "Culture of MFAT under Threat." *Dominion Post*. 2 April 2012.

30 Watkins, T. "Key hands-on in MFAT restructuring." *Dominion Post*. 8 May 2012.

31 Watkins, T. "Key hands-on in MFAT restructuring." *Dominion Post*. 8 May 2012.

32 "MFAT cutbacks 'shambolic'– Foreign Service Association." *TVNZ*. 17 May 2012.

33 "MFAT cutbacks 'shambolic' – Foreign Service Association." *TVNZ*. 17 May 2012.

34 http://pacific.scoop.co.nz/2012/03/mfat-partners-letter-to-ceo-on-proposed-restructuring.

35  This case was written by Scott Andrews, International Case Tutor and Principal Lecturer
    at the University of Worcester, UK. It was achieved with the collaborative support of
    Manisha Gandham, Ionut Grigorescu, Emma McQuaide, Sam Parkin and Alex Taylor.
    It is intended to be used as a basis for group discussion rather than to illustrate either
    effective or ineffective handling of a management situation. It was derived entirely from
    published materials. © 2018, The Case Centre. No part of this publication may be
    copied, stored, transmitted, reproduced or distributed in any form or medium whatso-
    ever without the permission of the copyright owner.

36  Direnç Erşahin, Scott Andrews and Nazli Wasti wrote this case study as a part of the
    Case-Study Alliance Turkey Erasmus+ Project. This case is based on the author's per-
    sonal experience. It was developed to provide material for class discussion rather than to
    illustrate either effective or ineffective handling of a management situation. The authors
    have disguised some identifying information to protect confidentiality. Copyright
    © TED University, University of Worcester, Middle East Technical University, 2018.
    No part of this publication may be copied, stored, transmitted, reproduced or distributed
    in any form or medium whatsoever without the permission of the copyright owner.
    Please address all correspondence to direnc.ersahin@tedu.edu.tr.

37  Direnç Erşahin, Scott Andrews and Nazli Wasti wrote this teaching note as a part of the
    Case-Study Alliance Turkey Erasmus+ Project. Copyright © TED University, Uni-
    versity of Worcester, Middle East Technical University 2018. No part of this publication
    may be copied, stored, transmitted, reproduced or distributed in any form or medium
    whatsoever without the permission of the copyright owner. Please address all corre-
    spondence to direnc.ersahin@tedu.edu.tr.

# INDEX

Printed in the United States
by Baker & Taylor Publisher Services